COMMUNITY PARTNERSHIPS WITH SCHOOL LIBRARIES

COMMUNITY PARTNERSHIPS WITH SCHOOL LIBRARIES

CREATING INNOVATIVE LEARNING EXPERIENCES

Bridget Crossman

Foreword by Paige Jaeger

LIBRARIES
UNLIMITED™

An Imprint of ABC-CLIO, LLC

Santa Barbara, California • Denver, Colorado

Library of Congress Control Number: 2019021184

ISBN: 978-1-4408-6891-7 (paperback)
        978-1-4408-6892-4 (ebook)

23 22 21 20 19   1   2   3   4   5

This book is also available as an eBook.

Libraries Unlimited
An Imprint of ABC-CLIO, LLC

ABC-CLIO, LLC
147 Castilian Drive
Santa Barbara, California 93117
www.abc-clio.com

This book is printed on acid-free paper ∞

Manufactured in the United States of America

Contents

Foreword

Somewhere between the birth of the Information Age and our current age of misinformation, the primary and prominent role of librarians being a reading advocate was marginalized. At the same time, we've seen a growth in testing, which relies on an ability to read, read well, and read critically. Recently the National Assessment of Educational Progress (NAEP) scores were released, and the International Literacy Association wrote a report, which began as follows:

> Concerns that reading scores of U.S. students have remained flat for the past decade have surfaced again along with suggestions about the source of this problem and how it might be remedied.[1]

Librarians all over America have been rallying for reading, but our voice seems to have been muffled by technology and test preparation. Dare we claim that the pendulum needs to swing back and recognize that our elementary students need to return to "learning to read and reading to learn"? Dare we advocate for increasing the volume of reading as a solution?

Don't get me wrong—I am a technology advocate and spent four years programming for an international company prior to getting an MLIS. I know the power and prominence of technology. But I also recognize that reading may be the weakest link https://www.literacyworldwide.org/docs/default-source/where-we-stand/ila-exploring-the-2017-naep-reading-results.pdf 20 March, 2019 in our educational chain right now. Reading well and reading critically will prepare kids for success as well as testing. It will also prepare them for life.

By building a stronger reading program in your school, you will be supporting your buildings' educational goals. Don't marginalize your role. Librarians are the keepers of the keys. Now is the time to strive for students to read more, to read deeply and critically, and to experience the joy of finding a great book.

If you are looking for ways to strengthen the reading program within your school or community, then this book is a must-read. If you are looking for ways to connect to your community and collaborate with classrooms, you will find a plethora of ideas to replicate. Bridget carefully explains and details the research and reasons behind her winning ideas.

From tapping into community experts to connecting globally via technology, her ideas are easy to replicate and will breath twenty-first-century ideas into your program.

As a successful classroom-teacher-turned-librarian, Bridget has been able to grow her building role into a leadership via a techno-literacy model. Some of her many standards-aligned connection ideas have been detailed in this book, offering a glimpse into purposeful planning. Successful curriculum connections take purposeful planning. If you are wondering how and where to start, get a few ideas here from the American Revolution to pollution in nearby habitats.

It is easy to see why she has won accolades from the NYS Reading Association. Her district's inquiry-based curriculum overhaul was largely spearheaded because of the two librarians (and supportive technology director) in the district. Bridget writes from successful experience.

If we are careful and purposeful to build a community that values literacy, our students will be successful—to say nothing of our programs. Why not learn from someone who has forged this path? Everything from marketing ideas to handouts is shared for your success. Enjoy these ideas, and weave a few into your library world.

Enjoy the journey!

—Paige Jaeger

NOTE

1. "Literacy Leadership Brief: Exploring the 2017 NAEP Reading Results," International Literacy Association, https://www.literacyworldwide.org/docs/default-source/where-we-stand/ila-exploring-the-2017-naep-reading-results.pdf.

Preface

Opportunity is here! The generation of learners who fills our libraries, classrooms, and school buildings has the vast ability to impact our world in ways other generations only dreamed about. Technology has changed how, when, and where we learn, connect, and engage, thus creating a "flat" world. As acknowledged by Thomas Friedman (2007), the "flat world" allows for a singularly connected field of knowledge that can bring with it an amazing era of innovation (8)—an era where individuals need to be prepared to not only compete with people all over the world but also work and collaborate with them (11). Schools must outfit our learners for success in today's globally connected world. Librarians are prepared to be the leaders in arming our schools with innovative learning experiences that equip our students for the future. It's time to unleash our skills, talents, and creativity to make a huge impact on learning and learners.

I am proud of our profession. The work done by *Future Ready Librarians* with the support of the *Alliance for Excellent Education* (n.d.). in defining the progressive role of a Future Ready Librarian™ is cutting edge and both inspirational and aspirational. Couple that with the rollout of the 2017 *American Association of School Librarians (AASL) National School Library Standards* and we have two powerhouse resources for meeting the needs of twenty-first-century learners. Kudos to the leaders in our profession for recognizing the need to adapt the standards and principles of our work to meet the changing needs and demands being placed on our learners. Now, it is the responsibility of each of us to embrace their work and use it to empower the creation of innovative learning experiences in our libraries and schools.

What are you doing in your libraries to meet the changing demands? In 2008, Dr. Tony Wagner published *The Global Achievement Gap: Why Even Our Best Schools Don't Teach the New Survival Skills Our Children Need—and What We Can Do about It*, where he shared his research that resulted in a list of "Seven Survival Skills for the 21st Century Learner." These skills focus on the need for schools to change their systems in order to produce innovative thinkers, communicators, and collaborators. Later, Wagner copublished *Most Likely to Succeed: Preparing Our Kids for the Innovation Era*, where he again touted the need to develop these skills in schools, emphasizing the fact that since the publication of *The Global Achievement Gap: Why Even Our Best Schools Don't Teach the New Survival Skills Our Children Need—and What We Can Do about It*, he had not received one objection to the need for schools to place value on changing their systems to address these essential skills (Wagner and Dintersmith 2015, 50). If we can agree that these skills are so important that we need to change our systems, then it is clear that we as librarians can start by embracing the new *AASL Standards*.

As established in the *AASL Standards*, the core of our work is built around the four domains of *Think, Create, Share,* and *Grow* through the Shared Foundations of *Inquire, Include, Collaborate, Curate, Explore,* and *Engage* (AASL 15). These support and reflect many of the essential "Seven Survival Skills for the 21st Century Learner." Our leaders have acknowledged the need for change. We have been armed with the resources to impact learners and improve their skills for success in an innovative world. Now it is up to us as individual librarians to create systems and experiences within our library programs that foster the development of these skills. So, I ask again, "What have you done to lead the way toward designing innovative learning experiences at your school?" Have you shifted your instructional practice, rethought your learning spaces, or reshaped your programs? The time in now; join me in leading the way.

We all need to be leaders in our schools through our library programs. I recognize and value that each of us is unique. Some of us are natural born leaders, while others shutter at the idea of leading. It is time to rethink leadership. You don't need to be standing up at the front of every faculty meeting to lead. You don't even need to be loud to lead. Leading in your school looks like one thing: *championing learning.* Once leadership is framed through this lens, you can begin to see opportunities everywhere.

In terms of *championing learning*, I lead every day through my work and my actions, and I would argue that most of you probably do, too. When I say that we need to lead our schools toward providing students with innovative learning experiences, there is no need or time to be apprehensive; instead, we need to use our passion and creativity to shape how we make it happen. In the chapters that follow, you are going to be provided with a treasury of community partnership opportunities and resources that will allow you to create innovative learning experiences. For each partnership, you will be provided with suggested actions that you can take to lead these learning experiences at your school. I recognize that each of us has access to varying degrees of resources and work in very different school cultures and structures, making some learning experiences more adaptable than others. Champions of learning and innovators will choose to accept the creative challenges each of our unique situations provide, and they will overcome roadblocks that prohibit success.

To get you started, here are some important factors to successful leadership. We need to build credibility, trust, and respect. The intention of our work should only come from one motive: to improve learning. When others witness this intention through our work and actions, we will start to earn the trust and respect we need to be valued as a leader. Simply put, lead by example. It is then that we will earn a captive audience that values and seeks our guidance.

Credibility, trust, and respect are certainly earned through our actions, but they can also be built through relationships. Relationships matter more than anything else in this profession. We need to foster strong relationships with community members, instructional partners, administrators, colleagues, and most importantly students. Within each relationship, we must continuously work to listen, connect, and support others in their growth. We can earn their trust through relentless efforts to support others and help them improve; we can seek their respect through our own successful practice and by modeling continual learning and personal growth; and, finally, we can motivate them with our passion and desire to improve learning. Nothing in the step-by-step action plans shared throughout this book will matter if you don't take the time to create and develop these strong relationships.

Let's also take a moment to acknowledge some basic truths that we can embrace. We are asking others to follow us as we prepare our learners for a changing world. That means we better be equipped to lead. We need to be honest with ourselves about the realities of our beliefs and our actions. We need to adopt a can-do mindset and work hard to live as a leader. Here are some essential truths for *champions of learning*.

- I aspire to be better.
- I am willing to lead.
- I place value in meeting the *AASL National School Library Standards*.
- I recognize the important work of *Future Ready Librarians*.
- I value the local and global learning community.
- I seek and value collaboration.
- I acknowledge and respect my responsibility to provide student learners with the skills, knowledge, and experiences necessary to be successful in their future.
- I acknowledge the shared responsibility to prepare our students for success in a global world.
- I view librarians as teachers.
- I embrace a growth mindset.
- I am willing to put in the work.

If you can, with conviction, say you live by these truths, you can be assured that you are fit to lead. However, that doesn't mean that leadership opportunities will just happen. I understand and recognize that these truths are often met with roadblocks that form barriers on the road toward success.

Roadblocks bring me to my final point. I would be remiss if I failed to discuss the need for grit, passion, and responsibility as underlying factors for success. I am the first person to recognize that our work is exhausting. So, what is it that makes me as passionate and as driven as I am to push through the difficult work that lies between me and the success of my learners? The truth is, I know my work is vital, and I own that responsibility. As cliché as it sounds, *we have the future in our hands*. We are developing the skills and knowledge of our future workforce and developing informed, responsible citizens. When we take time to invest in our learners, we will not only make an impact on them but also make an impact on our future (they are our future, right?). I own the shared responsibility of empowering learners to leave our classrooms with a continual thirst for learning and a desire to impact the world in a positive way. Passion and grit simply cannot be overlooked as essential components of our efforts to lead innovative learning experiences within our schools.

I hope you are willing to *roll up your sleeves* and embrace the new *AASL Standards* and Future Ready Librarian™ principles, and join me as we take the lead on developing innovative learning experiences. It is our craft, skills, and underlying efforts that will positively impact learning. For the sake of growth, we need to push ourselves, our learners, and our organizations out of their comfort zones. We need to welcome failure and cultivate a mindset of *failing forward*. We make forward progression toward growth when we learn from our mistakes and failures. I promise, if we can embrace these truths, attitudes, and mindsets that were outlined earlier, and will be in the following chapters, together we will be prepared to lead successful innovative library programs that effectively prepare learners for the future.

This book captures my practice of building a strong library program through community partnership–based learning experiences. It is my way of supporting you as you work toward leading innovative learning experiences in your schools and libraries. There is nothing that *fires me up* more than when people put forward valid concerns and do nothing to address them. I have listened to the concerns and voices from librarians across our profession and heard your cries for desired recognition in the field of education. You have communicated your concerns of being undervalued and underappreciated. I validate each and every one of your concerns; they are legitimate. This book is my attempt to support you in addressing your concerns. I must, however, point out that in order to earn the respect and appreciation of others, we must give ourselves the respect and appreciation that we deserve. During the same conversations where we complain about being undervalued, we can be heard minimizing our successes and doubting our abilities. Let's stop saying things like "I can't lead" or letting the incredible work of other librarians undercut our perceptions of our own work. We will never get the respect of others if we don't respect and value our own work. Start owning your value and communicating it in your language and behaviors. Together we must champion the work of one another and our efforts to improve learning and libraries. Let's take time to listen to one another's stories and grow collaboratively from each other, for the sake of our libraries and those we serve.

By sharing my stories, I hope to help you as you tackle the new *AASL Standards* and the *Future Ready Librarian*™ principles. Through a structured format of *Learn, Leap, & Grow*, I will provide you with the knowledge, understanding, and resources to create innovative learning experiences at your school. The shared learning experiences in this book are meant to be a guide for librarians as they work to develop innovative learning experiences through strong community partnership within their library programs. These experiences showcase how skills and knowledge within the *AASL Standards* can be developed through multiple types of community partnerships. Aspiring *Future Ready Librarians* will be excited to discover and explore the ideas, tools, and shared resources that they can use to enhance their practices, programs, and impact on learners.

Through publications, presentations, and mentoring, I have found success in leading others toward building innovative learning experiences that are learner centered. By no means does this make me an expert or pioneer. In fact, the thing I appreciate the most about our field is that we embrace collaboration and recognize that learning is a shared commitment and responsibility. This book is designed to support that philosophy. I hope you can learn from it, be inspired by it, and use it to seek and generate opportunities to lead powerful learning experiences at your school—experiences that will launch you, your students, your libraries, and your school toward a successful future.

Introduction

HOW TO THINK ABOUT AND USE THIS BOOK

Before accessing the treasury of innovative learning experiences that live in the chapters ahead, it is important to clarify and establish a common understanding of the persistent mindfulness and language used throughout the course of this book. This introduction will not only lay the groundwork for those understandings; it will also provide a breakdown of the structure used in each chapter that follows.

Defining Community Partnerships

A community partnership is a connection that is made between the learner and an individual, organization, or physical place outside of the school building. This connection can be made solely by the librarian or with the collaborative efforts of an instructional partner, to support student learning.

Types of Community Partnerships

There are two different types of community partnerships:

- Those that support learning inside the school building
- Those that support learning outside of the school building

The type of learning experience that is provided to learners is dependent upon the learners' needs, resources, the curriculum, standards, and goals and mission of the school. Partnerships are designed to support student learning, foster student engagement, expose students to broad experiences, and provide innovative student-centered learning opportunities.

INTERNAL LEARNING EXPERIENCES

During internal learning experiences, the connected learning between community partners and the learner most often takes place within a school building. However, there are cases when the learning happens in the building but the partner is not physically present (refer to Chapter 3).

EXTERNAL LEARNING EXPERIENCES

During external learning experiences, the connected learning experience between community partners and the learner takes place outside of the school building. Similar to internal learning experiences, external learning experiences don't always take on the same format. Oftentimes, students travel to connect with the community partner. However, in some cases, the learning is brought to the student when they aren't physically at the school (refer to Chapters 5 and 7).

Why Do Community Partnerships Matter?

We all work and live in unique communities. Some of our communities are filled with apparent opportunities for rich partnerships, while others are more hidden or sparse. However, potential partnerships exist in every community, and it is imperative that we invest our time and energy into developing them. When taking a close look at the benefits, they go far beyond their apparent surface value. Although partnerships are most often seen as informational resources, there is a beneficial value gained from the engagement, global awareness, empathy, and lifelong learning process they elicit.

Let us dive deeper into the benefits.

RESOURCES

Initially, community partnerships are sought out because of the value that can be gained when experts in the community are used as information resources. As educators we need to teach content, and generally we have members of our community who have expertise in a specific content area, making them an ideal resource for supporting the curriculum. Typically, when using partnerships for this reason, they can be most helpful to our students during the investigation stage of research, where learners are seeking and gathering information.

Utilizing community partnerships as resources can go beyond our initial perception. We need to push ourselves to think about learning beyond curricular content knowledge (although that is valuable). Partnerships cannot be restricted by a narrow vision of what a partner is. Why limit partnerships to physical people, when physical places can be excellent resources as well? Learning from seeing and experiencing a place or location can provide students with awareness and understanding that they would not be privy to without a connected partnership to a physical location. This will be highlighted further in Chapters 4 and 5.

Partnerships for the purpose of seeking resources provide learners with the understanding that resources go beyond books, databases, and websites. Learners can begin to appreciate that we live in a connected learning community that has shared value for each member. Through community partnerships, learners begin to recognize this and value the shared knowledge and understandings that can come through community resources. They also discover the impact this can have on their learning and others. Learning experiences that are built from these type of partnerships help to break down learning barriers and prepare students for future learning and experiences.

ENGAGEMENT

Having built many learning experiences around community partnerships, I can speak to the fact that experiences built from partnerships leave an imprint on students for years to come. Students can be heard clapping, cheering, and reminiscing when I refer back to a learning experience that was built through a community partnership. This response isn't because they loved the content and knowledge they acquired, although that would be great; it was because they were engaged. Students were active participants, engaged in authentic learning that was generated from their needs as learners. When we put learners and their needs at the center of the experience, it makes learning meaningful and relevant to them. There is no other weapon in education more powerful than that of relevancy. When you can make learning relevant, you have an engaged audience, and effective community partnerships will do just that.

GLOBAL AWARENESS

Since the explosion of technology and the internet, our world has become flatter (Friedman 2007, 8). We are connected all the time and connected all around the world. It is not only our job to teach our students how to live in a global world; it is our job to prepare them to thrive in it. We need to help develop global citizens who can communicate, collaborate, and create with others in an expanded and diverse learning community. We have a social responsibility to prepare and educate learners for the global world, by teaching them to appreciate and value the diverse perspectives and experiences that each learner brings (to a learning community). Through community partnerships, we begin to lay the foundation for this crucial work by exposing learners to different perspectives and experiences, ultimately impacting their schema moving forward. With increased exposure to community partnerships, learners begin to develop an appreciation for other learners' perspectives, and they develop the understanding that informed decisions require the voice and perspective of others.

EMPATHY

As already implied, in order for learners to succeed in life, it is not enough to simply teach content. We also need to teach our learners the skills to listen and understand others' perspectives. It is essential to their future success that they are capable of appreciating diverse perspectives and that they value the importance of understanding the *why* behind others' thoughts, beliefs, and actions. These skills are necessary for successful engagement in any work environment, but especially a global work environment where people aren't as inclined to share the same life experiences that shape their own perspectives. The more we expose our learners to community partnerships, the more we place value on seeking and listening to others and provide them with opportunities to develop these vital skills.

LIFELONG LEARNING PROCESS

We are preparing our students to become lifelong learners who possess the skills to continue to build knowledge and understanding throughout their lives. In order to do this, we not only need to equip our learners with these skills; we need to give them the opportunity to apply these skills in real-world experiences. Through community partnerships, authentic opportunities are created to do just that. Learners are put into safe learning situations where they feel comfortable to take risks and develop the skills to persevere, giving them the experience necessary to know that they are capable of meeting any learning challenge they are faced with, either in or outside of school.

Defining Innovation

George Couros (2015), author of *The Innovator's Mindset*, believes that learners need to focus on developing an *innovator's mindset*. Learners who acquire this mindset embrace the understanding that they have the abilities, knowledge, and talents that can be used to create something new (33). When we use the term *learners*, as the American Library Association (ALA) does in the 2017 *National School Library Standards*, to span beyond students, we can place ourselves as growing professionals in the role of learners (AASL 2018, 10). I believe we as *learners* need to embrace an innovator's mindset in our libraries. We need to use our knowledge, expertise, and talents to create new powerful learning experiences for our students.

Couros also describes innovation in his book as the ability to create not only something new but something better (2015, 34). I have no doubt that you are providing great opportunities and learning experiences in your library, but are you continually trying to improve those experiences and make them better? What are you doing that is new and relevant to today's learners? If the expectations for our learners are changing, then we better be changing our practice to meet those expectations. We can do this by redesigning the learning experiences that we provide and creating new and improved ones that captivate our learners and develop their continual growth for a prepared future.

Defining and Creating Innovative Learning Experiences

As one of the accepted truths in the preface, it was acknowledged that we need to prepare our students for a global world with shifting expectations. This is achievable when we expect nothing less than the best for our students and our libraries. Demanding higher expectations for the learning experiences that we provide is the key to keeping our libraries moving forward. We can begin to improve learning experiences by simply listening to the needs and interests of our learners. When you combine this knowledge, along with your skills and talents, it will lead to the creation of innovative learning experiences.

Do not undervalue the power of creating an effective learning experience! Experience has taught us that students are captivated and motivated to engage in learning when they see a reason to be invested. This challenge of building a captive audience can be met by building learning experiences around something that is relevant to them—their community. Communities provide a springboard for innovative learning—learning that is student centered and drenched with opportunities for skill and knowledge acquisition. These are the types of successful innovative experiences that I create in order to fuel my students for a lifetime of learning.

If we want our libraries and learning to progress, it is going to require you, me, and all of our colleagues to think differently about the experiences that we offer. Despite any and all roadblocks, we must prevail, by continually seeking opportunities to provide innovative learning experiences. If we don't, how can we say that we are preparing learners for the future? How can we say that we are preparing them for a global world? Let's be honest; using the same learning experiences and expecting to produce learners who are prepared for a new world is not going to be effective.

It's time to get innovative with the design of our learning experiences and challenge ourselves to build student-centered experiences that provoke critical thinking, require collaboration, and elicit creativity. Community partnerships are great launching pads for innovative learning. Use the ideas and experiences shared in this book to spark your creativity and help you design successful and innovative learning opportunities for your students. These shared experiences, combined with strong relationships, passion, and empathy toward your students' needs, will move your libraries forward.

Future Ready Librarians

In 2014, the *Future Ready Schools* initiative was launched as a means for schools to transform learning through digital tools and resources (*Future Ready Librarians* n.d.). This initiative addressed personalized student learning through several core areas of focus. *Future Ready Librarians* recognized the value librarians could bring to schools and districts as they work to meet the Future Ready goals. Through an expanded framework that utilizes the core areas of focus in the *Future Ready Schools* *Framework*, *Future Ready Librarians* (with the support of *Follett* and the partnership of *American Association of School Librarians*) created a framework to foster the collaborative work of librarians and school leaders in addressing Future Ready goals (Alliance for Excellent Education n.d.). This invaluable framework provides suggested actions, referred to as principles, that can be taken by librarians to facilitate the development of innovative learning experiences. When referring to the Future Ready Librarian™ gear icon (provided at the following link: https://1gu04j2l2i9n1b0wor2zmgua-wpengine.netdna-ssl.com/wp-content/uploads/2017/01/Library_flyer_download.pdf), the inner wedges provide the core areas of focus, while the outer edges refer to the actions or principles.

The *Future Ready Librarian™ Framework* is a leading resource for fostering the development of innovative libraries and learning. This prominent tool will guide your work toward digital transformation of learning and innovative practices. The experiences in this book are built around the core areas of focus identified in the framework: Literacy, Curriculum, Instruction, and Assessment, Personalized Professional Learning, Robust Infrastructure, Budget and Resources, Community Partnerships, Data and Privacy, Collaborative Leadership, and Use of Space and Time (Alliance for Excellent Education 2018). For each shared learning experience in the chapters that follow, a graphic will be provided to help identify the core areas that were addressed within each learning experience.

It is important to recognize our shifting role and responsibility as librarians and educators. We are tasked with preparing successfully equipped citizens who are informed and suited to participate in a global and digital world. This task requires urgency! It requires us, as well-positioned leaders in the building, to embrace our shifting role and prepare ourselves to be Future Ready Librarians. Although some of you may not feel that you are currently positioned to carry out this role, this book will help you to move toward that goal. Through persistent actions, you can position yourself to lead the facilitation between building or district leaders and classroom teachers, making your role instrumental in preparing learners for the future. The *Future Ready Framework* is a great resource that will help arm us with core actions for success. Remember, it is our job to successfully serve our students; let's start by becoming *Future Ready Librarians*.

AASL Standards

In 2015, the *American Association of School Librarians* (AASL 2018, 9) set out to remodel and revise their standards and school library guidelines. They conducted research and collected data, seeking the input of librarians and stakeholders across our field, in order to make informed decisions on how best to refine the standards. Our voices exposed a desire to have standards that are rigorous, valuable, and respected. Our input also revealed a common belief that the current guidelines were already relevant to today's learning environments and practices. What we did express was that we wanted new refined standards with rigor and relevance that would have a positive impact on learners and educators, but that also had improved clarity for ease of use (AASL 2018, 10–11).

As a result of our input, the American Library Association (ALA) published new *AASL National School Library Standards* in 2018, rolling them out in November 2017. These standards are the official position of our national association (AASL 2018, 10). They are clearly broken down into frameworks for learners, school librarians, and school libraries. Common language and a consistent structure is also utilized, making them easy to use. The standards are organized by four domains in which the roles and responsibilities of the respected users are embedded (15). The four domains of *Think, Create, Share,* and *Grow* reflect a process of inquiry that is presented in each of the three frameworks (*Learner, School Librarian,* and *School Library*) along with six shared foundations of *Inquire, Include, Collaborate, Curate, Explore,* and *Engage.* Each domain includes competencies that respect the uniqueness of each individual learner as they work to develop the desired knowledge, skills, and dispositions gained from a learning experience (19). The six foundations are the core values that should be reflected and promoted by school librarians and school libraries (17).

The learning experiences within this book were built upon appreciation, respect, and attention to the 2018 *AASL Standards.* Each learning experience embraces our valued multidisciplinary approach that allows for simultaneous application of each of our vital roles within the learning process. Each described learning experience is complete with a list of all three sets of standards (*Learner, Librarian,* and *Library*) that identify the applied standards for each respective group throughout the described learning experience. It is my hope that the experiences in this book will help guide you on your path to building valuable learning experiences in your programs that reflect and address the rigorous and critical *AASL Standards.*

How to Use This Book

Part I of this book will focus on internal learning experiences, while Part II will focus on external learning experiences. For the benefit of sequential learners, like myself, each chapter is structured as follows:

1. Identifying and describing the featured partnership
2. Describing important benefits of the partnerships
3. How to make it happen

This structure, with embedded examples, aims to show you how I delivered community partnership–based learning experiences within my school.

Each community partnership featured in Part I and Part II is structured in three parts: *learn, leap,* and *grow.* I start with *learn* to emphasize the *what, why,* and *how* behind the community partnership–based learning experience. Next, I invite you to *leap* forward toward creating a community partnership–based learning experience with a few basic suggestions for transferring your freshly acquired knowledge. These suggestions are followed by in-depth examples of my own personal work in developing the featured partnerships and learning experiences. At the conclusion of my shared stories, I encourage you to *grow*

IDEA BOXES PROVIDE USEFUL TIPS FOR CARRYING OUT COMMUNITY PARTNERSHIP BASED LEARNING EXPERIENCES.

Figure I.1   Idea Box

by providing bulleted suggestions that will help you move forward with creating the featured partnerships at your school, which is accompanied by a step-by-step action plan for creating partnerships and learning experiences within your programs. Refer to Table I.1 for a basic understanding of the chapter layout.

Throughout each chapter, a unique text feature is displayed as an *Idea Box*. These *Idea Boxes* provide useful tips for facilitating the learning experience. See Figure I.1.

Table I.1   Chapter Outline

Learn
Type of Partnership: The partnership is defined to provide an understanding of what the partnership entails.
Why Do They Matter?: Here you are provided with the justification for developing learning experiences through the featured partnership and the value it brings to the student learner.
Making It Happen: You are given a description of how you can begin to develop these partnerships and learning experiences in your library programs.
Leap
Leap (step) forward with . . . In the grey box, learners will be encouraged to *leap* toward creating the particular community partnership–based learning experience that was featured in the "Learn" section. There will be at least three suggested steps to help readers get started with integrating these learning experiences in their library programs. It is not necessary to apply all three suggestions, but it is encouraged to move forward with as many of the suggestions as possible.
Learning Experiences: In this section you will be provided with a detailed tutorial of how the featured community partnership and connected learning experience was carried out in my library program. There will be two or three learning experience examples for each partnership. These examples will be separated by the type of learning experience followed by a number in sequential order.
Named Learning Experience: The title of the connected learning experience will be provided . . .

(Continued)

Table I.1 (Continued)

Partnership: The connected community partner(s) will be identified. Depending on the need, sometimes this will appear in a list format, while at other times a detailed explanation will be provided.

Future Ready Framework: A checklist of Future Ready core areas of focus are featured, with check marks indicating the core areas that are focused upon throughout the community partnership–based learning experience.

AASL Standards:
AASL Standards for Learners: The 2018 *AASL Learner* competencies covered within the featured community partnership–based learning experience are indicated.
AASL Standards for School Librarians: The 2018 *AASL Librarian* competencies covered within the featured community partnership–based learning experience are indicated.
AASL School Standards for School Libraries: The 2018 *AASL Library* competencies covered within the featured community partnership–based learning experience are indicated.

Experience Summary: You are presented with a detailed tutorial of how within my library program, I prepared, delivered, and, when applicable, assessed and reflected on the community partnership–based learning experience.

Suggested Modifications: All the community partnership–based learning experiences featured in Part I and Part II of this book were carried out in a flexibly scheduled elementary (K–6) library program with a rich supply of resources, in a small school setting. This section is to provide you with suggested modifications that can help tailor the learning experiences so that it can be successfully applied to fit your school and library setting.

Resources: You are provided with resources to deliver the described learning experience featured in the "Experience Summary" section.

Grow

This section of the chapter is designed to help librarians take action and begin to grow their library programs by developing the featured community partnership–based learning experience featured in the chapter.

In this grey box, a short list of suggested action steps is presented for librarians to *grow* their library program. These steps are meant for librarians to put into action.

Action Plan
You are provided with a three-step action plan to guide your work in developing and delivering the featured community partnership–based learning experience. The action plan begins with "Setting the Stage," followed by "Establishing the Partnership" and concluding with "Delivering the Learning Experience."

Setting the Stage
You are provided with the criteria that need to be established prior to creating the community partnership–based learning experience. The criteria are presented in a three-column chart, divided by "Goals," "Key Players," and "Groundwork." Within each column, there is a list of bulleted suggestions that should be determined prior to developing the experience. The *goals* indicate what is expected of the community partnership–based learning experience. The *key players* help you determine who will be involved in the experience, while the *groundwork* outlines the work that needs to be done prior to developing the experience.

Setting the Stage		
Goals	**Key Players**	**Groundwork**
• Indicate what is expected of the community partnership–based learning experience.	• Identifies who will be involved in the experience.	• Outlines the work that needs to be done prior to developing the learning experience.

Establishing the Partnership
A table of ideas is presented to help guide your actions toward developing a community partnership. This table is broken down into five categories: Who, What, How, Where, and When.

Who	Suggestions for consideration when selecting a person, location, or organization for a partnership.
What	Suggestions for consideration when determining what the needs of the partnership.
How	Suggestions for consideration when creating a partnership.
Where	Suggestions for consideration when determining where the connected partnership will take place.
When	Suggestions for consideration when determining when the connected partnership will occur.

Delivering the Learning Experience
The reader is provided with an outline of suggested steps to follow when delivering a community partnership–based learning experience. This is displayed in an easy-to-follow sequential outline.

Finally, there is common language throughout the book that bares attention. Refer to the following box for a shared understanding of this language.

> *Community partnership–based learning experiences* are learning experiences provided to student learners through the creation of a connected community partnership.
>
> *Inquiry* is a learning process that students go through when acquiring new knowledge. According to the *WSWHE BOCES* model of inquiry, designed under the direction of Paige Jaeger and Mary Ratzer, learning progresses through the stages of Wonder, Investigate, Synthesize, and Express (2011), in a cyclical and iterative fashion.
>
> *Learners* refer to information seekers, including, but not limited to, students, teachers, librarians, and administrators.

PART I
Internal Learning Experiences

1

Curriculum Partnerships

LEARN

What Are Curriculum Partnerships?

Our local communities are filled with experts who can support our curricular content and should be seen as part of our learning network. These experts can be historians, professionals, public officials, directors of organizations, environmentalists, and beyond (refer to Table 1.1). Librarians have the important job of connecting our learners to these resources and bringing them into our schools to support learning across the curriculum and grade levels.

Curriculum partnerships support the learners' efforts during various stages of inquiry-based learning units. Partnerships look different depending on the intent of the learning experience. Curriculum partners could engage learners at the beginning of any inquiry by activating thinking on a curricular topic. They could also be a resource to answer learners' research questions during student investigation. Additionally, while students are creating knowledge products, they could provide expertise, or they could be a member of an authentic audience during delivery of a final knowledge product. The options are endless, but whatever their role is, the success of the learning experience is contingent upon their partnership.

Why Do They Matter?

According to the text *National School Library Standards for Learners, School Librarians, and School Libraries*, by providing learners with a diverse collection of resources, we as librarians can help learners progress toward valuing other learners' contributions. It can also broaden their awareness of global learning communities and resources that exist to support them in their acquisition of knowledge (American Association of School Librarians [AASL] 2018, 80).

Connecting local community experts with learners supports the development of skills that are crucial in the lifelong learning process, while also supporting knowledge acquisition and development. When we bring in experts to support learners as they inquire and curate, we teach our learners ways to *act on informational needs* by helping them to identify possible nontraditional sources of information. Helping learners see beyond traditional

Table 1.1 Potential Community Experts

Firefighters
Law enforcement officers
Emergency medical technicians
Community entertainment groups (theater, arts, etc.)
Chambers of commerce
Protective agencies
Family outreach program coordinators
Social services
Postal workers
Librarians
Historians
City officials
Medical professionals
Health officials
Dentists
Doctors
Therapists
Veterinarians
Business owners
Farmers
Lawyers
Professors
Engineers
Environmental protective agencies

print sources of information is important to their success. By introducing our students to community experts as resources, we are guiding them in the information selection process and modeling the exploration of innovative resources that support their learning needs. Our ultimate goal is that they will transfer this learning to their everyday lives, including outside of school.

Rich library programs are designed to support the needs of all learners, not just student learners. Building learning experiences that enrich the content area curriculum in the classroom provides curricular support to teachers and student learners. When we locate and connect community partners with teachers and classrooms, we are indeed supporting the curricular work of learners and teachers.

According to the *Future Ready Librarian™ Framework* (Alliance for Excellent Education 2018), *Future Ready Librarians* are responsible for cultivating community partnerships. These partnerships are undeniably beneficial to students. They provoke engagement, curiosity, and the desire to learn, which motivates learners to fill knowledge gaps, build on prior knowledge, and create new knowledge within sustained inquiry. These are all skills students need when preparing for success beyond our classrooms and libraries, solidifying the need for librarians to explore community partnerships in connection with curricular needs.

How Do You Make Them Happen?

Creating a curricular partnership with experts in the community is not terribly difficult. The challenge comes with co-constructing purposeful curricular learning experiences that build on curricular partnerships. Through informed instructional partnerships, teachers and librarians can collaborate to build a dynamic learning experience for students that cultivate community partnerships and address both content standards and *AASL Standards*. Librarians specialize in teaching skills; so, when given the opportunity to integrate skill building within content, we can construct rich and powerful learning experiences.

As leaders we have the important job of recognizing learning opportunities and engaging in collaborative efforts toward building innovative practices. Leading teacher learners and staff through the development of inquiry-based learning experiences, which address both content standards and *AASL Standards*, can certainly prove to be challenging work. However, without collaborating with teacher learners, opportunities to cocreate learning experiences would be lost. We must rise to the occasion and lead, by using learner and learning needs to guide collaborative discussions and curricular decisions. By embracing a positive mindset and the knowledge required to lead collaborative planning, you will produce the learning experiences you crave.

Understanding *AASL Standards* and the content standards is critical. Teachers will value and respect your perspectives and ideas when they trust in your knowledge and expertise. There are many ways to learn the standards and content across curriculum areas. Attending specific curricular conferences and professional development opportunities, joining curricular committees, and reading the content area standards across grade levels are all effective means for educating yourself on the standards. Once you feel comfortable with the standards and are knowledgeable about the grade level curricula, you are in a prime position to support learning in a way that is meaningful to both the teacher and the learner.

When we are aware of the standards and skills being addressed at each grade level, we become tuned into opportunities for integrated curricular learning experiences. This is not to say that you need to be proficient with all the content standards, but you certainly need to be knowledgeable about them. The better your understanding of the standards, the easier it will be to draw connections and collaborate. Choosing to initially focus your attention on one curricular content area can be the most efficient way to be an effective leader in designing these learning experiences (see Figure 1.1). Social studies is the perfect area of curricular focus when building experiences based on community partnerships. There are typically many natural social studies connections to local experts who can help meet curricular needs.

Being a curriculum expert is a good beginning, but it is not enough. The next step is taking the leap toward engagement. Engaging in building level curriculum design and instruction and positioning yourself on key (strategic) committees, where building and district level decisions are made, will help to place you at the table for important conversations. These conversations can lead to opportunities for your voice to be heard and for your expertise to be used to shape curriculum. For engagement strategies, refer to the journal article, "Are You at the Table? The Importance of Leadership in the Library," that I coauthored with Sarah Olson in the April 2018 edition of School Library Connection. We cannot underestimate the power and value of being engaged!

It is inevitable that active engagement in critical committees and conversations with key players will be lucrative for you as a leader. This instrumental role leverages your ability to lead or colead professional learning, creating the perfect opportunity to impact curriculum design. This is your *window* of opportunity to model what inquiry-based

Figure 1.1

learning experiences could look like within specific content areas. Capitalizing on this time to offer innovative ideas that will meet standards and enrich learning will energize teachers to collaborate with you on the creation and execution of these experiences. It may also lead to opportunities to launch impromptu inquiry-based minilessons in classrooms. It is through these processes that curriculum partnerships will evolve.

There are many different opportunities to provide professional learning (see Table 1.2) throughout your building and even your district. Those opportunities may consist of, but not limited to, whole-school professional development, committee level professional development, or modeling instruction within the classroom. It is during this time that collaborative work will lead to inquiry-based learning opportunities that can be supported by the utilization of community partnerships. It is up to us, the librarian, to leap at every opportunity to collaborate with teachers and design innovative learning experiences for our students. We must never forget our responsibility to serve our students and provide them with the best education possible to prepare them for the future. If we keep that in mind, it will make all the hard work worth it.

In a perfect world, all the groundwork stated here is in place, creating an ideal work environment to co-construct learning experiences. In this perfect world, curriculum partners seamlessly find their way to us, embracing our inquiry-based instructional units. Yet few of us can say we work in a perfect world. Do not let this limit you. Continue to work toward developing community partnerships that support learning. In truth, this work takes many years and may never be fully set in place—or perfect. You must continually aspire to improve yourself and lift others who are willing to come along with you. Embrace the instructional environment you are in, and work relentlessly to foster learning through innovative practices such as curricular partnerships!

Regardless of your work environment, when you are trying to develop community partnerships that support the curriculum, you need to be focused on what the needs are. You may not always be able to lead professional learning experiences, but you don't need to lead to be part of conversations. Simply being part of the conversations will keep you abreast of the needs and challenges within the curriculum. Engage in curricular conversations during scheduled planning times, grade level meetings, or committee meetings.

It is important to look with fresh eyes for opportunities to support the needs within the curriculum. For example, even within the inquiry model of learning, finding opportunities to connect outside resources within the process can be powerful. Do you know any experts in the community who can help activate thinking and spark curiosity in the *wonder* stage? Who are the experts in your community who can be a resource to answer student-generated questions in the *investigate* stage of research? Are there experts who can support learners in the creation of their knowledge product during the

Table 1.2   Professional Learning Leadership Opportunities

Lead professional development.
Allocate a portion of content-specific curriculum professional development to integrate inquiry-based instruction development.
Coplan professional development using the inquiry framework set by your school.
Collaborate with teachers on the design of inquiry-based units within the classroom.
Model inquiry-based instruction by "pushing" into the classroom.
Bring in an outside expert to train teachers and faculty on inquiry-based instruction.

synthesize stage? When students *express* or share their work, can a community partnership be generated for an authentic audience? These are a few of the many questions you can be asking yourself as you work to support curriculum through community partnerships. Each of these questions not only helps to focus your work toward supporting content curricular needs but also supports the four domains of the *AASL Standards*: *Think, Create, Share, Grow.*

Remember that curricular partnerships are not to be an add-on to the inquiry. If you were to remove the curriculum partner role, the unit would not be successful. The partnership is a critical element in the inquiry-based learning experience, filling a need within a particular stage of student inquiries. It is crucial that units are co-constructed in a way that the partnership meets the students' need at the appropriate time. Oftentimes, this requires flexibility within the unit, as the timing of students' needs alters based on the speed of their progression through the learning process.

Once a need is established within the appropriate inquiry stage, it is time to seek out potential curriculum partnerships within the community. The goal of the curriculum partner is to fill the existing need in the inquiry. When seeking curriculum partnerships, you may want to rely on the expertise of the community. Often the best tool for seeking partnerships is through networking. Personal and social networks in both digital and physical settings are equally as valuable and should be considered for use. Your local chamber of commerce is also a great resource.

Once a potential partner is identified, you should contact the person by both phone and email. I often contact my partner by phone first to establish the initial connection and then follow up our conversation with a detailed email. The follow-up email creates a nice form of communication that both the partner and you can refer back to for agreed upon details. During your phone conversation, you should (1) establish the date of the visit to your school, (2) set the time that works best for both parties, (3) provide a thorough description of the learning experience, and (4) state clear expectations of the curriculum partners role. This information should also be included within the follow-up email. You can think of it as a *receipt* of your conversation.

On the day of the partner's visit, be sure that the learners are prepared by having completed all the groundwork necessary for the work that lies ahead with the partnership. Additionally, ensure that all required resources are available and are taken care of (space, technology, permission for photographs, etc.). At the start of the learning experience, you will clarify the expectations for your learners and emphasize the value of the partnership. Once the work with the partnership begins, you will guide and support the learning, often moderating the exchanges between the partner and the learners when necessary. This might entail slowing the pace of the session, clarifying information, redirecting learners, and ensuring that all student graphic organizers are complete. Capturing photographs and learning during this time is important. These images can be used later to celebrate learning in the library through social media, newsletters, or other means of communication.

In the days that follow, students will spend time synthesizing their information and creating knowledge products. As learners begin to recognize knowledge gaps, encourage them to seek further information from the curriculum partners by contacting them directly. In cases where students don't have the ability to utilize email or other communication tools, you can communicate the questions to the partners for the learner. Once the knowledge products are complete, they should be shared.

LEAP

Leap (step) forward by. . .

1. Asking to join a grade level, committee, or administrative meeting where curriculum is being discussed.
2. Identifying potential teachers and curricular areas to work with.
3. Brainstorming opportunities in the curriculum where "experts" could help support the curriculum.

CURRICULUM-BASED LEARNING EXPERIENCE #1

Named Learning Experience
American Revolution Inquiry

Partnership
Saratoga Battlefield Expert Reenactor and Sociologist, Fort Ticonderoga Expert Reenactor, Librarian

Future Ready Framework (refer to Figure 1.2)

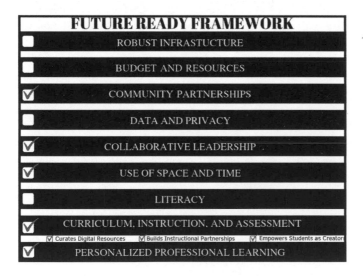

Figure 1.2

AASL Standards

AASL Standards for Learners: I.A.1., I.A.2., I.B.1., I.B.2., I.B.3., I.C.3., I.C.4., I.D.1., I.D.2., I.D.3., II.A.1., II.B.1., III.A.1., III.A.2., III.A.3, III.B.1., III.B.2., III.C.1, III.C.2, III.D.1., III.D.2., IV.A.1., IV.A.2., IV.A.3., IV.B.1., IV.B.2., IV.B.4., IV.D.1., IV.D.2., V.A.3., V.C.1.,V.C.2., V.C.3., V.D.1., V.D.3., VI.A.1.,VI.A.2., VI.B.1., VI.B.2., VI.B.3.,VI.C.2., VI.D.1., VI.D.2.

AASL Standards for School Librarians: I.A.1., I.A.2., I.B.1., I.B.2., I.B.3., I.C.1., I.C.2., I.D.1., I.D.3., II.A.1., II.B.1., III.A.1., III.A.2., III.A.3., III.C.1., III.C.2., III.D.1., III.D.2., IV.A.1., IV.A.2., IV.A.3., IV.B.1., IV.B.2., IV.B.4., IV.D.1., IV.D.2., V.A.3., V.C.1.,V.C.2., V.C.3., V.D.1., VI.A.1., VI.A.2., VI.B.1., VI.B.2., VI.B.3.,VI.C.2., VI.D.1., VI.D.2.

AASL School Standards for School Libraries: I.A.1., I.A.2., I.B.1., I.B.2., I.C.1., I.C.2., I.D.1., I.D.2., II.A.1., II.A.2., II.A.3., II.B.3., II.C.1., II.D.2., III.A.1., III.A.2., III.B.1., III.B.2., III.C.1., III.C.2., III.C.3., III.D.1., III.D.2., IV.A.1., IV.A.3., IV.B.1., IV.B.2., IV.B.5., IV.D.3., V.A.1., V.A.2., V.B.1., V.B.2., V.B.3., V.C.1., V.C.2., V.D.1., V.D.2., V.D.3., VI.A.1., V.A.2., VI.A.3., VI.B.1., VI.B.2., VI.C.2., VI.D.1., VI.D.2.

Experience Summary

All learning experiences collaborated with me and the classroom teacher are inquiry based. We follow the WISE model of inquiry at our school, adapted from our local *WSWHE (Warren, Saratoga, Washington, Hamilton, Essex) BOCES Library System* (2011). We use this framework to structure inquiry units (learning experiences) and deliver content. To support students as they work through the inquiry process, learners refer the WISE visual poster (see Figure 1.3) that I, along with my aide, Lynn Gauger, created for each classroom. This is also used as a tool for instructors to reference while teaching.

We now use the WISER model when designing and delivering the two units that follow. There are four stages to the inquiry model—wonder, investigate, synthesize, express—and we added *reflect* to make the acronym WISER. We use two tools called *blueprints* when coplanning and constructing our units. Both blueprints are equally valuable. One is tailored for designing social studies units that address all components of the New York State Social Studies Framework; this Social Studies blueprint, with permission, was modified from the original *C3 Teachers Inquiry Design Model Blueprint* (C3 Teachers 2018), while the other blueprint is used for all other curricular units (refer to Figure 1.4).

Each year our fourth-grader students research the American Revolution as part of the New York State Social Studies Curriculum. Following the WISER model of inquiry, students are charged with creating an American Revolution eBook, which is then shared with next year's fourth graders. This innovative approach to learning allows the students to acquire knowledge and develop and apply their skills toward creating a meaningful knowledge product to be shared with an authentic audience. A knowledge product, which once shared through a class webpage, will help build and develop future learners' understanding of the American Revolution in New York State.

I was able to recognize both curricular needs and opportunities to coplan an *American Revolution* inquiry-based unit with our fourth-grade team of teachers. This unit has taken on many formats over the years to meet the needs of shifting standards and English language arts programs that have been adopted by our school. With each change, our unit of inquiry shifted from a free-flowing student-centered inquiry to a guided inquiry. These changes altered the needs and resources, reshaping the learning experience each time. Refer to Table 1.3 to see the cocreated blueprint of this unit.

The final version of our unit created a need for support during the *investigate* stage of the inquiry. Students were expected to examine and explore multiple aspects of the American Revolution in New York State, which proved to be a challenging topic for students to locate information at their reading level. This created a circumstance where I was able to introduce our teachers to the idea of seeking community resources through curricular partnerships. The curricular partnerships would be between community experts on the American Revolution and the students, with the community experts providing information to support our learners' research needs.

The groundwork was already in place to establish one curricular partnership. The grade level teachers currently held a small session each year with an expert from Fort Ticonderoga, but they had never considered using the experts as an active part of student inquiries. Together we altered our unit to coordinate the timing of the expert with the *investigate* stage of research. Creating this change allowed learners to use the information presented by the expert to support their research.

Next, a follow-up curricular partnership, with a second community expert, was established. It was designed to help fill any knowledge gaps that still existed after students

WONDER
- Activate thinking
- Generate curiosity
- Build background knowledge
- Tap prior knowledge
- Frame questions for investigation
- Identify purpose for using information

Adapted from WSWHE BOCES

INVESTIGATE
- Manage search process:
  locate, gather, select, & analyze information
- Construct meaning from text
- Note-take and paraphrase
- Determine relationship between ideas

Adapted from WSWHE BOCES

SYNTHESIZE
- Use facts to build meaning
- Make connections between ideas and
  determine relationships
- Determine important and main ideas
- Draw conclusions
- Identify whether more information is needed
  or if new questions need to be answered
- Design & create a product that conveys new
  understanding

Adapted from WSWHE BOCES

EXPRESS
- Communicate and share new knowledge
- Select appropriate format and tool that best suits
  presenter & audience
- Self assess & revise product based on audience
  feedback

Adapted from WSWHE BOCES

Figure 1.3 WISER Model of Inquiry

Inquiry Planning Template

Theme/Project Title:
Content/ Standards:
Essential Question:
Students will know or will be able to:
Resources:
Knowledge Product:

Step	Activity/Task	Who	Prep Work
	Hook:		
	Wonder:		
	Investigate:		
	Synthesize:		
	Express:		

Figure 1.4 Inquiry Unit Blueprint

Table 1.3 Example American Revolution Social Studies Blueprint

Unit of Study		
Compelling Question (Essential Question)	"How can you help me construct a knowledge product to teach next year's fourth graders about the role New York State and New Yorkers played in the American Revolution?"	
SS Framework Key Idea(s) & AASL Standards for Learners	4.3 COLONIAL AND REVOLUTIONARY PERIOD IN NEW YORK: European exploration led to the colonization of the region that became New York State. Beginning in the early 1600s, colonial New York was home to people from many different countries. Colonial New York was important during the Revolutionary Period. (Standards: 1, 3, 4; Themes: MOV, TCC, GEO, SOC, GOV) *AASL Standards for Learners*: I.A.1., I.A.2., I.B.1., I.B.2., I.B.3., I.C.3., I.C.4., I.D.1., I.D.2., I.D.3., II.A.1., II.B.1., III.A.1., III.A.2., III.A.3., III.B.1., III.B.2., III.C.1., III.C.2., III.D.1., III.D.2., IV.A.1., IV.A.2., IV.A.3., IV.B.1., IV.B.2., IV.B.4., IV.D.1., IV.D.2., V.A.3., V.C.1., V.C.2., V.C.3., V.D.1., V.D.3., VI.A.1., VI.A.2., VI.B.1., VI.B.2., VI.B.3., VI.C.1., VI.C.2., VI.D.1., VI.D.2.	
Stimulus for Staging the Question (Maps, charts, images, etc.)	Share these three images of stressed people: This is what Mrs. Crossman looked like the past two weeks, because I have been trying to find resources for you on New York State and the American Revolution and I am getting great information for high-school and college students to use but nothing at your reading level. So I looked like these three women, until I got an idea. We need to create a book for fourth graders so that they have resources to learn all about the role of New York State and New Yorkers during the American Revolution. Then I thought that the best people to write that book would be fourth graders. So, you guys are going to help me create a resource for next year's fourth graders.	
Supporting Question 1 (Wonder)	Supporting Question 2 (Investigate-synthesize-investigate-synthesize)	Supporting Question 3 (Synthesize)
Conceptual Understanding:	Conceptual Understanding:	Conceptual Understanding:
4.3d Growing conflicts between England and the 13 colonies over issues of political and economic rights led to the American Revolution. New York played a significant role during the Revolution, in part due to its geographic location.	4.3d Growing conflicts between England and the 13 colonies over issues of political and economic rights led to the American Revolution. New York played a significant role during the Revolution, in part due to its geographic location.	4.3d Growing conflicts between England and the 13 colonies over issues of political and economic rights led to the American Revolution. New York played a significant role during the Revolution, in part due to its geographic location.
Question:	Question:	Question:
If we were going to make a book on the role of New York and New Yorkers in the	Where are we going to find our information (especially since Mrs. Crossman already	How can we use the information we gathered to create our own unique digital

Unit of Study		

American Revolution, what information would we need to include in that book? (Padlet activity)
• Who lived in New York (groups of people), and what were their role?
• What was life like for New Yorkers, in and out of the war?
• Were there any battles, and where were they located? What was the result?
• What circumstances existed to cause battles?
How can we use our questions to create chapters for our book?
• Create a row for each potential chapter based on answers to "What should go in our book?"
• Under each of the chapter topics, students will generate questions they will need to know the answers to in order to write a chapter about that topic.
	had trouble finding resources that were at a fourth-grade reading level)?
	• Experts
	• Maps
	• Primary Sources: art, artifacts, journals, graphs
		eBooks to share with next year's fourth graders?
		  ○ Book Creator
		    i. Make a page for each chapter.

Formative Performance Task	Formative Performance Task	Formative Performance Task
Practices: 4.A.1. Develop questions about NYS and its history & geography.	Practices: 4.A.2. Recognize, use, and analyze different forms of evidence used to make meaning in social studies (including sources such as art and photographs, artifacts, oral histories, maps, and graphs).	Practices: 4.A.2. Recognize, use, and analyze different forms of evidence used to make meaning in social studies (including sources such as art and photographs, artifacts, oral histories, maps, and graphs). 4.A.3. Identify and explain creation and/or authorship, purpose, and format for evidence; where appropriate, identify point of view.
Activity: Whole group: Develop what sections we would need in our book. Break into small groups with teacher leaders. We will develop questions in our groups	Activities: • Day 1: Generate a list of potential experts in our community who can help us learn more about life as a New Yorker during the	Activities: • Focus on one chapter at a time. Each day teach students about different digital and media literacy skills.

(*Continued*)

Table 1.3 (Continued)

Unit of Study		

to answer for each section in our book. Fill out the graphic organizer with our "wonder" questions.	American Revolution and experts who might be able to help us learn about the battles fought in New York. Guiding kids toward:
	  ○ Fort Ticonderoga experts
	  ○ Saratoga Battlefield experts
	• Develop a plan for taking notes:
	  ○ Digital tools—Notes App., Noteabiliy, Popplet
	  ○ Physical graphic organizer
	• Day 2: Expert from Fort Ticonderoga will share about New Yorkers and each group's role as soldiers.
	• Day 3: Reflect on information as a group, refer to questions on Padlet that we received information on, and identify what information we still need. Develop gaps in knowledge, and prepare notes for next expert. Use note evaluation form.
	• Day 4: Expert from Saratoga Battlefield
	  ○ Reflect on information as a group, refer to questions on Padlet that we received information on, and identify what information we still need. Develop gaps in knowledge.
	• Day 5: Research unanswered questions using *History Happened Here: The American Revolution in New York State* by New York Historical Society.
		○ Chapter 1: Organizational layout of information—consistency (font colors, sizing, and spacing)
		○ Chapter 2: Digital text features—adding images
		  ▪ Legal images
		  ▪ Citations
		  ▪ Labeling images
		○ Chapter 3: Video
		  ▪ Sharing knowledge by explaining information through a recorded video
		• Independently create books, by adding information, reflecting, and responding on feedback to improve work.

Featured Source(s)	Featured Source(s)	Featured Source(s)
Nearpod: https://share. nearpod.com/jANjYJY84L Add questions to Padlet Teacher #1 Teacher #2 Teacher #3	Expert from Fort Ticonderoga Expert from Saratoga Battlefield—Note-taking sheet Note evaluation form *History Happened Here: The American Revolution in New York State* by New York Historical Society (editor)	Book Creator

Unit of Study		
Formative Assessment	Formative Assessment	Formative Assessment
Padlet activities	Notes, shared Padlet, note evaluation form	Book Creator chapters
Summative Performance Task (Express)	Students will share books with class and complete Reflection Cards.	
Taking Informed Action (Express)	Books will be added to a class website to share with next year's fourth graders.	

synthesized their notes from the first round of investigation. This is no easy task for anyone, let alone a young researcher. However, this clearly put the *re* in *research*. It required students to be persistent by going through the inquiry cycle one more time and searching again, providing an important lifelong skill.

Leading up to the delivery of this unit, the teachers took several weeks to build students' background knowledge on colonization in New York State and the events prior to the American Revolution, providing a solid foundation to launch the inquiry unit. We established a teaching schedule that allowed me to work in each of the three classrooms, throughout a two-week time period. This typically entails pushing into the classrooms for back-to-back forty-five-minute sessions. At the start of the unit, I set the stage by creating a *need* for the work that lay ahead. Presenting a challenge through an essential question that asked "How can you help me construct a knowledge product to teach next year's fourth graders about the role New York State and New Yorkers played in the American Revolution?" proved to be an energizing tactic.

When structuring the delivery of the essential question and work of the inquiry, I wanted to create an engaging and collaborative work environment, subsequently leading toward the use of the digital app Nearpod. This innovative tool helps to improve the delivery of instruction. It has an interactive platform that can be used on any device. The tool allows for student participation and gives students a voice through simple-to-set-up lessons. Through utilization of this tool, I was able to keep students on task, while sharing all my resources from one platform. I embedded a collaborative Padlet (digital tool) activity within my Nearpod lessons that activated thinking, curiosity, and problem-solving strategies. These activities challenged learners to think about what information we needed to know about New Yorkers and New York State during the American Revolution.

Learners also developed a comprehensive list of questions that covered a broad range of topics within the American Revolution. However, we needed to stop and pause. We knew our purpose for gathering the information, but we still hadn't established how we were going to share our information. Collectively we agreed that the best way to share the information was through the creation of an eBook. All our students have iPads, making this a logical and appropriate choice. They were also comfortable with using Book Creator, which is a free application that can be used to create eBooks on iPads, Chromebooks, and the web.

Determining the format for sharing our information allowed us to move forward with organizing our questions in a more meaningful way. We began grouping all of our questions that were similar together in one column on our *Padlet*. In the end we had several columns of questions. The students were arranged in groups to coincide with the number of columns. Each diverse group of learners was tasked with creating a name for their column that would ultimately be the name of our chapter.

It was impressive to see the organizational structure we had cocreated among the class. Once we had our structure for gathering information, we collectively problem-solved how and where we could acquire our information. I shared with students that it was difficult to find resources within our databases on the American Revolution specific to the questions that they asked on New York State. Together, learners problem-solved and developed a list of potential sources, one of which was to ask an expert. This suggestion opened conversation to potential experts within our community who might be able to help us retrieve valuable information to answer our research questions.

The grade level teachers established a curricular partnership with an expert from Fort Ticonderoga who was extremely knowledgeable about the soldiers of the American Revolutionary War while I established a curricular partnership with an expert on the battles of the American Revolutionary War from Saratoga National Historical Park. When scheduling these curricular partnerships, we staggered their visits to strategically allow students time to synthesize the information they had gathered from the first partnership and then determine whether they still had gaps in their knowledge. This drew on the learning skills we were trying to develop and gave them the experience of participating in a sustained inquiry where they needed to revisit the initial stages in the inquiry process iteratively before they were ready to express their information. It required the student learners to go back and search for new information; in other words, they needed to "re" search. This not only helped them to recognize that learning is a cyclical process but allowed them to actually engage in the process, giving them the opportunity to gain deeper understandings and continually develop questions and pursue knowledge.

Learners and classroom teachers were accustomed to guest speakers visiting our school, but this experience would prove to be different. It was a learner-centered experience that grew from the needs of the learners and their voice. During the learning experience, the students were actively engaged. They were empowered to seek answers to their questions and gather information that they would later use to apply to their knowledge products. Throughout the experience, learners were participating in conversations with curricular partners, both critically thinking and preparing follow-up questions to expert responses. These curricular partnerships were extremely successful because of the learner-centered nature of the experience.

As a class we collaboratively shared the information we learned from our community partners by recording the answers to our questions on our *Padlet* notecards. This allowed learners to contribute to shared research within our classroom learning community, helping others to acquire valuable information that they may have overlooked during the presentation. In some situations, there were still areas where we lacked information. In this case, students used specific text resources that we had available on specific elements of their research.

Once we had the questions filled in on our virtual notecards with information from our research, it was time for students to begin independently designing and creating their own knowledge products. For several days, students spent time synthesizing their information and embedding their newly formed knowledge into an eBook. Each time students started a new chapter, I would take time to focus on media and digital literacy skills, teaching learners to recognize how to share information effectively through media. I placed value on using consistent structure, font, and color choices within the pages of their eBooks and discussed the need to be conscientious and purposeful in the selection of images. I also taught students that it is pertinent to keep their audience in mind when creating knowledge products by ensuring that they are valuable to the users' needs. Additionally, I took time each day to present a minilesson on the safe, legal, and ethical use of information during the creation and sharing of their knowledge products. By integrating these skills at meaningful and appropriate times, the learning became relevant and purposeful for the students.

Throughout the construction of the learners' knowledge products, the teachers and I visited with each of the students, monitoring their progress and providing feedback to help them improve their work and develop their growth mindset. Once the eBooks were complete, students shared their products with the class. This was a time for celebration and reflection. Students displayed their work on the classroom interactive board, highlighting both their information and text features and structures. During this time, classmates, the teacher, and I asked questions, recognized student successes, and made suggestions for improvement. Additionally, both the student and I filled out reflection cards (see Table 1.4) as a tool to analyze and evaluate the student work. This step allowed the student to deliberately identify areas of improvement that would pave the success of future work, making reflection a catalyst for growth.

Table 1.4 Example Reflection Card

Name:_____	
Attribute	**Librarian Feedback**
You included research that supported facts in each of your chapters.	
The main idea is clearly presented in each of your chapters.	
Your book was organized in a clear and easy-to-read format.	
Your book is visually appealing (it is not distracting to the reader or too plain).	
Your book is free of spelling and grammar errors.	
You included accurate citations when necessary.	

Name:_____	
Attribute	**Student Reflection**
I included research that supported facts in each of my chapters.	
The main idea is clearly presented in each of my chapters.	
My book was organized in a clear and easy-to-read format.	
My book is visually appealing (it is not distracting to the reader or too plain).	
My book is free of spelling and grammar errors.	
I included accurate citations when necessary.	

Sharing and reflection are two significant stages in the inquiry process that cannot be overlooked. Unfortunately, it is too often an area where I see inquiry units fall short. Teachers feel rushed to wrap up units and move on. If we deprive our learners of the opportunity to share, then we are taking away the one thing that they worked for the entire unit. This time places value and gives purpose to the student work. We must honor this time and ensure to give it the proper attention it deserves; otherwise, students will be reluctant to continue to invest in work that we deem as meaningful. Take time to celebrate their success. This is their moment . . . let them shine!

Suggested Modifications

- Due to the nature of schedules, it can be difficult to be involved in each stage of the inquiry process. Start by focusing on the stage of the inquiry process that the curricular partnership is supporting as your priority. Then, if time allows, identify areas of instructional needs within your curriculum, and select those areas within the inquiry process that can be used to address those needs.
- If you do not have the luxury of a flexible schedule, there can be other creative ways to make this learning experience happen. Although the instructional component is most meaningful when integrated into the content area curriculum, it can also be delivered effectively within a fixed library time. However, under these circumstances, it is essential that units are strategically planned and delivered at the appropriate times, allowing the learning experience to flow in a natural progression. Clear dates must be established between the classroom teacher and the librarian. Student work done within the library can carry over to the classroom (and vice versa), making it possible to continue with the next portion of the lesson. Digital platforms such as *Google Classroom* and *Nearpod* can help facilitate a successful learning experience. These platforms will make it easier to communicate and share resources and student work.
- This learning experience can take place in multiple locations. To help maximize the use of your time at the elementary level, consider implementing the delivery of instruction in a large space to accommodate an entire grade level, not simply one class at a time. Then, when it becomes time to work, classes can disperse back to their rooms, while you roam between classrooms to provide support and feedback.
- At the middle- and high-school level, your schedule is often more flexible, providing time to push into classrooms during scheduled periods. However, when curricular partners are invited to support student research, consider hosting a one-time session in the library on an assembly schedule.
- These particular partnerships are contingent upon working with an instructional partner to support content curriculum. It takes time to develop integrated inquiry-based learning experiences to the level of the example experience provided earlier. However, focusing on the partnership portion of the inquiry can and should be your focus.
- If being part of committee conversations and coplanning experiences are not leading to opportunities to integrate curricular partnerships into content-based learning experiences, I suggest reviewing the district's mission, vision, and values to build a case for these partnerships. Extract any part of the those statements that support these type of learning experiences and strategically share your plan for helping to meet your district goals with your administration. This conversation should be followed up with ideas for ways your administration could support you in creating these partnerships at your school.
- Curricular partnerships do not need to be restricted to social studies curriculum. There are opportunities within each content area. Sometimes, it can be easier to start by looking at the resources of expertise that exist in your community and then seeing what curriculum they could support.

- Throughout the learning experience, I utilized a rich amount of digital resources, all of which were free digital tools that can be used on any type of device. These experiences are not restricted to these specific tools, and oftentimes, the suggested activities can be carried out without the use of technology. However, I would caution that purposeful use of integrated technology and instruction is the best practice for teaching technology skills and resources. If you were to remove one of the tools and replace it with another tool or activity, be certain to consider the skills that were being addressed through the means of the tools. See Table 1.5 for suggested alternative tools.

Table 1.5 Alternative Digital Tool Options

Tool	Needs & Skills	Alternative Tool(s) (with similar capabilities)
Nearpod	Collaborative, allows for student voice, requires participation, allows to share resources in one place, synchronized lessons	Google Classroom Seesaw
Padlet	Collaborative, allows for student voice, organized notecards	Pinup Lino NoodleTools EasyBib
Book Creator	Creativity; allows embedding of text, video, audio and images; ability to publish to an authentic audience	Little Bird Tales I-book Author

Resources

Digital Resources, Tools, and Links
Book Creator: https://bookcreator.com/
C3 Teachers Inquiry Design Model: http://www.c3teachers.org/ inquiry-design-model/ (C3 Teachers n.d.)
Nearpod: https://nearpod.com/
Padlet: https://padlet.com/

CURRICULUM-BASED LEARNING EXPERIENCE #2

Named Learning Experience
Lake Inquiry

Partnership
New York State Park Commission Director, New York State Park Commission Police Officer, Captain of Steamboat Company, Librarian

Future Ready Framework (refer to Figure 1.5)

AASL Standards
AASL Standards for Learners: I.A.1., I.A.2., I.B.1., I.B.2., I.B.3., I.C.3., I.C.4., I.D.1., I.D.2., I.D.3., I.D.4., II.D.1., II.D.2., II.D.3., III.A.1., III.A.2., III.B.2., III.C.2, III.D.1., III.D.2., IV.A.1., IV.A.2., IV.A.3., IV.B.1., IV.B.2., IV.B.4., IV.D.1., IV.D.2., V.A.3., V.C.1., V.C.2., V.D.1., V.D.3., VI.A.1.,VI.A.2.,

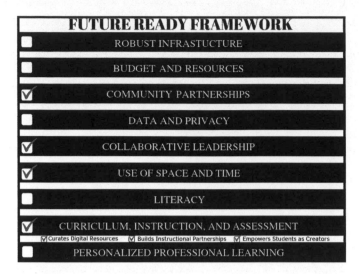

Figure 1.5

VI.B.1., VI.B.2., VI.B.3., VI.C.2., VI.D.1.
AASL Standards for School Librarians: I.A.1., I.A.2., I.B.1., I.B.2., I.B.3., I.C.1., I.C.2., I.D.1., I.D.3., II.A.1., II.D.1., II.D.2., II.D.3., III.A.1., III.A.2, III.A.3., III.B.2., III.C.1., III.C.2., III.D.1., III.D.2., IV.A.1., IV.A.2., IV.A.3, IV.B.1., IV.B.2., IV.B.4., IV.D.1., IV.D.2., V.A.3., V.C.1., V.C.2, V.D.1., V.D.3., VI.A.1., VI.A.2., VI.B.1., VI.B.3., VI.C.2., VI.D.1., VI.D.2.
AASL School Standards for School Libraries: I.A.1., I.A.2., I.C.1., I.D.2., II.A.1., II.A.2., II.A.3., II.B.3., II.C.1., II.D.2., III.A.1., III.A.2., III.B.1., III.B.2., III.C.1., III.C.2., III.C.3., III.D.1., III.D.2., IV.A.1., IV.A.3., IV.B.1., IV.B.2., IV.B.5., IV.D.3., V.A.1., V.B.1., V.B.3., V.C.1., V.C.2., V.D.1., V.D.2., V.D.3., VI.A.1, VI.A.2., VI.A.3., VI.C.1., VI.D.1., VI.D.2.

Experience Summary

There are learning experiences that can rely on both internal and external partnerships. Each of these partnerships is equally important, but support different stages within the inquiry process. I will feature a site-based learning experience within both this chapter and Chapter 4 for that reason. Within this chapter, I will strictly provide the basis for the unit and highlight a unique internal partnership created to support the investigation stage of our students' inquiry. In Chapter 4, I will provide an external partnership that was also utilized to make this inquiry-based learning experience possible.

Truly meaningful learning experiences have the learners' interest at the heart of their design. During this experience, second-grade students study one way the physical lake, located in our village, impacts our community. After engaging in a site-based learning experience at our community lake (Lake George) and developing questions about things that they were curious to learn more about, our students had established a need to investigate the answers to their questions.

When beginning the pursuit of their answers, they very quickly discovered that we do not have books and resources in our library about their areas of research specific to Lake George and the surrounding community. This became a window of opportunity to teach students about the different types of resources that exist for gathering information, such as community experts. It is worth noting that what made this learning experience so significant is that the students discovered the need for further resources on their own. By letting them discover that they have a need for different resources, they are motivated to discuss and identify other resources that exist.

Once I had a captive audience, one that had a need for information, I could begin to brainstorm different sources of information with them. Collaboratively students began to build off one another's ideas and generate a list of experts within the community who were knowledgeable about the lake and the community.

The students selected the types of experts (partners) from our community who could help us learn about the animals, safety, jobs, rules and laws, and entertainment and businesses on the lake. As the librarian, I researched community organizations in those fields through a basic internet search. I then reached out to the organizations, explaining our needs as learners, and inquired about seeking a potential partnership. The three organizations promptly replied to my request with a resounding *yes*, and we quickly established partnerships with a sergeant of the *Lake George Marine Patrol*, a captain at the *Lake George Steamboat Tour Company*, and the executive director at the *Lake George Park Commission*.

After sharing the list of curriculum partners with the classroom teachers, we created a list of potential dates and times for the experts to visit our school. We felt it was critical to the learning process to have all three curriculum partners visit our school at the same time. This provided the learners experience with making appropriate choices when selecting sources of information. Once these decisions were made, I shared the expectations and potential dates and times with the partners in a joint email. Together, we were able to settle on a one-hour visit on a select day. During that time, we would meet in the classroom (we have an open-classroom design with no walls), with one expert and teacher stationed in each room.

Prior to the experts' visit, I pushed into the students' classrooms and taught them how to take their current questions and turn them into higher-level questions. Each of the students' questions started as questions that elicited a *yes* or *no* response. This was the perfect opportunity to meet the students where they were at in their curriculum and embed *AASL Learner Standards*, which ask learners to develop questions about curricular topics (Standard I.A.1.).

I started by showing students a picture of my daughter that was featured in the local newspaper. I told them that they had ten questions, as a class, to try and figure out as much information as they could about the picture (of my daughter) that was in our local newspaper. Students asked questions like "Do you know her?" "Is she in Lake George?" "Is she running a race?" I then *shook things up a bit* and gave them ten more questions, but this time I presented them with the *Wonder Grid* (see Table 1.6) to give them options for

Table 1.6   Wonder Grid

Who	When	Why	What
Which	Where	How	Identify
Define	Would	Could	Should
Describe	Predict	Compare	Explain

Adapted from the chart created by Laurie Alden, Library Media Specialist at Harrison Avenue School District, South Glens Falls, New York.

deeper question starters. After just one question, they were able to gain more information than they had with any one of their previous ten questions. After several rounds of practice using the *Wonder Grid*, students were able to modify their original question with excellent starter questions, such as *describe* and *explain*.

After students learned how to generate good questions for soliciting rich information, they worked to develop their own quality questions for their research. Once students developed their questions, they received instructional feedback from the classroom teacher or me and worked diligently to improve their questions. While students were developing good questions, the teachers and I would coach students through the questioning process. It was important throughout the process that we held true to our job as coaches and ensured that the students were doing the work, not us. When a student would create a question that we knew would not solicit enough information, we would ask them what the possible responses would be to their question, often getting the student to realize that either they didn't ask a question that was deep enough or they asked a question that would not help them answer the essential question. We would then refer them back to the *Wonder Grid* to help them while working on developing a stronger question. This activity challenged students to critically think about what it is that they needed to know and how they could refine their questions so that it would elicit information that would help them answer the essential question. This was a critical skill in the learning process, and it should be consistently practiced throughout curricular work.

We followed up our questioning activity with transferring our questions to a graphic organizer (see Figure 1.7) that students could use to take notes while the experts visited the classrooms. These organizers had a place for students to record the answers to their questions and gather additional supporting facts for their research. We discussed the roles of each of the experts, when the experts came. Students analyzed their topics, and, with the support of the teachers and me, they identified the expert who would be the best source of information for their research. I had instructed the curricular partners ahead of time to provide the students with a brief introduction followed by an open invitation to use them as a resource. I made the deliberate statement that the experts are physically in front of them to help them with their research project and they are always available as resources within the community as well. See Figure 1.6 for an additional tip.

Students peppered the experts with questions for forty-five minutes. One teacher was assigned to each group during this time. The teachers and I filled the role of coach during this process by slowing the pace of discussion so students could record the wealth of information that was shared with them on their graphic organizer (see Figure 1.8 and 1.9). We also called for time-out when students needed a

IT IS EXTREMELY HELPFUL TO RECORD WORK SESSIONS WITH COMMUNITY PARTNERS. STUDENTS WILL FIND THEM BENEFICIAL TO REFER BACK TO IN THE FOLLOWING DAYS AFTER THEIR VISIT.

Figure 1.6

Name:_____

Wonder Question:

Facts

Figure 1.7   Wonder Question

break to refocus and reflect. We spent time walking around and assessing the students' graphic organizers and made sure everyone had what they needed before the experts left. In several cases, this required students to repeat questions that had already been answered.

Post community partner visit, students spent time distinguishing which facts supported their essential question. Students then transferred their facts to a graphic organizer (see Figure 1.9) with a preset topic sentence. This allowed them the freedom to synthesize their notes in a clear and concise format. They analyzed which facts they would use to support the topic sentence and what information they would still need. After transferring their facts to their organizer, many students also recognized that they didn't have enough supporting facts. As a class we built an entire discussion around where we would find remaining supporting facts for our research. Some students acknowledged the fact that we could contact our community partners and ask them follow-up questions, but most of the students verbalized the need to use websites. As the librarian, I followed up this discussion with a lesson on keyword searching and a structured search process, where students researched their topics with the support of classroom teachers and me.

After students had all their facts, they synthesized their information by transferring their facts into statements that would support their topic sentence (_____ is important to the lake and the community). Again, the classroom teachers and I worked individually with each student, guiding them as they synthesized their notes and created supporting statements.

Once the students had completed their graphic organizers, students were motivated to begin creating their knowledge products. Each year this inquiry is offered, students chose to make a different knowledge product. Some years students chose to make eBooks, other years students chose to make posters, and some years they chose to do both. Once the knowledge products are created, they are shared with our community partners and displayed in their places of work. In addition, the final knowledge products are also printed and shared in the library. Having an authentic audience places value on the student work and gives students a sense of purpose.

Suggested Modifications
- When looking at this inquiry unit, there are a series of valuable lessons structured before and after the partnership. For librarians working on a fixed schedule in an elementary school, start by identifying lessons that can be delivered during scheduled library time with each class. Sequentially deliver these lessons so that the appropriate skills are addressed and work is completed in a logical order.
- If your library operates on a fixed schedule, it is important that the work between the curriculum partner, your instructional partner, and yourself is still completed together at the appropriate stage of the inquiry process, and not in isolation. Therefore, it is important to seek out time for all classes to take part in the active research session with the curriculum partners. A great place to house this partnership session is in the library, depending on the space. If the library is not conducive, consider a large instructional space within your building.
- If you are in a middle-school or high-school setting, it might be most effective to deliver instruction and the curriculum partnerships during class time. However, if the curriculum partners are not available to work within the time frame of all your classes, it might be best to try and develop a one-shot class period where all students can meet with experts.
- If your students do not have iPads, this work can be carried out on computers.
- If time does not allow for the extensive research within the inquiry, consider having students work within groups based on learner interest.

Name:_____

+--+
| Question #1: |
| |
| _____ |
| |
| _____ |
| |
+--+

+--+
| Facts: |
| |
| |
| |
| |
| |
| |
| |
+--+

+--+
| Statement:_____|
| |
| _____ |
| |
| _____ |
| |
| _____ |
| |
| _____ |
| |
+--+

Figure 1.8 Lake Inquiry Graphic Organizer

Name: _____

Essential Question: Why is/are _____ important to the lake and community?

Fact:	Statement: _____
	_____
	_____
	_____

Fact:	Statement: _____
	_____
	_____
	_____

Fact:	Statement: _____
	_____
	_____
	_____

Fact:	Statement: _____
	_____
	_____
	_____

_____ is/are important to the lake and community

because _____.

Figure 1.9

- When looking for an instructional partnership for this work, consider someone whom you can have a sustained inquiry with since this is a two-part experience (the other part is explained in Chapter 4) that will require a solid collaborative working relationship. Additionally, instead of focusing on all classrooms at a grade level, focus on working with one class or section of a class. After delivering the experience for one year on a smaller scale, it will be easier to manage more classes. Additionally, other instructional partners will be more empowered to collaborate once they witness the success of another class.

- It is ideal to find several curriculum partners who can meet a range of learner needs. However, if you can't locate multiple partnerships, locating a partner who has a broad range of knowledge on the topic will be needed. Under these circumstances, it will be beneficial to spend extra time preparing the curriculum partner. By sharing student-generated questions prior to their visit, the research session will be more successful for the expert and the learners.

- Consider bringing in several curricular partners, but not on the same day or time. It can be much easier to facilitate these learning experiences when you aren't trying to manage several schedules that need to connect on the same day and same time.

- If your students don't require the use of paper graphic organizers for taking notes and have the ability to take notes on a device, there are several great digital tool options (refer to Table 1.7).

Table 1.7

Digital Tool	Platform
Notability	iPad, iPhone, iPod Touch, Mac
Notes	iPad, iPhone, iPod Touch, Mac
Google Keep	Android, Chromebook
Evernote	Android, iPad, iPhone, iPod Touch, Kindle Fire, Nook HD, Chromebook, Windows Phone, Apps for Windows
Google Docs	Website
EasyBib (notecards)	Website
NoodleTools (notecards)	Website
Skitch	iPad, iPhone, iPod Touch

Resources

Digital Resources, Tools, and Links
Lake Inquiry Question Record Sheet: http://bit.ly/InquiryQuestionsrecord
Lake Inquiry Notes Graphic Organizer: http://bit.ly/InquirynotesGO
Lake Inquiry Unit: http://bit.ly/LakeInquiry

GROW

Grow your library program by . . .

1. Teaming up with a teacher or grade level to develop an inquiry-based learning experience that is supported by a curriculum partnership.

> 2. Determining a need in your curriculum and inquiry unit that can be supported by local or global experts.
> 3. Establishing a connection with an expert(s) and coordinating a learning partnership where together you deliver an innovative learning experience to learners.

ACTION PLAN

Setting the Stage

Approach this learning experience by determining the following criteria for your work (refer to Table 1.8):

Table 1.8

Setting the Stage		
Goals	*Key Players*	*Groundwork*
• What content standards are you hoping to address? • What *AASL Standards* are you hoping to address? • What Future Ready Principles are you trying to address?	• Who is your audience (specific classroom or grade level)? • Who will be your instructional partner(s)?	• What content area are you going to focus on? • How will you learn the standards? • How will you become part of curricular conversations? • In what ways can you lead? • What instructional method are you going to use for designing the learning experience?

Establishing the Partnership

Use the bullets featured in each section of Table 1.9 to guide you in your actions toward developing a community partnership.

Table 1.9

Who	• Determine how many curriculum partners are needed for the learning experience. • Seek curriculum partner(s) within the community who can fill a content-specific need within the desired stage of inquiry. • Select a curriculum partner who is engaging. • Ensure that the curriculum partner(s) is capable of working with the needs and abilities of the student audience.
What	• Identify what it is that you need the curriculum partner to do and communicate that to them. • Distinguish what it is the curriculum partner needs to know prior to agreeing to the partnership and the established visit, and communicate that to them. • Determine any needs the curriculum partner(s) may have.

How	• Decide if learners or the teachers are going to select the curriculum partners or type of partner. • Research potential partners. • Seek potential partnerships through personal and professional networks. • Determine the best way to reach out to curriculum partners (email, letter, phone, website contact form, etc.). • Contact potential partner with details about learning experience and expectations of curriculum partnership.
Where	When determining the most conducive learning environment consider . . . • Size of the group • Access to resources (technology, books, tables, etc.) • Work of the learners (interactive, stationary work, small group, large group).
When	• Identify at what stage in the inquiry process that the partnership is needed. • Collaborate with classroom teachers to determine when the best opportunities are for the learning experience with the curriculum partner. • Communicate preferred days and times for the curriculum partner to work with the students. Offer several options, and be flexible when possible.

Delivering the Learning Experience

Table 1.10 provides an outline of the suggested steps you can take when delivering a curriculum-based learning experience with the support of community partnerships.

Table 1.10

Steps to Developing Learning Experiences with Curriculum Partnerships
1. Be a leader!
2. Choose a curriculum area to build an inquiry-based learning experience.
3. Learn the standards and curriculum for that content area.
4. Join curricular conversations for that content area by inviting yourself to committee meetings, where curriculum is being discussed.
5. Lead or colead professional learning opportunities.
6. Highlight potential inquiry-based learning experiences in collaboration with curriculum partnerships.
7. Collaborate with teachers on creating an inquiry-based learning experience that is supported by curriculum partnerships.
8. Determine the curricular needs of the inquiry-based learning experience.
9. Identify what stage of the inquiry process a curriculum partner(s) is needed.
10. Seek curriculum partnerships that can meet the needs of the inquiry-based learning experience.
11. Establish curriculum partnerships (time, date, method of delivery, expectations, etc.).
12. Deliver unit as planned out in the blueprint, making adjustments where necessary.
13. Build in reflection time for both students and instructional partners.

2

Literacy Partnerships

LEARN

What Are Literacy Partnerships?

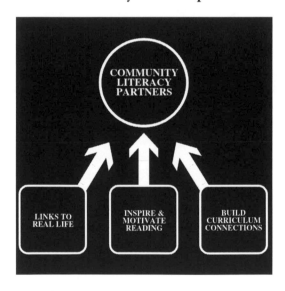

Figure 2.1

When community members and the librarian work together to create an inviting literacy-based learning experience, a powerful partnership is formed as represented in Figure 2.1. These partnerships and their influential experiences encourage and nourish a student's love of reading. Literacy partners are used as motivational tools and resources for generating positive and memorable experiences with literature. These partners are considered resources based on their knowledge and skills, experiences, or product they provide. These partnerships occur within the library at various times of the year, separate from classroom curricular experiences.

Why Do They Matter?

Our passion for literacy is reflected in the experiences that we create. We have the ability to set the tone, attitudes, and perceptions associated with reading and other future literacy-based activities. We cannot take this responsibility lightly. For far too many students, the thought of an additional literary experience at school is intimidating and daunting, especially for our most vulnerable readers. Reading does not come naturally for so many and is often laborious. I know this feeling all too well, being a child who was a reluctant reader myself. I also know from experience that the only way to get better at reading is to read more. This here presents a challenge. How can we get students to partake in something that isn't fun for them? The answer is . . . make it fun!

Literacy partnerships make reading fun. They create nonthreatening learning experiences by placing student joy at the core of the development. When designing these partnerships and experiences, two questions are at the center of every decision: (1) Will the students be engaged? (2) Will the students have fun? When experiences are approached in this way, students are compelled to join, and learning inherently falls into place.

How Do You Make Them Happen?

The key to a successful literacy learning experience is rooted within the partnership. Partners provide the grounds for fun and engaged learning. There are a couple of angles to consider when selecting partnerships, each resulting in ripe learning experiences:

- Will they have the time?
- Will they want to participate?
- Does anyone have a connection to a potential reader?
- Will this result in a "fun" connection?

Finding eminent partners to join in literacy-based learning experiences will consistently result in increased participation. Sometimes the partner themselves is not the attraction, but the activities that they afford are. These partnerships equally elicit strong participation.

Approaching partnerships from the angle of choosing community partners to lead activities draws the focus on the partner and disguises the intentional purpose of generating a love of literacy. This is not to diminish the value of literacy experiences; it's actually quite the opposite. It's to attract reluctant participants and allow them to choose to become involved and discover that reading can be enjoyable.

Seeking distinguished partners may seem like a challenge at first, but remember our standards for eminent figures are much different than our students'. If you have ever been spotted in the grocery store by a student, you know what I mean when I say that we have *celebrity status* in their eyes. Once you begin to shift your paradigm, you will start to develop an extensive list of distinguished figures in your community who can fill this role. For a list of potential partners, refer to Table 2.1.

Developing promising ideas into viable learning experiences sometimes takes the wisdom to seek partners who have capabilities that you don't. These partners help to move your innovative ideas forward through their resources: knowledge and skills, experiences, or product. When designing literacy learning experiences, don't limit yourself to what you can solely provide; instead think about the opportunities that you want to provide, and identify partners who can make them possible. Refer to sample suggestions in Table 2.2.

Table 2.1

Potential Literacy Partners
Dentist
Business owners
Bakers
Athletes
Meteorologists
Newcasters
Veterinarians
Public officials
Mascots
Rangers
Ice cream shops
Law enforcement
Animals
Members of the military
Farmers
Auto-body professionals

Table 2.2

Partnership	Learning Opportunity	Resource
Local business	Provide resources for a literacy event (refreshments, books, giveaways, etc.).	Product
Engineer	Teach students how to build and design structures to meet the needs of characters in books.	Knowledge and skills
Olympian	Share personal experiences of how reading helped them to become one of the best athletes in the world.	Experience

Regardless of how a partnership is selected, literacy experiences should create a wave of enthusiasm. These experiences play a pivotal role in shaping the mindset of young readers. We want readers of all abilities to feel welcome and equally as excited to participate. These experiences should not be built around working on specific reading strategies or improving specific skills; rather, the focus should be on championing reading as a fun and enjoyable activity. When designing these experiences through community partnerships, start by building relationships with students and discovering what excites and motivates them. Understandings gained from successful relationships with students will give you the fuel you need to ignite a powerful learning experience. They will lead you toward a path of favorable partnerships. A perfect example of this is when I heard students talking about the video game *Zelda* in the library. I had never heard of it, not being a gamer myself, but I knew that we had the series of *Zelda* graphic novels by Akira Himekawa in the library. I began to learn a little more about the game from my students and then reached out to one of the technology specialists in my building who was a gamer. I asked him if he would be willing to partner with me to offer a literacy experience for these boys and all other interested students in the building. This partnership led to an engaging and successful learning experiences where students read the book *The Legend of Zelda: Ocarina of Time* and then played the Zelda video game on the big-screen television in the library with our technology specialist.

By listening to and learning about the students' interests, I was able to generate a connected experience with a partner whose resources and skills stretched beyond my capabilities. This partnership provided the opportunity for several reluctant readers to engage in a fun and memorable literacy learning experience. Imagine the impact we can have on students' perceptions of reading if we begin to approach literary experiences in this way. It could be life changing for so many students.

Once you have built strong partnerships that were influenced by students' likes and interests, you can move forward with planning the literacy partnership–based learning experience. I recognize that this won't be easy and that innovation can be untidy. I challenge you not to succumb to the roadblocks; be an innovator, and get creative.

Scheduling is typically the most common obstacle for everyone. Many of us don't have extra time during the school day and don't have access to students outside of their scheduled class times. These are real legitimate concerns but are not excuses worthy of denying students these experiences. Consider using lunch periods (yes, at the elementary level too), study halls, summer, evening, and after-school hours. Keep in mind that you also don't need to be present for all opportunities that involve partnerships; you simply need to provide the time, space, and activities. Perhaps, you might also consider giving up something old, which could free up time to replace it with something new and innovative. This open and flexible mindset will be imperative while planning all the fine details such as time, location, and resources. If you choose not to embrace this mindset, you will struggle to have a successful literacy experience come to life. Be creative. Be persistent. Be an innovator!

Once you have established an innovative literacy-based learning experience through a connected partnership, it is time to market the experience. When marketing, always consider your audience and what attracts them. This should be easy because a great deal of thought was put forth in finding partnerships that would be attractive to the students. The key is to take those appealing features and sell them to your desired audience through multiple modes. For a list of ideas, see Table 2.3.

Table 2.3

Mode	Digital Tool
Social media	Facebook, Twitter, Instagram, Snapchat
Video	Animoto, iMovie, Adobe Spark Video, Powtoons, DoInk
Posters	Canva, Smore, Easily, Adobe Spark

Invest time and thought into the marketing and rollout of your learning experiences; otherwise, your good intentions and ideas will fall short of success. Students will not attend even the best-designed learning experiences if they don't know about them or if they don't see the value it will bring to them. Setting aside time during a school day or during a scheduled class period to launch the fun and exciting details of a learning experience will result in increased participation. Relying solely on informational flyers to market your learning experience will not be fruitful. Take the extra time to build students' understanding and anticipation of the experience through a lively rollout.

The most exciting part of any learning experience is the delivery. To ensure a successful experience, be as prepared as possible. Spend time anticipating the needs that might occur, and properly prepare for them. You don't want to be running around missing out on the experience while it is happening. You are the face of the experience. You should be fostering a love of literacy and building relationships during the learning experience, not be in the back office looking for supplies and resources.

Finally, take time to celebrate the successes of your learning experiences once they are over. Plaster images on your webpage, social media, and hallway bulletin boards, recognizing both the experience and the supporting partner(s). These images will continue to foster the positive feeling we want students to associate with reading. Additionally, this will also help to publicize the successful experiences and progressive practices taking place in your library to all school and community stakeholders.

LEAP

Leap (step) forward by . . .

1. Creating a list of potential literacy partners whose knowledge and skills, experiences, or products can be used to motivate readers to partake in a fun and engaging literacy-based learning experience.
2. Listening to your students and identify potentially engaging partnerships that can meet their needs and interests.
3. Brainstorming existing literacy experiences that you could support and improve through literacy partnerships.

LITERACY LEARNING EXPERIENCE #1

Named Learning Experience
Sip and Read

Partnership
Local Café, Parents, Librarian

Future Ready Framework (refer to Figure 2.2)

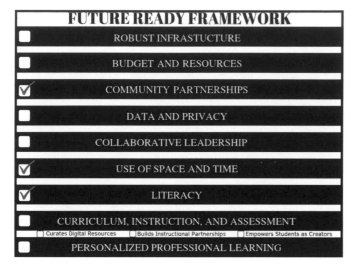

Figure 2.2

AASL Standards

AASL Standards for Learners: V.A.1.

AASL Standards for School Librarians: V.A.1.

AASL School Standards for School Libraries: II.D.2., II.D.3., V.B.3., V.C.2., V.D.2.

Experience Summary

Each year our school celebrates Parents as Reading Partners (PARP) during the month of March. This is a program in which students are required to read each night with their families and track their time spent reading. Our reading department does a fantastic job of partnering with outside groups to kick off the PARP program with an entertaining opening ceremony built around the yearly PARP theme. They also reward students throughout the process to keep them focused and motivated. Each year the program is carried out with successfully high participation.

As a supportive colleague and a promoter of literacy, I wanted to help make this a memorable experience for our students and families. I know on a personal level how difficult it can be to find uninterrupted and stress-free time to read with your children each night. Between nightly sporting events, family obligations, and backpacks full of homework, children and families are overloaded, creating the perfect storm for an unenjoyable nightly reading experience. This reality haunted me a bit. Despite our positive intentions, might we be creating unhappy experiences with reading rather than enjoyable ones? This question spurred me into action. I decided to create the conditions for a positive literacy experience that would support our PARP program and the participating families. With parent help and a key community partnership, I was able to host a successful "Sip and Read" event in the library.

Ironically, the parents planted the seed for this program. Through our *Facebook* page, parents shared an interest in an evening event in the library. I took this idea and coupled it with the desire to support our school's PARP program. Out of it grew a new and improved learning experience that supported a need. I partnered with a local café to build an inviting experience in the library, where families could meet their required nightly minutes for reading in a relaxing and stress-free environment.

There were many details that went into making this experience just as I had envisioned it. In order to cultivate the warm and enjoyable feeling that I was aiming for, I needed to focus on both the kids and the parents' needs. I strategically secured a partnership with a popular local café catering to the interests of parents. This partnership allowed me to provide a warm and inviting environment for families to sip on free hot cocoa and coffee while nestled up with their child and a good book.

This perfectly coordinated event was housed in the library from 5:30 p.m. to 7:00 p.m. on a Thursday night before a long weekend. Since the students had the following day off, they were able to relax and enjoy their time, versus being rushed to fit in an event before bedtime. This created the desired tone that I had hoped to generate; families spent hours nestled in the *nooks and crannies* of the library, reading books from our well-stocked collection. Additionally, they had a plethora of comfy furniture and pillows to choose to *cozy up* on. I had borrowed bean bags, sleeping bags, cushions, large pillows, and blankets for families to choose from.

The night was magical and positive in every way. It provided a great change of pace for students and families as they reached the midpoint in the PARP program. One of the greatest perks to me was the ability for students and families to browse the shelves for the perfect book. The process of exploring the shelves not only contributed to the joy of the experience but also provided access to a larger selection of books than students had at home for their required nightly reading.

This wonderful event wouldn't have happened without marketing. I went into each classroom and energized students by sharing all the captivating details (coffee, cookies, comfy furniture, time to read for PARP, friends to share in the experience, etc.) and sent them home with informational flyers to share with their families. I also created an informational poster using the digital tool *Canva*, shared the flyer across all the library social media platforms (*Twitter* and *Facebook*), and hung them throughout the school. See Figure 2.3 to view the informational poster.

As crucial as marketing this experience was, it was equally as valuable to publicly reflect the success of this literary experience. It is important for the world to see the positive impact the school library plays in the lives of families and students. I built a short *Adobe Spark Video* that featured heartwarming images of children, parents, and friends side-by-side enjoying a good book. The video reflected the joy one can get from reading while supporting my efforts to build positive perceptions of literacy experiences.

The final important detail is to recognize our partners in this experience. It is not only necessary to publicly thank your partners for their

Figure 2.3   "Sip and Read" Informational Poster

generosity; it also elicits a powerful message. It showcases to students, parents, members of the school community, and beyond that reading is valued not only by you but also by significant and respected members of the community. Public recognition can be broadcasted through school mailings, district newsletters, websites, social media, presentations, and beyond. I chose to publicly recognize my partner through social media, on my school website, and in a presentation to the Board of Education.

Suggested Modifications

When considering timing and coordination of similar partnership-based literacy learning experiences at your school, some of the following options may be helpful:

- Host this experience on a Saturday or Sunday morning, and partner with a local bakery to offer bagels and donuts.
- If your school doesn't participate in PARP, consider hosting an end-of-the-year event that will kick off your school's summer reading campaign/program. Partner with a local ice cream shop that can serve sweet treats to families as they read on picnic blankets in the library.
- Coordinate this experience in conjunction with an evening event that is already happening at the school. For example, if students are already going to be at the school for a sporting event or concert, open your doors before or after the event. If families are going to the school anyway, this opportunity will help them in their efforts to meet the nightly reading goals and attend their other activities.
- If you work in a junior or senior-high building, host a morning coffee shop in the library once a month. Students could visit the library before the start of the school day and enjoy an iced coffee, donut, or bagel provided by a community partner, while resting in a quiet corner enjoying a book.

Resources

Digital Resources, Tools, and Links
Sample Adobe Spark Video: https://spark.adobe.com

LITERACY LEARNING EXPERIENCE #2

Named Learning Experience
Celebrity Summer Reading Circles (CSRC)

Partnership
Local Celebrities, Librarian

Future Ready Framework (refer to Figure 2.4)

AASL Standards
AASL Standards for Learners: III.B.2., III.D.1., V.A.1., V.C.1.
AASL Standards for School Librarians: III.B.2., III.D.1., V.A.1.
AASL School Standards for School Libraries: II.D.3., III.C.1., III.C.3., III.D.1., V.C.1., V.C.2., V.D.2.

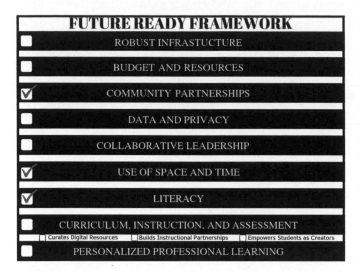

Figure 2.4

Experience Summary

Keeping students motivated to read over the summer is a challenge. Ignoring the valuable role we can play in assisting with this challenge is unfair to students. Similar to my concerns associated with requiring students to read a set amount of time each night during PARP, I also fear that programs that require students to read a set amount of books over the summer are missing the fun factor that generates a positive association with reading. Although both of these programs are effective at keeping students committed to working toward developing their reading skills, they can unconsciously, in the minds of children, place a seclusive association between reading and work. We cannot ignore this reality, reading is work for so many, but we can acknowledge the reality that reading can be both work and fun. As skilled librarians we have the ability to create innovative and fun literacy-based reading experiences to offset students' negative perceptions.

In order to support both positive literacy experiences for students and my school's efforts to keep students reading over the summer months, I designed weekly summer learning experiences in our library called *Celebrity Summer Reading Circles (CSRC)*. *CSRC* are focused not on the amount of reading but on the *Celebrity Readers* and activities connected to the reading. As a result students develop an association between reading and the fun activities, not the work of reading. This energizes students to participate, helping meet my goal of supporting both positive literacy experiences and continual summer reading.

Celebrity Summer Reading Circles are completely student centered. They are solely designed based on the likes and interests of our students. Each week over the summer, we invite multiple *celebrity readers* into the library to host an activity related to a book that both the *celebrity reader* and the students have read prior to the gathering in the library. *Celebrities* and students meet for thirty minutes in the library, where they participate in an engaging activity loosely based on events in the book and the talents of the celebrity reader. The *celebrity reader* uses the book at the beginning of the session as a conversation piece to connect and engage all the participants in the room, but there is not an in-depth discussion or analysis of the book. The focus is meant to be placed on the fun activity associated with the book, not reading skills or comprehension, creating a playful element to reading.

The celebrity reader is not what you or I might consider to be a celebrity, but in the eyes of a student, they are seen as one. Celebrity readers are community partners who hold a position or skill that brings them attention or status. Refer to Table 2.4 for examples of *celebrity readers*. In some cases the celebrity themselves do not attract attention, but the activity they provide is attention worthy. Your community is full of potential celebrity readers; you just need to shift your lens to see them as your students do. Stop thinking

Table 2.4

Celebrity Summer Reading Circles		
Celebrity Reader	*Book*	*Activity*
A doctor of veterinary medicine	*Bad Kitty Goes to the Vet* by Nick Bruel	Students learned about veterinary care, examined animal x-rays, and then used veterinary equipment to examine their own stuffed animals.
Local creamery owner who makes his own ice cream	*Should I Share My Ice Cream?* by Mo Willems	Students discovered how ice cream is made and then made their own ice cream sundaes with the creamery's ice cream.
Ballet instructor	*Ballet Cat Dance! Dance! Underpants!* by Bob Shea	Students participated in basic ballet dance with a trained instructor.
Meteorologist from local news station	*I Survived the Children's Blizzards, 1818* by Lauren Tarshis	Students inquired about the weather, snowdays, and major storms as the meteorologist explained the science behind weather.
Baker from a local bakery	*The Chocolate Chase* (*Geronimo Stilton* #67) by Geronimo Stilton	Students learned how to decorate yummy cakes and indulged in their own bakery treats.
Professional minor league hockey team and mascot	*Jim Nasium Is a Hockey Hazard* by Marty McKnight and Chris Jones	Students made hockey stick bookmarks with a picture of themselves and the team mascot.
Horseback rider	*The War That Saved My Life* by Kimberly Brubaker Bradley	Students went to a local ranch and learned how to groom and ride a horse.
Officer and canine partner	*Max: Best Friend. Hero. Marine* by Jennifer Li Shotz	An officer came to the library with his canine partner. Students watched the canine in action as he was tasked with certain jobs by his partner. Each student had their picture taken with both partners.
A New York State congresswoman	*House Mouse, Senate Mouse* by Peter Barnes and Cheryl Shaw Barnes	Students learned all about life in the House of Representatives and took pictures with the congresswoman.
STEM teacher	*Whoosh!: Lonnie Johnson's Super-Soaking Stream of Inventions* by Chris Barton	Students played squirt-gun tag on the lawn of the school.
Via Aquarium	*Surprising Sharks* by Nicola Davies and James Croft *Ready Freddy: Second Grade Rules* by Abby Klein *Shark Attack: A Survive! Story* by Jake Maddox	The Via Aquarium hosted an interactive informational session on sharks. Students were able to touch shark artifacts and replicas.

of the doctor in the community as someone who cares for children's health, but as a significant role model in your students' life who would make a great *Celebrity Reader*. What about the local barber? Students love getting their haircut by them, so wouldn't they also love having them as a *Celebrity Reader*? Once you begin looking at your community members this way, the possibilities for readers will become endless.

When creating a robust schedule of *Celebrity Readers* and activities for the summer, I have the challenging job of selecting a list of approximately thirty perfectly fitting books (and readers as discussed earlier). Each week I work to provide at least one book for each grade span (kindergarten to second, third to fourth, fifth to sixth, or a similar combination) of readers, which is both high-interest and conducive for generating follow-up activities. I also like to provide a variety of genre choices each week to keep a balance of book selection choices throughout the summer.

Strong student relationships guide the selection process of celebrity readers, books, and activities. It is through interactions with students that I am able to discover what it is that they love to read, what their hobbies are, and what the newest craze is. I also often discover what it is that they are curious about, what type of lifestyle they live outside of school, and what it is that they are aspire to be. All of this information factors into my decisions when creating Summer Reading Circles that pique the interest of students. If I want students to be invested, then I must start by investing in them!

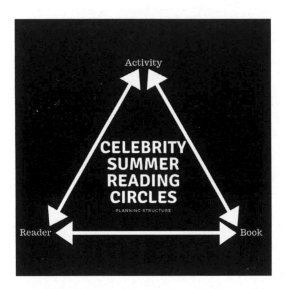

Figure 2.5

Using students' interests to develop a strong summer line-up of *Celebrity Reading Circles* is the best starting point, but the organizational flow of steps beyond that is not at all linear (refer to Figure 2.5). Sometimes students' interest in a particular author guides the book selection, and then an event in the book sparks an idea for a celebrity reader. However, sometimes an event might take place in the book that sparks the idea for an activity that would be fun for kids, at which point I would search the community for a partner (celebrity) to fill that role. The lack of structure can get messy and does require both creativity and persistence, but the results are worth every ounce of energy and passion I pour into the process.

Table 2.4 showcases a variety of Celebrity Summer Reading Circles that I have created at my school library, highlighting the three main elements needed to create these experiences in the library. Hopefully this table can help you as you begin to

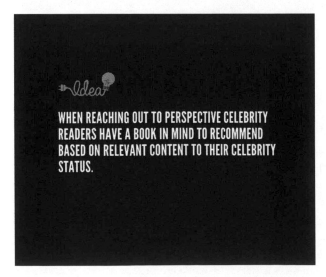

Figure 2.6

1. Name _____

2. Email address: _____

3. Would you like to choose the book or have Mrs. Crossman select the book for your group?
   - I would like to choose the book.
   - I would like Mrs. Crossman to choose the book.

   If choosing your own book, what book would you like to read? Please list the title and author. ____
   _____

4. Would you like to create your own activity for your session or have an activity created for you that you will lead?
   - I will create my own activity and bring my own supplies for the activity.
   - I will create my own activity but will need Mrs. Crossman's help with getting supplies.
   - I would like to have an activity created for me, which I will lead on that day.

5. What date would you like your group to meet?
   - July 11th, 2019
   - July 18th, 2019
   - July 25th, 2019
   - August 1st, 2019
   - August 8th, 2019
   - August 15th, 2019
   - August 22nd, 2019

6. What time would like your group to meet?
   - 8:30–9:00
   - 9:00–9:30
   - 9:30–10:00
   - 10:00–10:30
   - 10:30–11:00

7. Which type(s) of book would prefer to read? (You can choose more than one.)
   - Picture Book
   - Leveled Reader (Beginning Readers)
   - Junior Fiction (Beginning Chapter Book)
   - Fiction Chapter Book (Fantasy)
   - Fiction Chapter Book (Realistic Fiction)
   - Fiction Chapter Book (Historical Fiction)
   - Nonfiction Science
   - Nonfiction History
   - Biography
   - Graphic Novel
   - No Preference
   - Other (specify)_____

8. Do you know of someone else who might be interested in leading a group? (Please add email address of person to contact.)
   _____

9. Please leave any questions or comments below:

Figure 2.7

gain an understanding of *CSRC* and assist you in designing a similar learning experience at your school.

To help in the process of developing a list of *Celebrity Readers*, books, and activities, I utilize several methods. I begin by generating an online survey using *SurveyMonkey* (refer to Figure 2.7) that I share through school email and social media. I encourage teachers, administrators, faculty, and parents to share the survey and help me in soliciting *Celebrity Readers*. In the survey I ask for potential *Celebrity Readers* to join in the learning experience and offer them the choice of selecting their own book or having me choose the book for them (see Figure 2.6 for a helpful tip). This form of communication has proven to be extremely fruitful. The second-most successful method has been contacting prospective *Celebrity Readers* directly through email, telephone, or formal letters in the mail. My final method is to have a sign-up sheet available in the library for parents, teachers, *Board of Education* members, and administrators to volunteer (refer to Table 2.5 for sample template). I have this available at our end-of-the-year Open House so that I can reach as many potential celebrity readers as possible. These three methods combined have been sufficient for producing a comprehensive list of celebrity readers each summer. It is unbelievably gratifying to see how many community members understand the importance of creating a true community of readers and are willing to support the students and the important work we do.

Table 2.5

Summer Reading Circles Sign-Up

Available dates:

Various book types are available. If you have a preference, please indicate that below; if you'd prefer, a book can be selected for you.

- Fiction Chapter Book (grades 2–4 or grades 4–6)
- Fiction Chapter Book (beginning chapters/grades K–3)
- Easy Reader (grades K–3)
- Picture Book (grades K–3)
- Nonfiction
- Graphic Novel

Activities can be planned by you or the librarian. Please let us know which you prefer.

Thank you for volunteering! We look forward to working with you this summer!

Name	Contact Info (email or phone #)	Date You'd Like to Read	Book Type	Create your own activity?

As information begins to flow in with potential readers, books, and activities, I track all the information on a digital spreadsheet. I then begin creating individual planning forms for each of the celebrity summer reading circles, which house all the valuable information in one resource: book information, activity information, celebrity reader, supplies needed, and participants. Refer to planning Figure 2.8 for a sample planning form. All this information is then condensed into one master schedule that I share with families and readers (refer to Table 2.6 for a sample schedule). For suggested tips for designing a schedule, refer to Figure 2.9. As I build each of the *CSRC*, I also create a separate list of supplies and resources I need for purchase. I later present this list to the school's *Parent Teacher Student Organization* (PTSO) through a minigrant, in hopes for their support in funding our activities.

Celebrity Summer Reading Circles

Book Information
Title: Bad Kitty Goes to the Vet
Author: Nick Bruel
Genre: Fantasy, Humor
Age Group: 7-10yrs, 2-4 grade
Description: Kitty is an energetic and playful kitty when she feeling well, but when she is sick she just lays in her bed. That means that Kitty is going to have to go the Vet even if she doesn't want to.

Activity
Day: August 10
Time: 8:30 - 9:00
Description:
The students will learn from Dr. Oswald, how to take care of their animals. She will show them some of her tools for caring for animals and answer any questions. Students will practice a routine check-up on a stuffed animal and see x-rays of actual animals.

Celebrity Reader
Dr. Oswald, DVM

Supplies
Veterinarian Tools
Small Animal X-rays
Stuffed Animals to practice on

Participants

Student #1
Student #2
Student #3
Student #4
Student #5
Student #6
Student #7
Student #8
Student #9
Student #10
Student #11
Student #12
Student #13
Student #14
Student #15

Figure 2.8   Sample Celebrity Summer Reading Circle Planning Form

Table 2.6

Name: _____ Teacher _____ Email _____

Please circle the session/s you will be attending, and return this form to the library by June 21st. Books will be provided on a first-come-first-serve basis for the first 10 students to sign up for each session/book. For information on specific sessions and more detailed book descriptions, please visit the library website.

July 18th

8:30–9:00	9:00–9:30	9:00–9:30	9:30–10:00	10:30–11:00
Celebrity Reader: Baking Co. **Title:** *Geronimo Stilton: The Chocolate Chase* **Type:** Chapter Book **Interest Level:** 2–6	**Celebrity Reader:** Mrs. D **Title:** *Please Write in this Book* **Type:** Chapter Book **Interest Level:** 3–5	**Celebrity Reader:** Meteorologist Tim **Title:** *I Survived the Children's Blizzard, 1888* **Type:** Chapter Book **Interest Level:** 3–6	**Celebrity Reader:** Magician **Title:** *The Magician's Hat* **Type:** Picture Book **Interest Level:** K-2	**Celebrity Reader:** Zookeeper **Title:** *The One and Only Ivan* **Type:** Chapter Book **Interest Level:** 4–6

July 25th

8:30–9:00	9:00–9:30	10:00–10:30	10:30–11:00
Celebrity Reader: Woodcrafter **Title:** *Pax* **Type:** Fiction **Interest Level:** 3–6	**Celebrity Reader:** Horseback Rider **Title:** *The War I Finally Won* **Type:** Ch Book **Interest Level:** 3–6	**Celebrity Reader:** Dance Instructor **Title:** *Giraffes Can't Dance* **Type:** Picture Book **Interest Level:** K-2	**Celebrity Reader:** Bunny Farmer **Title:** *Battle Bunny* **Type:** Beginning Reader **Reading Level:** K-3

August 1st

8:00–8:30	8:30–9:00	9:00–9:30	10:00–10:30	10:30–11:00
Celebrity Reader: Nursery Owner Title: *Wishtree* Type: Chapter Book Interest Level: 3–6	**Celebrity Reader:** Mrs. Martineau **Title:** *French Teacher* **Type:** Picture Book **Interest Level:** K-2	**Celebrity Reader:** High School Librarian **Title:** *The Land of Stories* **Type:** Fantasy Chapter Book **Interest Level:** 3–6	**Celebrity Reader:** Seamstress **Title:** *Sew Zoey: Ready to Wear* **Type:** Chapter Book **Interest Level:** 4–6	**Celebrity Reader:** Dentist **Title:** *Pete the Cat and the Lost Tooth* **Type:** Beginning Reader **Interest Level:** K-2

August 8th

8:30–9:00	9:00–9:30	9:30–10:00	10:00–10:30	10:30–11:00
Celebrity Reader: Engineer **Title:** *Whoosh* **Type:** Nonfiction **Interest Level:** 2–4	**Celebrity Reader:** School Psychologist **Title:** *Because of Mr. Terupt* **Type:** Chapter Book **Interest Level:** 3–6	**Celebrity Reader:** Science Teacher **Title:** *The Magic School Bus and the Electric Field Trip* **Type:** Picture Book **Interest Level:** 1–3	**Celebrity Reader:** Dr. Fronhofer **Title:** *Philomena's Glasses* **Type:** Picture Book **Interest Level:** K–3	**Celebrity Reader:** Rent'em Games **Title:** *Pig the Winner* **Type:** Picture Book **Interest Level:** K–3

August 15th

8:00–8:30	9:00–9:30	9:30–10:00	10:00–10:30	10:30–11:00
Celebrity Reader: Art Teacher **Title:** *A Color of His Own* **Type:** Picture Book **Interest Level:** K–2	**Celebrity Reader:** Technology Specialist **Title:** *The Legend of Zelda* **Type:** Graphic Novel **Interest Level:** 5 & 6	**Celebrity Reader:** Police Officer **Title:** *The Bad Guys* **Type:** Chapter Book **Interest Level:** 2–4	**Celebrity Reader:** Principal **Title:** *Mr. Klutz Is Nuts* **Type:** Beginning Chapter Book **Interest Level:** 2–4	**Celebrity Reader:** BMX Club **Title:** *BMX Bully* **Type:** Chapter Book **Interest Level:** 2–6

August 22nd

8:30–9:00	9:00–9:30	9:30–10:00	10:30–11:00
Celebrity Reader: Local Diner Cook **Title:** *Frank Pearl in the Awful Waffle Kerfuffle* **Type:** Beginning Chapter Book **Interest Level:** K–3	**Celebrity Reader:** Comedian Teacher **Title:** *Knucklehead* **Type:** Nonfiction (Humor) **Interest Level:** 4–6	**Celebrity Reader:** Knitter **Title:** *Extra Yarn* **Type:** Picture Book **Interest Level:** 2–4	**Celebrity Reader:** Food Truck Co. **Title:** *Home Sweet Hotel* **Type:** Chapter Book **Interest Level:** 4–6

TIPS FOR DESIGNING A CELEBRITY SUMMER READING SCHEDULE

TIMES

Sessions should be a half hour in length and should be scheduled so that multiple sessions targeted for the same grade span are not at the same time.

READERS

Ask readers for their preferred days and times. Build the schedule around those times and strategically blend in the readers who don't have a preference of day and time.

BOOKS

Ensure that each week there is at least one book for each grade span and that there are a variety of genres offered.

ACTIVITIES

Although all activities should be engaging, some activities are inevitably more motivating than others. When possible create a balance in activities, providing at least one extremely high-interest activity each week.

CREATING & SHARING SCHEDULE

It can be challenging to create a schedule that can fit onto one sheet of paper, but you want to avoid making a schedule that requires multiple pages. To assist in this process consider accompanying your hardcopy schedule with a more detailed digital schedule that is housed on the library website. Families can be referred to these sites to view the expanded schedule.

Figure 2.9

Gathering books becomes the next big challenge. I provide the first ten students who sign up for each *Celebrity Summer Reading Circle* a book to borrow. After that, families have the option to purchase the book themselves or share with a friend who has a copy of the book. I use our interlibrary loan to borrow as many of the titles as I can, in addition to borrowing from our local Board of Cooperative Educational Services (BOCES) MultiMedia Services collection. I also use Scholastic Book Fair Dollars that I earn from our annual Book Fair to purchase multiple copies of titles.

Marketing and rolling out this event go *hand-in-hand*. A tremendous amount of thought and energy is placed into getting this right. If the goal of this literacy partnership experience is to make literacy experiences fun and engaging for all students, then this kick-off experience needs to be electrifying. In the last weeks of the school year, our school allocates an entire day to have a school-wide summer reading kick-off event. During this time, students rotate through the classrooms, playing literacy-related games and learning all about summer reading opportunities, such as *Celebrity Summer Reading Circles*. This day is full of laughter, excitement, and positive energy.

Each year we have a theme for our event with an opening ceremony. The opening ceremony is my first opportunity to market *Celebrity Summer Reading Circles*. In the past we have had several themes, but one of my favorite themes was an Olympic theme. It was a year of the World Summer Olympics, which made for a perfect summer reading program theme. To complement our theme, we hosted former Olympians who came to our school and presented on the valuable role reading had on their Olympic success. We then held a parade of athletes featuring our *Celebrity Readers*. The gymnasium roared with excitement as our line-up of readers was announced over the microphone and readers marched up to the front of the stage. Once the last *Celebrity Reader* took their spot on the center stage, the lights were dimmed, and I revealed the book choices for the summer reading program through an entertaining movie trailer created using *I-Movie*. Students were pumped with energy as they clapped and cheered for popular book titles that were part of the CSRC. As the students proceeded through the days' activities following the opening ceremony, they visited the library for forty-five minutes, where they would scan QR Codes that led to book trailers for each of the CSRC books, and learned more about the activities and celebrities who would accompany each title. When students left, I distributed informational letters with an attached schedule of the *Celebrity Summer Reading Circles* so they could sign up.

In the days following the school-wide kick-off, students return their sign-up permission sheets indicating the session(s) that they plan to attend. I track student participants on each of the *Celebrity Summer Reading Circle Planning Forms* and on a digital spreadsheet. I then assign the students a copy of the book for each of their registered *Circles* and put them in a special *I Love Reading* themed bag (for purchase through *Demco*). During the last week of school, I deliver each bag of books to the classrooms, delivering happiness and cheer to eager readers throughout the building. It is heartwarming to watch our students proudly carry their books home for everyone to see that they are readers.

As students and *Celebrity Readers* fill the library throughout the summer, I take time to capture the positive energy through photos. These photos prove to be a powerful means of displaying my commitment to community partnerships, literacy, and engaged learning. I share these photos through social media, with the hashtag #enjoyyourlearning, and on our library website. Oftentimes I will see these photos pop up on district calendars, newsletters, and presentations.

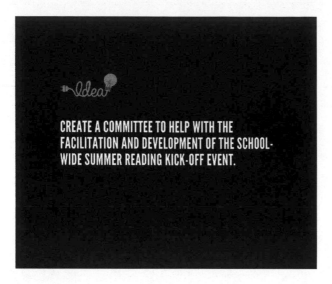

Figure 2.10

During the days leading up to the weekly *Celebrity Summer Reading Circles*, I use social media to remind families of the upcoming sessions for that week. I also find it to be helpful to send a reminder email to the *Celebrity Readers* as well, confirming their time and offer my assistance in preparing for the upcoming session. This alleviates any anxieties I might have about being prepared for their arrival. On the actual day of the session, I have everything prepared for the activity (when necessary), and during the session I walk around supporting the *Celebrity Readers* and students. I collect each of the books from the students and pack them up for return delivery to their proper school at the end of each session.

This experience may seem beastly, but when organized and managed well, it is not as overwhelming (refer to Figure 2.10 for a helpful tip when planning this kick-off experience). I typically begin planning for this learning experience in March, giving myself plenty of time to find readers, books, and activities, and plan the end-of-the-year kick-off event. There is no denying that this learning experience requires work, but you are an innovator! Innovators are creative, persistent, and dedicated to improving learning through meaningful and engaging experiences such as *Celebrity Summer Reading Circles*.

Suggested Modifications
- **Books.** Locating enough books for this learning experience can be challenging as not everyone has access to outside collections or additional funding. If this is the case for your school, consider some of the following options:
  - If your school participates in *Scholastic Book Clubs*, consider asking teachers to donate some of their *Scholastic Points* from their classroom book orders to put toward multiple copies of books for CSRC.
  - Hold a *Celebrity Summer Reading Circle* fundraiser where families, classrooms, community members, and local businesses can sponsor a particular *Celebrity Summer Reading Circle*.
  - Consider using an online fundraising tool such as GoFundMe or DonorsChoose.
- **Compensation.** Getting paid for your summer hours is important. Look into getting a stipend or alternative means of compensation, perhaps with designated funds from your teachers' union. If there is no option for compensation, consider developing the learning experiences in conjunction with a public library and having the public librarian deliver the experience at their library.
- **Scheduling.** If scheduling multiple *Celebrity Summer Reading Circles* is too much each week, then create one learning experience each week, alternating the targeted grade ranges and genres from week to week.
- **Summer Kick-off**
  - When planning a school-wide event, use the school's mission and goals to build an argument for collaborative efforts in planning and delivering this event.

- When looking for themes, consider aligning your theme with your state's summer reading theme, if they have one.
- If it is not possible to host a school-wide event during the day, consider hosting an evening event where families can experience a fun night of reading activities and learn all about the *Celebrity Reading Circles* planned for the summer.

Resources

Digital Resources, Tools, and Links
Celebrity Summer Reading Circle Planning Template: http://bit.ly/CSRCplanningtemp
Celebrity Summer Reading Circle Schedule Template: http://bit.ly/CSRCscheduletemp

GROW

Grow your library program by . . .

1. Determining a program at your school that could use the support of a literacy partnership.
2. Designing a literacy learning experience that would support a program in need.
3. Connecting with community partners who can support your literacy learning experience.

ACTION PLAN

Setting the Stage
Approach this learning experience by determining the following criteria for your work (refer to Table 2.7):

Table 2.7

Setting the Stage		
Goals	*Key Players*	*Groundwork*
• What would you like the literacy experience to be able to provide or support? • What AASL Standards are you hoping to address? • What Future Ready Principles are you trying to address? • How can you build a literacy partnership–based learning experience that fosters a positive perception of reading?	• Who are the potential community partners who can effectively support your goals? • What do you need your partner to be able to do for you? • What community partnerships would be appealing to students? • Who is your audience?	• What is the best time of the year to access students for this experience? • Will you need permission before planning and launching your learning experience? • How many community partnerships will you need to form? • Will you need the support of other colleagues, administrators, parents, and beyond? • How are you going to foster a positive literary experience for everyone, including your most reluctant readers?

(Continued)

Table 2.7 (Continued)

Setting the Stage		
Goals	*Key Players*	*Groundwork*
		• How are you going to build relationships to better understand the students' needs and interests upon which a partnership should be built? • What are the needs and interests of the students? • What activities would motivate students to participate? • What types of experiences can you create where students are engaged the entire time?

Establishing the Partnership

Use the bullets featured in each section of Table 2.8 to guide you in your actions toward developing a literacy partnership.

Table 2.8

Who	• Seek partners who will motivate students to participate or partners who can afford students opportunities that you could not on your own. • Ensure that the partners meet the needs of students' likes and interests. • Identify potential partners who will make literacy experiences fun.
What	• Identify the role(s) of the partner, and communicate their responsibilities to them. • Ask the partner what resources they will need (supplies, technology, books, etc.).
How	• Seek potential partnerships through personal and professional networks. • Determine the best way to reach out to partners (email, letter, phone, website contact form, etc.). • Contact potential partner(s) with details about learning experience and expectations. • When applicable, create a survey for potential partnerships to sign up to be a partner. Share the link to the survey digitally.
Where	• Identify any special needs, such as seating, resources, or space, required for the partner to carry out a successful literacy experience. • Identify the best environment for you or your partner to generate a positive literacy experience.
When	• Determine what time of the year the partnership is needed. • Determine the amount of time the partner needs to be present (if applicable). • Determine the best time period for the experience to occur during the day, keeping in mind both the needs of the students and the partner. • Be flexible and accommodating to the partner's needs when possible by providing multiple options when scheduling.

Delivering the Learning Experience

Following is an outline of the suggested steps you can take when delivering a literacy-based learning experience with the support of a community partnership (refer to Table 2.9).

Table 2.9

Steps to Developing Literacy Learning Experiences
1. Identify a need within your school where partnership-based literacy experiences could support an existing program.
2. Develop relationships with students, and listen to their needs and interests.
3. Identify and establish fun and engaging literacy partnerships that can meet the needs and interests of the students. a. Choose an eminent or beloved partner. b. Choose a partner who can turn your ideas into action.
4. Plan details for learning experiences (permission, scheduling, location, resources, etc.) while keeping a flexible and open mindset.
5. Choose multiple paths for marketing that reach and appeal to your target audience.
6. Create a rollout event that will energize students and motivate them to participate.
7. Analyze and review activities prior to the delivery of the learning experience. a. Be organized. b. Prepare for anticipated needs.
8. Deliver the learning experience. c. Be present and engaged. d. Develop relationships. e. Foster a love of literacy.
9. Celebrate success publicly.

3

Virtual Partnerships

LEARN

What Are Virtual Partnerships?

These partnerships take place virtually and allow learners to communicate with the world outside of their classroom through digital means. Although each form of communication is executed digitally, the type of communication can occur through oral, written, or visual means. Through these learning experiences, librarians can enhance and support the classroom curriculum and provide experiences that help increase global awareness.

Why Do They Matter?

Virtual learning experiences are the epitome of innovation. They allow students to engage with and discover new cultures, perspectives, and locations without having to leave the classroom. When trying to reach new heights in the *SAMR Model* of technology integration, these learning experiences will help you climb to the *redefinition* step of the framework, where learning is transformed. Through technology integration and virtual partnerships, students are capable of engaging in learning experiences that were once impossible.

If we are tasked with preparing students to develop empathy through understanding and appreciation of various perspectives, then we must expose our students to new places and people near and far. Telling students that there is a vast world outside the walls of our school buildings and borders is important; however, there is no finer learning opportunity than when students can come to this conclusion on their own. Virtual learning experiences allow students to observe, interact, inquire, and develop new understandings and appreciations for people and places that would not be possible without technology and dynamic virtual partnerships.

How Do You Make Them Happen?

There are a multitude of opportunities that exist for connecting virtually with classrooms, people, and places outside of your school, such as *Google Earth*, *Google Expeditions*, and *safariLIVE*. However, similar to any other experience that you create, you must start with the *why* behind the learning experience. Yes, the obvious *why* is to expose students to new perspectives and experiences, but we must provide richer and more connected experiences. Making a digital connection to information being taught in the classroom not only can help to meet content curriculum standards but can magnify the experience. Additionally, we can make a huge impact on the movement of the school's *mission, vision,* and *values,* when we build learning experiences that support and align with the school's goals and strategic plan.

In order to build virtual learning experiences that support the work of the district's strategic plan, the curriculum, and the standards, we need to ensure that we have a good understanding of all three. As discussed thoroughly in Chapters 1 and 6, the best way to build understanding is to be involved. Join curriculum and district strategic planning committees; attend professional development opportunities to stay abreast of new information; continue to build relationships with teachers, administrators, and curriculum leaders; and vocalize your desire to support them in their work. Through these means, you will be able to identify opportunities to create connected and meaningful virtual learning experiences.

Once the *why* behind your learning experience has been determined, it becomes easier to identify which virtual learning experience to partake in. In many cases, you will create your own virtual learning experience based on the unique needs of the classroom. Other times, you might find it useful to rely on digital sites that are designed to assist in the connection of learners across the world. There is not a singular approach that is better for making connections, and oftentimes a blended approach is needed. Table 3.1 can help provide resources for making connections.

Table 3.1

Digital Tool	Purpose
Classroom Bridges	Connects teachers with other classrooms around the world that are looking to connect. (free)
Skype in the Classroom	Provides free live connection opportunities for classrooms.
Field Trip Zoom	Facilitates the connection of learners and educational content specialists through live video. (membership fee)

Librarians are the linchpin that holds this learning experience together. Developing tools and systems for effective and clear communication will have a significant impact on the success of the learning experience. Some experiences require more involved levels of interaction with virtual learning partners than others. Each experience will require a system and structure that helps facilitate a seamless and easy learning experience for all parties. When facilitating communication, it helps to focus on the *when, how,* and *what.*

- *When:* Establish the date and time of *when* the learning experience will occur, and when applicable, ensure that the time zones fit your schedule.
- *How:* Identify the tools that will be used to connect virtually.
- *What:* Determine *what* students will need to know or be prepared for prior to the connected learning experience, and determine *what* will happen during the learning experience.

In order to generate a powerful and enjoyable learning experience for all students, it helps to focus on the following details when facilitating the delivery of the learning experience:

- Having a structure and process for connected communication set in place.
- Ensuring that all learners have an active, engaging role. In many experiences this will occur naturally, while other experiences will require you to create roles and responsibilities for the learners.
- Generating a smooth flow between instruction and student active participation.

LEAP

Leap (step) forward by . . .

1. Identifying a curricular need that could be supported by a virtual learning experience.
2. Identifying a goal of your district's strategic plan that could be supported by a virtual learning experience.
3. Exploring digital tools and resources available to virtually connect learners to the world outside their classroom.

VIRTUAL LEARNING EXPERIENCE #1

Named Learning Experience
WildEarth Schools: safariLIVE

Partnership
Africa Safari Expert Guide, Librarian

Future Ready Framework (refer to Figure 3.1)

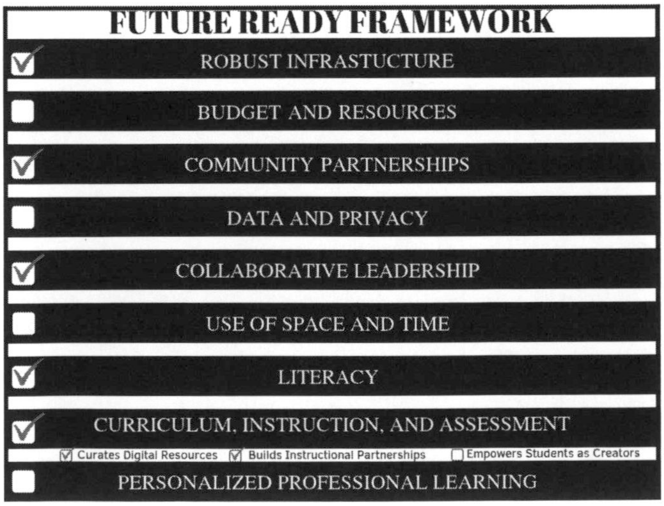

FUTURE READY FRAMEWORK

- ☑ ROBUST INFRASTUCTURE
- ☐ BUDGET AND RESOURCES
- ☑ COMMUNITY PARTNERSHIPS
- ☐ DATA AND PRIVACY
- ☑ COLLABORATIVE LEADERSHIP
- ☐ USE OF SPACE AND TIME
- ☑ LITERACY
- ☑ CURRICULUM, INSTRUCTION, AND ASSESSMENT
  - ☑ Curates Digital Resources ☑ Builds Instructional Partnerships ☐ Empowers Students as Creators
- ☐ PERSONALIZED PROFESSIONAL LEARNING

Figure 3.1

AASL Standards
AASL Standards for Learners: I.A.1., I.A.2., I.D.1., I.D.3., I.D.4., III.A.1., III.A.2., III.B.1., IV.A.1., IV.B.1., IV.B.2., V.C.1., V.C.2., VI.A.1., VI.A.2.

AASL Standards for School Librarians: I.A.1., I.A.2., I.A.3., I.B.1., I.B.2., I.D.1., I.D.3., III.A.1., III.B.1., III.B.2., III.D.1., IV.A.1., IV.A.2., IV.B.1., V.C.1., V.C.2, VI.A.1., VI.D.1.

AASL School Standards for School Libraries: I.A.1., I.B.1, I.C.1., I.C.2., I.D.1., I.D.2., III.A.1., III.A.2., IV.A.1., IV.A.3., IV.B.1., IV.B.5., V.A.1., V.A.2., V.B.1., V.B.2., V.B.3., V.C.3., V.D.2., V.D.3., VI.C.2., VI.D.1., VI.D.2.

Experience Summary

I took my kindergarten students on a live African safari with an expert guide who drove through the Savanna, looking for animals in their natural habitat. This free experience provided students with an understanding and appreciation of safari animals and allowed them to experience Africa's climate and geography *with their own eyes*. With the guidance of an expert safari tour guide (virtual partner) and digital tools (*Skype* and *YouTube Live*), students were able to interact, inquire, engage, and learn. This virtual learning experience not only provided an opportunity for students to visit a world beyond their classroom; it also gave them an appreciation, awareness, and concrete understanding of a location that was vastly different than their own.

I had first learned about *safariLIVE* at a conference. Being part of an innovative school that works to transform and redefine learning through the integration of technology, I instantly began to inquire more about this experience. As I began my research, I discovered that through this virtual learning opportunity, I would be able to help meet several curricular needs and standards. Additionally, I would also be able to address several of the target goals our district had set in place so that we could reach our new district-wide mission. It was at that point that I decided to take the leap and build a virtual partnership with *WildEarth Schools*.

WildEarth Schools makes it easy to establish a connection. Once you visit their official website (https://wildearth.tv/schools/), you can view a calendar of safaris by date and time. Three schools are allowed to participate in each of the live safaris, with the first school to sign up being the school to set the age range of the experience. Once you find a session that works for you, they provide an easy-to-use *Google Form* to book your safari. After your safari is confirmed, you will receive guidelines for establishing a connection through *Skype* to their *WildEarth Schools Project* account. They will also send you a link to connect with their live broadcast on *YouTube*. The stress of creating a structure for establishing communication and a virtual connection are almost nonexistent with this experience because of the structure already put into place by *WildEarth*.

As the teacher you are able to communicate with their expert guide during the *LIVE safari* through Skype. While students are viewing the safari in action through *YouTube Live*, the guide shares information about the animals you are seeing and their behaviors. During this time, you as the instructor can type in the students' questions on *Skype*, and the guide will answer your students' questions during the live session. This simple communication format is extremely easy and straightforward. However, in order to effectively engage all students and address each personal inquiry, a structure must be set in place.

The major challenge for this experience lies in the preparatory work. Since you are only able to ask one question at a time, it is not effective to have each student shouting out questions at once. Depending on the grade level and your purpose, you will surely establish a structure that meets your class needs.

A questioning structure I found successful for younger classes was periodically asking, "Raise your hand if you have a *what* question." After receiving a response to our question, I might say, "After learning what was just shared, does anyone have a follow-up question?" I would continue this structure by next asking, "Raise your hand if you have a *why* question?" This structure not only kept the students engaged, critically thinking, and learning, but it also gave them practice with developing good questions using question starters. This structure certainly took practice in order for us to be successful at it. Luckily each *safariLIVE* is archived for later viewing, so we were able to practice as a class prior to our actual connection. This preparatory work was instrumental in the monumental success of our learning experience.

This virtual experience was strategically planned to align with the content standards being covered in the kindergarten science and English language art's curriculum and with the information literacy skills in our library curriculum. Each year our kindergarten studies animals, and typically we use databases to gather basic facts about behavior, habitat, and life cycle of an animal of their choice as part of a basic inquiry. This simple research allows me to guide the students through the inquiry process while addressing information literacy skills as well as both science and English language art's standards. As valuable as the skills were that I was teaching the students, it wasn't innovative, and it certainly wasn't authentic or engaging. By utilizing *WildEarth safariLIVE*, I was able to improve and enhance the learning experience to make it more meaningful for the students. During the learning experience, we still went through the stages of the inquiry model, but our discussions and knowledge products were richer and more meaningful since the work became more relevant to them.

After experiencing *safariLIVE*, students were invested and curious about the animals we saw. I decided to build off this momentum and read to them Paige Jaeger's book *Who Will Roar if I Go?* This book about endangered species became personal to them. They had just witnessed some of the same majestic animals in their natural habitat, and now they were learning about their potential extinction. Students became charged and empowered to help. This led to amazing discussions and collaborative brainstorming sessions about how we can make a difference and help animals. Even at the youngest grade level, I was able to build empathy, create a desire to learn more, and ingrain the need to be socially active.

Through social media, conversations with administration, and scrolling slideshows on the library website, I was able to showcase this virtual learning opportunity. I drew attention to the fact that students were engaged in an innovative and diverse learning experience with the global learning community and that it was aligned with our school's mission and vision to "empower all students to be global citizens." This experience was later featured by our administration to our *Board of Education* in a reflective video that highlighted the successful work we have done to help reach our school's goals. As time-consuming as marketing can be, I recognize the importance of being not only the face of the library but also the voice of the library. The time invested in marketing has undeniably shaped and impacted the success of the library program.

Suggested Modifications

The initial structure of this partnership has been established by *WildEarth*, so no matter your grade or schedule, the same format for booking a virtual learning experience is followed. Where learning experiences will differ is in the instruction.

- The content for my experience focused on animals in their natural habitat and resulted in authentic action. While at higher levels, inquiries can be much richer and provoke action from the onset. Starting an inquiry with Paige Jaeger's book at any level could lay the grounds for a great action-based inquiry. If the goal of your unit is activism, perhaps start the learning experience with the question "Who will roar while I am still here?"
- This virtual learning experience is great for any school age. They offer programs in the following age groups: four to six, six to eight, eight to eleven, ten to thirteen, thirteen to fifteen, sixteen plus. Although the experience I shared was for four- to six-year-olds, it could be a more powerful learning experience for students at a higher age.
- Kindergarten is the only fixed class in my schedule, so for this experience, I did not utilize a collaborative instructional partner. However, this experience could create the perfect opportunity for you to support instruction in the classroom. At all grade levels, you could push into a

science (animal behaviors and habitats, ecology, biodiversity), social studies (Africa, activism, human activity), or English language arts (connection to a story, writing for a purpose) classroom depending on the curricular connection.

- The structure that I established during the virtual learning experience was simplified to meet the needs of kindergarten students. If you are working with a classroom at a higher level, students can individually write their questions on a notecard for you, and you can type them as they are presented. Students could also work in groups to develop questions as well.

- At the kindergarten level, our final product resulted in making informational posters, but students could take action in many ways. Having students explore different organizations that already exist to help protect endangered animals and reaching out to them to see how they can help support their cause could be a powerful experience that would meet many *AASL Standards*.

Resources
Jaeger, Paige. *Who Will Roar if I Go?* Virginia: BQB Publishing, an imprint of Boutique of Quality Books Publishing, 2018.

Digital Resources, Tools, and Links
safariLIVE Educator Guide: http://media.nationalgeographic.org/assets/file/SafariLIVE_Educator_ Guide.pdf
WildEarth Schools Project: https://wildearth.tv/schools/

VIRTUAL LEARNING EXPERIENCE #2

Named Learning Experience
Global Read Aloud

Partnership
Teachers, Partner Classroom (from an outside location), Librarian

Future Ready Framework (refer to Figure 3.2)

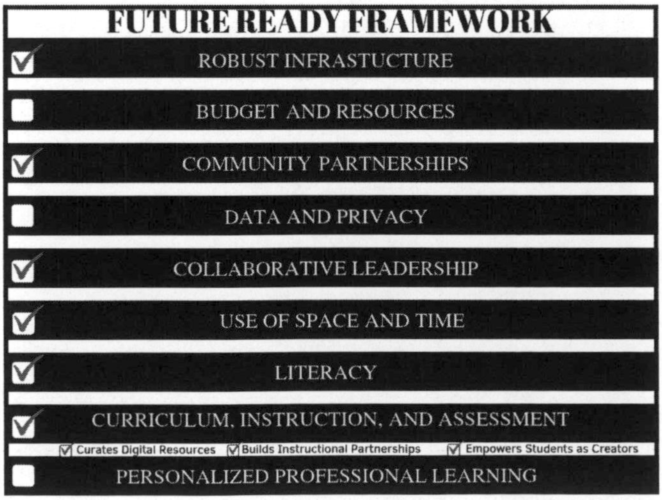

Figure 3.2

AASL Standards
Each of the addressed *AASL Standards* for learners, librarians, and school libraries will vary based on the weekly activities associated with the reading for the *Global Read Aloud*. However, through the weekly reading activities associated with the *Global Read Aloud*, students will encounter all the competencies within the *AASL Standards* through thinking, creating, sharing, and growing.

Experience Summary

The *Global Read Aloud* (*GRA*) is an amazing opportunity, generously established by Pernille Ripp, to digitally connect students around the world through a book. This six-week experience is free for all schools and builds rich conversations and an awareness and appreciation of others. Participating schools follow a set schedule established through the *GRA*, but they create their own classroom connections to other participants through the Global Read Aloud *Facebook* Community or designated *Twitter* hashtags.

This global learning experience was the perfect opportunity for me to meet the new *AASL Standards*, Future Ready Librarian™ Principles, and my school district's mission and goals. After researching the GRA, I gained an understanding of the structure and requirements. The GRA provides several selections of book choices for participants to choose a book title from for the GRA. Each week all participants who chose the same book will read the designated chapters of the book, or if they chose the picture book author study, they will read a specific title by that author each week. Throughout the week, students engage through the use of technology with students around the world who are reading the same book. Teachers are responsible for establishing a connection with other schools and developing the activities that will take place between partnering schools.

Once you sign up for the Global Read Aloud on the *GRA* website (theglobalreadaloud .com), you will receive an email from the creator of the GRA, Pernille Ripp, who shares valuable information and resources for making connections.

During my first year in this learning experience, I took time to *get my feet wet* by choosing just two grade levels in my school to participate. This made it more manageable and helped to produce a positive experience for the classroom teachers, students, and me. Teachers quickly became invested in this opportunity once I highlighted ways that this experience could support them with: (1) the meaningful integration of technology and (2) meeting our district's mission and goals. By facilitating and managing all digital connections and activities with our partner schools, I was able to model an effective virtual learning experience and a series of powerful digital learning tools for teachers to emulate in the future.

The structure that I set in place was extremely effective for the first year and allowed me to gain the experience that I needed to eventually create a more dynamic and powerful structure. In the first year of the experience, I used the suggested *Facebook* Global Read Aloud Community to find interested classrooms around the world to collaborate with. This process was a little tedious and required me to be extremely organized. For each person whom I contacted and established a connection with, I needed to track their contact information, the scheduled activities, and the schedule for shared communication (refer to Table 3.2). Although each classroom experience was meaningful and exciting for students, the behind-the-scene management of six different connecting schools and classes became overwhelming.

Through reflection, I learned from my initial experience and developed an innovative structure that proved to be helpful not only for me but also to each of my connecting partners. I created a collaborative website through *Google Sites* (http://bit.ly/gra2018Flett) where participants could connect with partners, share weekly work, and receive suggested ideas for weekly activities. This collaborative resource not only alleviated work and time; it expanded the amount of connections and learning opportunities for participants.

In order to find participants to share in using the collaborative site, I posted a link to my *Google Site* on the Global Read Aloud Facebook Community, select library ListServs, and

Table 3.2

Classroom Teacher	Connecting Teacher	Contact Information	Location	Day & Time	Connecting Platform	Notes
Mrs. A's Second Grade Class	Mrs. D	email@spsprinceton.org	Saint Paul School of Princeton	Friday Time: ?	Skype & Padlet	Friday's work, still waiting to hear back on time from partner.
Mrs. K's Second Grade Class	Mrs. F	email@georgetown.k12.me.us	Georgetown Maine	Fridays 1:40–2:00	Skype & Padlet	Mrs. F would like to connect at 1:40. Asked about possible Wednesday/Thursday. Sent plan for *Nana in the City* activity.
Mrs. D's Second Grade Class	Mrs. M	email@penncharter.com	Quaker School in Philadelphia	Thursday 1:30–2:00	Skype & Padlet	Sent plan for *Nana in the City* activity.
Mrs. K's First Grade Class	Mrs. S	email@penncharter.com	Quaker School in Philadelphia	I have a conflict on Thursday??	Skyping, blogging, Padlet	Sent plan for *Nana in the City*.
Mrs. Z's First Grade Class	Mrs. R	email@aol.com	Philadelphia	Thursdays @1:30	Skyping, blogging, Padlet	Sent plan for *Nana in the City*.

my social media feeds. Participants quickly joined onto the site. I also included the partner teachers whom I was working with at my school so that they could be instrumental in choosing the activities and sharing their student work each week. I continued to push into classrooms, read the books each week, and share in the instructional responsibilities, but the management was much easier for all parties.

At the lower grades, the *GRA* features a different picture book by the same author each week. To help facilitate an effective structure that would work for all classes, each week I would

- read and discuss the book on Monday or Tuesday;
- help students create a digital product or connection on Wednesday or Thursday;
- respond to our partner classrooms' work on Friday, if applicable;
- be flexible and *allow room* in the schedule to condense two activities into one day when needed (read the book and create a digital product); and
- manage the activities and communication through a tracking tool (refer to Table 3.2).

Throughout the six-week program, we utilized a multitude of digital tools to connect and share with our partner schools. It was important to me to feature a variety of communication tools so that classroom teachers could experience them and potentially integrate them into future instruction. The beauty of the *GRA* was that I wasn't alone in selecting and learning new tools to use and share. I had a community of experts within my network of *GRA* partners who would share their ideas for communication with the group, allowing me to preview and discover new digital tools for communication. Refer to Table 3.3 for a list of suggested virtual communication tools or Table 3.4 for app smashing ideas. We are each other's best resource. Take advantage of it.

Generating weekly lessons can take on all different formats. Having participated in the *GRA* for many years, I have used several different approaches. See Figure 3.3 for a helpful tip when approaching your weekly lesson plans. When experiencing the *GRA* for the first time, I partnered with a veteran of the program and relied on her expertise to guide our weekly work. In the years that have followed, I have taken the reigns and designed the lessons for rookie partners, and I have also collaborated with virtual partners to develop lessons together. However, most recently, I have found free, consistently structured, and strong lessons on the

Table 3.3 Example Virtual Communication Tools

Padlet
Skype
FlipGrid
FaceTime
Blogs
Twitter
Google Docs
Google Slides
Google Classroom
Google Hangouts
Seesaw
Websites (Weebly or Google Sites)
ThingLink
Smore

Table 3.4 Example App Smashing Ideas

ChatterPix → Post to Padlet
PicCollage → Post to Blog
Picture from Camera Roll → Post to Twitter with GRA hashtag
Draw and Tell Video → Post to website
Google Drawings → ThingLink
Videos → Upload to Smore
QR Codes (linked to work) → Upload to Google Slides

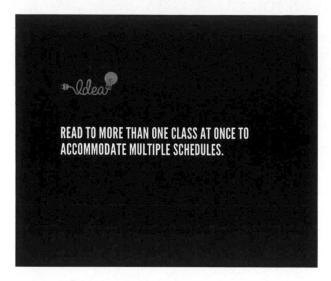

Figure 3.3

internet that have reshaped the experience for me and my virtual partner schools. We no longer need to have constant back-and-forth exchanges, trying to settle on lessons and activities; we now use the free lessons as the foundation for our weekly activities and make tweaks where necessary. It is important to emphasize that all the activities, lessons, and resources used for the *GRA* are free, as that is the beauty and intention behind the work of the GRA.

As accustomed as I became with using the shared lessons, I did not lose sight of my responsibility to build tools and resources for assessing student awareness of diversity between us and our partner school. This step was important to me because the *why* behind my work was to support our strategic plan, and one of the goals in our plan was to provide learning opportunities where students can develop an awareness and appreciation for diversity. By building learning activities where students were deliberately asked to think about and acknowledge differences, I was able to assess their understanding and progress toward meeting our district goals. Refer to "Digital Resources, Tools, and Links" for a sample assessment.

As students participate in the weekly activities, they will engage in creating their own personal work and enjoy sharing about their connections to the book. As valuable as their work is, we want to expand this experience beyond themselves and include the views, experiences, and perspective of others. What makes the *GRA* powerful is the shared connections and diverse understandings that matriculate from the activities associated with the book. You cannot miss out on these opportunities to develop students' understandings and appreciation for others. I deliberately facilitate discussions that build an awareness and respect for diverse interests, ideas, perspectives, and cultures. It is through these rich learning experiences that we will prepare informed global citizens who have empathy, tolerance, and appreciation for the diverse global community.

Participation in the *GRA* brings innovative learning experiences to our students. This is reflected and celebrated on the global stage through *GRA*-specific hashtags and digital communication networks. The shared information through these platforms brings attention to the valuable work teachers and librarians are doing, and it is our responsibility to foster these digital conversations and use them as tools to champion the merit of virtual partnerships. We must showcase the rich learning that each experience brings.

Suggested Modifications

- The GRA mostly consists of chapter books and not picture books. For chapter books, consider building a collaborative website that is organized by chapters.
- Oftentimes, especially with the chapter books, it can be difficult to stay up with the pace of the reading. In these cases it might be advantageous to seek out partners ahead of time that are also looking to commit to an extended partnerships and together build a schedule that works for both of you.
- When participating in the GRA for the first time, choose one digital tool for communication with your partner school(s) instead of trying a new tool each week.
- If timing is an issue based on time zones or class schedule, use means of connection that don't require you to be present at a specific time. Perhaps create work and share knowledge through a QR code exchange, or seek a virtual communication tool in Table 3.1 that doesn't require both partners to be present at the same time.
- In the upper grades, empower students to make their own connections through their own preferred means of communication, and have them reflect on not only the experience but also the preferred tool.
- If you find difficulty in selecting the digital communication tool, collaborate with a technology savvy teacher or instructional technology specialists who can help support the communication process of the *GRA*.
- If your district has technology integration goals and initiatives set in place that some teachers are reluctant to embrace, use the *GRA* as a way to support them in reaching their goals.
- If it is difficult to arrange this virtual learning experience for an entire class, consider creating a book club for interested students.
- Consider working with your reading specialists to offer this experience to students who require academic support services for reading. This unique opportunity might be engaging and meaningful enough to help motivate struggling and reluctant readers.
- If you have a fixed schedule and work in an elementary school, it might be easier for you to select the picture book study, because you will not need to participate in each book.

Resources

Digital Resources, Tools, and Links
Digital Planning Form Template: http://bit.ly/virtualplanningtemplate
Diversity Awareness Informal Assessment: http://bit.ly/GRAsampleassessment

GROW

Grow your library program by . . .

1. Deciding which group of students and instructional partners you will be working with internally.
2. Selecting a virtual learning experience that meets students', curriculum, or district needs.
3. Delivering a virtual learning experience through a connected partnership.

ACTION PLAN

Setting the Stage

Approach this learning experience by determining the following criteria for your work (refer to Table 3.5):

Table 3.5

Setting the Stage		
Goals	*Key Players*	*Groundwork*
• What curricular needs are you trying to meet? • How will the virtual learning experience support district initiatives? • What AASL Standards are you planning to address? • What Future Ready Principles are you planning to address?	• Who will be your target audience for this experience? • What virtual learning partnerships are available to support your goals? • Who will be your instructional partners within the school?	• What content area is your virtual partnership going to support? • How much time do you have to work with students (a day, a week, a month)? • What equipment, technology, and space do you have for a virtual connection? • What skills do students need prior to the virtual learning experience? • What content do students need to know prior to the learning experience? • What structure needs to be set in place to ensure a smooth experience that is not overwhelming?

Establishing the Partnership

Use the bullets featured in each section of Table 3.6 to guide you in your actions toward developing a virtual partnership.

Table 3.6

Who	• Seek virtual partners who meet the needs of the learning experience. • When applicable seek recommendations for virtual partnerships. • When building potential partnerships, discuss goals and needs of the learning experience with several potential partners before confirming your partner. • Research quality virtual partnerships before reaching out to potential partners.
What	• Identify what will happen during the learning experience. • Determine what needs to be done by you, your virtual partner, and your students prior to the learning experience. • Identify what technology is needed for both partners to make the virtual partnership possible. • Identify if there are any costs or requirements associated with the learning experience. • Determine if there is a set amount of students that the learning experience can accommodate.

How	• Determine where to seek out virtual partners. • Identify the desired digital tool (video, blogging, digital knowledge product sharing) of virtual connection with your potential partner. • Identify what digital platform will be needed for communication.
Where	• Identify a place in the building that has adequate resources (technology, quiet space) for the virtual connection with your partner. • Determine where your virtual connection will take place online.
When	• Determine when in the school year the partnership is needed. • Collaborate with classroom teachers, when applicable, to see when would be the best time for a virtual partnership. • Determine if you and your potential virtual partners' schedules allow for a time where you are both available to connect virtually.

Delivering the Learning Experience

Use the information in Table 3.7 to guide you in your actions toward developing a virtual learning experience with the support of a community partnership.

Table 3.7

Steps to Developing Virtual Learning Experiences

1. Begin with the *why*.
  • Determine which standard(s) the learning experience will support.
  • Determine which curricular need(s) the learning experience will support.
  • Determine how the experience can support the work and goals of the district's strategic plan.

2. Connect with a virtual learning partner.
  • Use personal and professional learning networks to elicit a connection.
  • Use a digital site to help facilitate a connection.

3. Develop a structure and system for the facilitation of clear communication between you and the connected partners (both inside and outside of your building).
4. Develop a structure for learners to effectively communicate during the virtual learning experience.
5. Develop and embed an inquiry or lesson within the virtual learning experience.
6. When applicable, build extension activities to further learning and understanding based on the virtual connection experience.
7. Make learning visible by marketing the learning experience to stakeholders.
8. When applicable, build and utilize assessments that inform you on student understanding.

PART II
External Learning Experiences

4

Site-Based Partnerships

LEARN

What Are Site-Based Partnerships?

Site-based partnerships allow librarians, oftentimes in collaboration with a classroom teacher, to purposefully engage with an outside entity as a site for personal and academic-based inquiry. These sites can be hosts during any stage of learning in the inquiry process and can oftentimes serve as a host for more than one stage, much like a physical library would. They are oftentimes gold mines filled with primary and secondary resources and act as an incubator for exploration and curiosity.

Locations for site-based learning vary. Physical structures or simply the physical environment can be host sites for learning. The worth or value of a site is determined by the needs of the user and the way in which they interact with the site. It can be surprising how every day places within our community are ideal locations for site-based learning. Take a local municipality, for example. These locations are filled with opportunities to make curricular connections across all grades. Once you begin looking at the standards and viewing sites in and out of your community as resources for learning, a whole new world of learning opportunities will develop.

Host sites provide a rich breeding ground for learning, and those learning experiences can be magnified when partnered with an expert. A majority of sites have experts who work within the location and who are willing to accommodate the content needs of the student learners. However, there are sites where experts are not readily available, and partnerships may need to be created. If a site is being used during the *investigate* stage of inquiry, there can be a more significant need to partner with an expert. In these situations, learners are purposefully seeking and gathering information, in which case experts would be meaningful to that particular stage of the learning process. If a site is being used during the *wonder* stage of inquiry, the emphasis is being placed not on gathering answers to their questions but on developing questions, in which case you might strategically decide not to utilize an expert.

Why Do They Matter?

Well-designed libraries support the six Shared Foundations of the *AASL Standards* and their Key Commitments. Libraries are incredible venues meticulously designed to meet the academic and personal needs of learners and fill their desires to inquire, explore, and engage. As essential as the physical library is, there is also extreme value in the physical spaces outside of the school library. When properly utilized in collaboration with a strong school library program, these external learning environments can become ideal launchpads for site-based learning, making them the perfect classroom.

By shifting the learning environment from the physical library or classroom to a site, student learners can meaningfully engage with the larger community and truly experience the value of community resources and experts. When we provide learners with these innovative experiences, we are modeling, teaching, and promoting the use of personal learning networks that will be applicable and meaningful throughout their lives.

Experts not only bring knowledge to the learner but also expedite the learning process by providing on-demand information and feedback to the learner. The learner can be brought through the inquiry cycle several times within one visit. As they ask and receive information from an expert, new questions and curiosities develop, leading to new understandings. By seeking out nontraditional resources and reflecting on their value, learners can delineate the significance of one resource from another.

In addition to supporting the teaching of valuable resources and the utilization of the inquiry process, site-based partnerships also support authentic opportunities for application of digital skills. A Future Ready Librarian™ who is leading their districts toward the digital transformation of learning can bring the ultimate innovative learning experience to their learners by infusing technology. With the use of digital technology, teachers can completely redesign the site-based learning tasks to elicit higher level thinking and achievement. Ideally, with a mobile learning experience such as site-based learning, tablets and cellular phones are most conducive for recording notes, voice, and videos and capturing images while traveling throughout a learning space.

How Do You Make Them Happen?

Site-based learning experiences can look very different and fill many different (learning) needs. When creating these experiences, it is important to consider your purpose and the purpose of those you are potentially collaborating with. It can be exciting to think about all the opportunities that exist for site-based learning. But, if there is not a need for this experience, it will be hard to get others to invest at the same level you are. As librarians we can think of a million different ways to capitalize on host sites for learning. A striving Future Ready Librarian™ needs to place value on building instructional partners and being leaders in innovative learning experiences that transform teaching and learning. We need to think broader than ourselves and our standards and seek out opportunities to integrate *AASL Standards* with other content area standards and beyond.

There is not one singular approach to getting started with developing a site-based experience. It is oftentimes easier to see where needs exist, if you look within the grade level and content area curriculum. With any recent rollouts of new standards and initiatives within a building, great opportunity can be created for librarians. It seems that every year something new is being delivered, yielding teachers who have an urgency to develop curriculum. This is where we can step in and support teachers and building leaders in the design of engaging learning experiences that can meet both our needs. To be an effective leader during these opportunities, we must be prepared with high-interest learning experiences, such as site-based learning, that create the perfect window of opportunity for instructional partnerships.

It is imperative that you have an understanding of the curricular standards and are abreast of the current and innovative teaching and learning practices when developing partnerships through site-based learning. Through this you will not only be able to create meaningful connections and opportunities but also be able to respectfully lead discussions and planning of innovative learning experiences.

Utilizing professional learning networks, attending conferences across disciplines, being an active member on school-wide committees, joining online classes and webinars, and immersing yourself in standards are best ways to stay ahead and become a trusted leader of curriculum development. Refer to Table 4.1 for suggested professional learning opportunities.

Through curriculum development, you will be able to integrate *AASL Standards*, Future Ready Librarian™ Principles, and content standards into the design of innovative and engaging learning experiences such as site-based learning inquiries. It is the hope that these units can be created collaboratively during professional development, but at times

Table 4.1 Professional Learning Opportunities

Conferences	Dates and Locations
AASL National Conference	Held every two years in alternating cities across the nation.
EdTechTeacher Innovation Summit	Held in November in Boston, Massachusetts. Held in February in San Diego, California.
International Society for Technology in Education (ISTE) Conference	Held in June in alternating cities across the nation.
State Content-Specific Conferences	Varies from state to state.
State Library Conference	Varies from state to state.
Professional Learning Networks	
Twitter	@aasl: American Association of School Libraries @SLC_Online: School Library Connection @AAPSFRLibs: AAPS Future Ready Libraries @EdTechTeacher21: EdTechTeacher @iste: International Society for Technology in Education @edutopia: Edutopia @CommonSense: Common Sense Media @BIEpbl: Buck Institute for Education @curriculum21: Curriculum21 #futurereadylibs #tlchat #globalclassroom
Facebook	Learning Librarians Future Ready Librarians American Library Association WebJunction Library Journal School Library Journal International School Librarian Connection

(*Continued*)

Table 4.1   (Continued)

Online Learning	Details
School Library Connection Workshop and Webinars	https://schoollibraryconnection.com/
ISTE Librarians Network & ISTE U	https://www.iste.org/learn/librarians
WebJunction	https://www.webjunction.org
Professional Reading	**Details**
Rx for the Common Core	Coauthors: Mary Boyd Ratzer & Paige Jaegar https://www.abc-clio.com/ABC-CLIOCorporate/product.aspx?pc=A4235P
Think Tank Library	Coauthors: Paige Jaegar & Mary Ratzer K–5: https://www.abc-clio.com/ABC-CLIOCorporate/product.aspx?pc=A4592P 6–12: https://www.abc-clio.com/ABC-CLIOCorporate/product.aspxvapc=A4591P

they will be designed collaboratively during planning periods. There is also the reality that there won't be time to get everyone together to collaborate on the unit. In these cases, you may need to independently create the structure of the unit prior to meeting with teachers and share your vision with teachers individually to gather their feedback for suggested modifications.

Once the unit is developed, roles and responsibilities should be established, and all parties should have a clear understanding of the integral work that lies ahead. Contact should be established with the partner site, if needed, and all accommodations should be made with the school district for travel. If technology is being used for the learning experience, be sure to have a clear vision for transporting and maintaining care of the devices.

As students begin to partake in the learning experience and teachers and librarians work to guide them through their inquiry, take time to capture their learning. These opportunities enrich and expand their learning experiences and provide them with the skills they need for success. It is important for parents, teachers, students, administrators, and community members to witness the value the library program brings to a student's education.

LEAP

Leap (step) forward by . . .

1. Brainstorming opportunities for a site-based learning experience that would allow the integration of *AASL Standards* with other content area standards.
2. Seeking out internal professional learning opportunities where you can collaborate with teachers and building leaders on curriculum development or unit design.
3. Investing time in educating yourself on new standards, new technology, and best practices so that you are prepared to lead the design of site-based learning experiences that meet the curricular needs of the students.

SITE-BASED LEARNING EXPERIENCE #1

Named Learning Experience
Local Community Site (Lake George)

Partnership
Classroom teacher, Librarian, Physical Site (Lake George)

Future Ready Framework (refer to Figure 4.1)

FUTURE READY FRAMEWORK

☐ ROBUST INFRASTUCTURE

☐ BUDGET AND RESOURCES

☑ COMMUNITY PARTNERSHIPS

☐ DATA AND PRIVACY

☐ COLLABORATIVE LEADERSHIP

☑ USE OF SPACE AND TIME

☐ LITERACY

☑ CURRICULUM, INSTRUCTION, AND ASSESSMENT
  ☑ Curates Digital Resources   ☑ Builds Instructional Partnerships   ☐ Empowers Students as Creators

☐ PERSONALIZED PROFESSIONAL LEARNING

Figure 4.1

AASL Standards
AASL Standards for Learners: I.A.1., I.A.2., I.D.1., I.D.2., I.D.3, II.A.1, II.D.2., III.A.3., III.B.2., III.D.1., V.C.1., VI.A.1., VI.D.1.

AASL Standards for School Librarians: I.A.1., I.A.2., I.C.1., I.D.2., I.D.3., II.A.1., III.D.1., III.D.2., VI.A.1., VI.A.2., VI.D.1.

AASL School Standards for School Libraries: I.A.1., I.B.1., I.B.2., I.C.2., I.D.1., I.D.2., II.A.2., III.A.2., IV.A.1., IV.A.3., IV.B.1., IV.B.2., V.D.3.

Experience Summary
This is one of my favorite and most unique inquiries that I collaborate on each year. The idea for this experience was generated from a session that I attended at the *Boston Innovation Summit*. A group of teachers and their instructional technology director presented site-based learning and the benefits of using sites in the local community as resources for learning. Having been familiar with the social studies standards, an instant connection with the second-grade curriculum came to mind for me. Upon my return to school, I reviewed the social studies standards, previewed our English language arts units, and studied the ISTE and *AASL Standards* to draw connections for a possible cocurricular unit focused on the lake within our community.

I presented the idea of a site-based learning experience to our second-grade teachers, and they were intrigued to learn more. They loved the idea of using the lake in our community as a resource for learning, but they were reluctant to take on this experience without a better understanding of what it would look like. Together, during limited common planning time, we created a blueprint for the experience (refer to Table 4.2). To help support teachers and the success of this experience in its birth, I took any extra responsibilities associated with the experience, such as establishing partnerships, organizing technology, seeking administrator approval, and booking a field trip through our transportation department.

Table 4.2 Lake Inquiry Blueprint

Second-Grade Lake Inquiry		
Compelling Question (Essential Question)	Why is the lake important to our community?	
SS Framework Key Idea(s) & AASL Standards	*Social Studies:* 2.5 Geography and natural resources shape how urban and suburban and rural communities develop and sustain themselves. *AASL Standards for Learners:* I.A.1., I.A.2., I.B.1., I.B.2., I.B.3., I.C.3., I.C.4., I.D.1., I.D.2., I.D.3, I.D.4, II.D.1., II.D.2., II.D.3., III.A.1., III.A.2., III.B.2., III.C.2, III.D.1., III.D.2., IV.A.1., IV.A.2., IV.A.3, IV.B.1., IV.B.2., IV.B.4., IV.D.1., IV.D.2., V.A.3., V.C.1., V.C.2., V.D.1., V.D.3., VI.A.1.,VI.A.2., VI.B.1., VI.B.2., VI.B.3., VI.C.2., VI.D.1.	
Stimulus for Staging the Question (Maps, charts, images, etc.)	Do you want to go on a field trip to the lake?	
Supporting Question 1 (Wonder)	Supporting Question 2 (Investigate)	Supporting Question 3 (Synthesize-Investigate-Synthesize)
Conceptual Understanding:	Conceptual Understanding:	Conceptual Understanding:
2.5 Geography and natural resources shape how urban and suburban and rural communities develop and sustain themselves.	2.5 Geography and natural resources shape how urban and suburban and rural communities develop and sustain themselves.	2.5 Geography and natural resources shape how urban and suburban and rural communities develop and sustain themselves.
Question:	Question:	Question:
What about the lake interests me? What about the lake do I want to learn more about?	Where can I find more information about my interests with the lake?	How can I take what I have learned about the lake and teach others?
Formative Performance Task	Formative Performance Task	Formative Performance Task
Practices: • Develop Questions about the community. • Ask geographic questions about where places are located and why they are located there, using geographic representations, such as maps and models. Describe where places are in relation to each other, and describe connections between places.	Practices: • Recognize different forms of evidence used to make meaning in social studies (including sources such as art and photographs, artifacts, oral histories, maps, and graphs). • Identify and explain creation and/or authorship, purpose, and format of evidence.	Practices: • Recognize the relationship between geography, economics, and history in his or her community. • Describe how his or her actions affect the environment of the community; describe how the environment of the community affects human activities. • Describe how human activities alter places in a community.
Activities: *Day 1:* Prepare students for a site-based field trip to the lake. Discuss what we know about our lake, and recognize that	Activities: *Day 5:* Brainstorm as a class about where you are going to find the information to your questions. Develop a list:	Activities: *Day 8:* As a class, collectively review the information that we learned and the value of utilizing experts

Second-Grade Lake Inquiry

although we see the lake every day, there are lots of things that we don't know about our lake. Introduce EQ, and establish the need to visit the lake. Teach students how to use Educreations to capture notes through images, voice, and drawing. Take images, and ask "wonder" questions. Share expectations for using devices at the lake.

Day 2: Visit the lake (one hour). Start at Shepard's Park, and walk down to Dog Beach. Students should take up to ten pictures on their iPads, using Educreations to record their thoughts. For each picture they should ask a question about what they want to learn more about.

Stop and visit Sergeant on the Marine Boat.

Day 3: Within each room, students will review their notes. They will determine the one thing they were interested in learning more about. Collaboratively, as a class, interests will be sorted into topics.
- Businesses
- Transportation
- Recreational
- Animals and plants that are impacted by the lake
- Services
- Jobs

Day 4: Mrs. Crossman will teach students how to develop good questions. Beginning with sharing an image in the newspaper and giving students twenty questions to try and determine all they can about the image. Then teach them how to use the "wonder" grid to develop good questions that solicit more information.

Activities:

Day 5: Brainstorm as a class about where you are going to find the information to your questions. Develop a list:
- Experts within the community
- Websites
- Printed materials (brochures, pamphlets, etc.)

Begin with community experts, and identify people who might be able to help in each of the topic areas we are studying.

(Mrs. Crossman will reach out to potential partners.)

Day 6: Explain the experts who will be coming in and their role. Learners will determine which expert will help them most. After making their selection and reviewing it with the teachers, they will join that expert on the day of the visit. Teachers will model how to take notes during the visit by the expert.
- Okay to use incomplete sentences.
- Ask that information is repeated when necessary.
- Record any extra information that is beneficial, even if you didn't have a question for that information.

Day 7: During the expert's visit, learners will bring their questions on a clipboard to the expert session that best suits their needs. Students will ask their questions and record their answers on their graphic organizers.

One teacher will be paired with each expert (curriculum partner). Teachers will help moderate and guide the learning experience, ensuring

to help us learn. Recognize the responsibility that we now have to teach others about what we have learned. Brainstorm ways that we can share what we have learned.
- eBooks
- Posters
- Pamphlets
- Websites

Students will then synthesize their notes and reflect on whether they have enough information to create their knowledge products.
- Identify information that will help them to answer the EQ.
- Transfer useful information to the Lake Inquiry graphic organizer.
  - Record facts.
  - Turn facts into statements.

Day 9: Students will determine what they still need to know. They will use information websites to fill in knowledge gaps.
- Mrs. Crossman will instruct students on keyword searching.
  - Use *Lake George* with each keyword search.
    - Model with the topic of beaches.
  - Teach students how to cite information found on websites.
- Students can choose to contact experts (curriculum partners) with follow-up questions.

Day 10: Continue researching on websites. Students will record information on Lake Inquiry graphic organizer and turn facts into supporting statements. They will complete the topic sentence and concluding statement.

(*Continued*)

Table 4.2 (Continued)

Second-Grade Lake Inquiry		
Review the EQ with the students. Have students use the "wonder" grid to create questions about their topic that will help them to answer the EQ. Record questions on Question Record Sheet. Teachers will work with each student to provide guidance and challenge students to create deep questions.	that all students have their questions answered and have recorded responses on their graphic organizers.	*Day 11:* Students will create knowledge products in PicCollage and share with Mrs. Crossman. Depending on students' choice of knowledge products, Mrs. Crossman will collectively assemble all student work in the desired format. Students will reflect on learning with partners.
Featured Source(s)	Featured Source(s)	Featured Source(s)
Wonder Grid Question Record Sheet Educreations App	Question Record Sheet	Lake Inquiry graphic organizer PicCollage Book Creator
Assessment	Assessment	Assessment
Question Record Sheets	Notes on Question Record sheet graphic organizer	Graphic organizer
Summative Performance Task (Express)	Knowledge Product	
Taking Informed Action (Express)	Students' final products will be shared with experts to be put on display at their various locations within the community. A copy of the class final knowledge product will be housed in the school library.	

The experience itself is unique in that it relies on both internal and external learning partnerships. As shared in Chapter 1 (when we discuss the internal partnership associated with this experience), we rely on curriculum partners to help with the *investigate* stage of our Lake Inquiry. However, during this stage, the stage prior to student investigations, we spend time letting students *wonder* about what they want to *investigate*. Here is where we rely on external partnerships developed through site-based partnerships that support and enhance our students learning experience.

The Lake Inquiry is built around a specific social studies standard that addresses students' understanding of the impact natural resources have on shaping communities. Lucky for us, we have a beautiful natural resource in our community, Lake George. We begin the *wonder* stage of the inquiry process by discussing Lake George and what we know and don't know about it. After a brief discussion where we activate students' thinking and build their background knowledge, we introduce the essential question: "Why is the lake important to our community?" This question typically creates a lot of chatter and leaves students with a lot of curiosity about the lake and our community. This curiosity activates our students' interest in learning more about the lake and leads us to a purposeful site-based partnership with Lake George.

As a Future Ready Librarian™ and a supporter of meaningful technology integration, I built an instructional day into our lesson plans for this inquiry prior to visiting the lake. During their visit to the lake, students are tasked with developing *wonder* questions about things they are curious about in relation to the lake. It was important that students not only knew how to capture their questions and ideas related to what they were curious about, but that they also recognized the need for a tool to record their thoughts. I helped them discover this need and shared the digital tool *Educreations*. This tool allowed them to capture a picture, sketch on their image, and record questions and thoughts using their voice. This valuable instructional time allowed me to address several skills and standards that were critical to the success of our learning at the lake. It also provided students ample time to practice prior to our trip the following day.

When students visited the lake the following day, they were tasked with three responsibilities:

- Use *Educreations* to take a maximum of ten pictures of things around the lake that you are curious about.
- Use the *Educreations* drawing tool to indicate the section of the image that you are most curious about.
- Use the microphone on *Educreations* to record your *wonder* questions associated with the image.

During our trip, we walked a half of a mile along the shore of the lake with our iPads, stopping to let students capture thoughts, photographs, and notes. We also built in a special stop along the way to meet with a patrol boat sergeant. He took time to let students view his boat and share about his job on the lake. I had established this partnership ahead of time so that students could see firsthand the jobs that are needed because of our community's natural resource. Naturally, this sparked several students' curiosity that later became the focus of their inquiry. In addition to guiding students through their thinking and curiosity, I also spent time capturing the learning experience. I later used these photos to celebrate our learning on social media and the library website.

Immediately after returning from the field trip at the lake, we shared the things we were most interested in learning about and grouped our ideas into categories. This experience gave students an opportunity to not only share their interest but also gain an awareness of what other students found to be intriguing. After grouping each of the student's interests, narrowing down our topics of interest to animals, safety, jobs, rules and laws, recreation, and entertainment and businesses on the lake came next. We were then prepared for the move into the next stage of inquiry that was discussed in Chapter 1.

This two-day process of allowing students to discover and wonder through a site-based exploration is monumental in setting the stage for meaningful student-centered work throughout the rest of the inquiry. It gives the learning that follows relevancy and allows students' own self-interests to guide their learning. If the site-based partnership were to be removed from this learning experience, students would not be as invested and not as driven to actively engage in the learning.

Suggested Modifications
- **Site-Based Partnership Location.** Not everyone has a significant natural resource in their community, but that should not stop you from creating a site-based partnership with a location in your community. To determine the location, be sure to consider the standard and the need for

the learning experience. Some options worth consideration would be historical buildings or grounds, businesses, and emergency service buildings.

- **Schedule.** This inquiry does require the use of an absence from school for a short period of time (the length of the field trip). If you do not have flexible scheduling in your library, I encourage you to seek approval for a substitute so that you can participate in the site-based learning experience.
- **Technology.** iPads are certainly a great tool for capturing thoughts, images, and questions while mobile, but a simple paper and pencil with a clipboard could also work. If you choose to go this route, it would be valuable to have a place where students can sketch an illustration or diagram and a place where they can write a question.
- **Apps.** I chose to use Educreations with my students, but there are many great apps for taking notes. *Notability* is another amazing note-taking tool that allows students to add pictures, take notes, and record their voice.

Resources

Digital Resources, Tools, and Links
Educreations: https://www.educreations.com/
Inquiry Blueprint (blank): http://bit.ly/InquiryBlankBlueprint
Lake Inquiry Unit (full version): http://bit.ly/LakeInquiry
Notability: https://apple.co/2ORzhE7

SITE-BASED LEARNING EXPERIENCE #2

Named Learning Experience
Museum Site

Partnership
Classroom Teachers, Baseball Hall of Fame, Librarian

Future Ready Framework (refer to Figure 4.2)

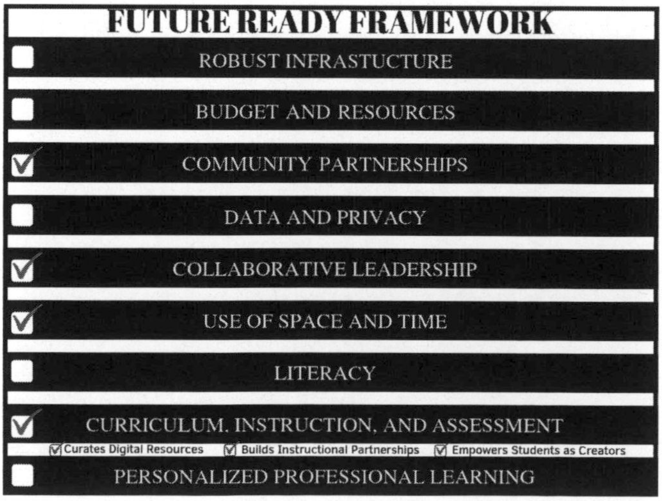

Figure 4.2

AASL Standards

AASL Standards for Learners: I.A.1., I.A.2., I.B.1., I.B.2., I.B.3., I.C.1., I.C.2., I.D.1., I.D.2., I.D.3., III.A.1., III.A.1., III.A.2., III.B.2., III.D.1., IV.A.1., IV.A.2., IV.A.3., IV.B.1., V.C.1., V.C.2., V.D.3., VI.A.1., VI.A.2., VI.B.1., VI.B.2., VI.D.1.

AASL Standards for School Librarians: I.A.1., I.A.2., I.B.1., I.B.2., I.B.3., I.C.1., I.C.2., I.D.1., I.D.3., II.A.1., II.D.1., II.D.2., II.D.3., III.A.1., III.A.2., III.B.2., III.D.1., IV.A.1., IV.A.2., IV.A.3,

IV.D.1., IV.D., V.A.3., V.C.1., V.C.2, V.D.3., VI.A.1., VI.A.2., VI.B.1., VI.B.2., VI.D.1.

AASL School Standards for School Libraries: I.A.1., I.A.2., I.B.1., I.B.2., I.C.1., I.C.2., I.D.1., II.A.1., II.A.2., II.D.2., II.D.3., III.A.2., III.B.2., III.C.1., III.C.2., III.D.1., IV.A.1., IV.A.3., IV.B.1., IV.B.2., V.A.1., V.A.2., V.B.1., V.D.1.,V.D.3., VI.A.3., VI.C.2.

Experience Summary

My desire and obligation to design opportunities for our students to engage in authentic inquiry, while also exploring a variety of information sources and meaningful digital tools, led (me) toward the facilitation of a site-based learning experience for our fifth-grade students. Through a deep understanding of curricular standards, I was able to identify a connection in our social studies and English language arts curriculum, where we could build a site-based learning experience with the *Baseball Hall of Fame*. This experience would suit my curricular needs as the librarian and the curricular needs of the classroom teacher. In addition, this was another opportunity to meet the needs of our district's strategic plan by creating a community partnership. Refer to Figure 4.3 for a tip to help you with this stage of planning.

IN ORDER TO BE AN EFFECTIVE LEADER DURING PROFESSIONAL DEVELOPMENT AND CO-PLANNING SESSIONS IT IS CRITICAL TO HOLD YOURSELF ACCOUNTABLE TO A GROWTH MINDSET. EMBRACE NEW STANDARDS, SKILLS, TECHNOLOGY AND INNOVATIVE TEACHING PRACTICES, AND STAY ABREAST OF CHANGES WITHIN ALL RELATED DISCIPLINES. THIS WORK WILL ALLOW YOU TO MAKE CONNECTIONS, SEE OPPORTUNITIES AND ULTIMATELY TO BE AN EFFECTIVE AND RESPECTED LEADER THAT IS SEEN AS AN ESSENTIAL RESOURCE.

Figure 4.3

I began by having discussions with our curriculum director and content-specific curriculum leaders to look for opportunities where I could work with teachers on designing this experience for our students. These discussions led to the coplanning of professional development for our teachers in both English language arts and social studies. These professional development sessions occurred both during the school year and over the summer. During a portion of the professional development, I provided teachers with direct instruction about the following:

- Site-based learning
- Inquiry
- Literacies (information, digital, and media)
- Integration of cross-curricular standards (social studies, English language arts, AASL, and Instructional Society for Technology in Education)

Providing this foundation enabled the remaining time to be used efficiently. We were then able to coplan a cross-curricular site-based learning experience for students that integrated a multitude of standards. We continued our work outside of our professional development session, during monthly social studies curriculum meetings and after-school meetings.

Our collaborative work looked for connections across curriculum areas:

- In our reading and writing units, we found opportunities to integrate required content and skills through historical book clubs and a poetry unit.
- For social studies, we focused on meeting standards through student opportunities to "build knowledge through Inquiry"—best practices according to AASL and the C3 Social Studies Framework.
- Five of the six *Shared Foundations* of the *AASL Standards*: *Inquire, Collaborate, Curate, Explore*, and *Engage* would be addressed through the social studies individual student-centered inquiries.
- Within the social studies inquiry, we found purposeful opportunities to integrate technology and technology standards.
- Particular attention to media and digital literacy skills, along with the ethical use of information and technologies, could be employed through the social studies inquiry. All of these helped to address our district-wide strategic goal.
- Through student acquisition, creation, and sharing of knowledge.

Next, we were ready to design a cocurricular unit. Reading and writing units were created by the teachers to build understanding about minorities in baseball. It then became very easy for me to design a baseball-themed inquiry where students would build knowledge of important social studies *Key Ideas* about struggles that minorities in our nation faced with equality, civil rights, and sovereignty. I strategically designed the inquiry part of the unit so that I could also teach students specific skills addressed in the *AASL Standards* and our school's Innovation Standards (which were adopted from the *ISTE* Standards). Student would then need to apply their learned skills in order to acquire knowledge, create knowledge products, and share understandings.

Together, we created an essential question that has changed over time to better suit the learning circumstances. Through a site-based learning experience, students would need to discover "What inequalities existed in baseball for minorities?" It is important to recognize that this essential question was not the ideal essential question. It did not require a deep level of synthesizing; however, it best suited the concerns of the teachers who felt the original essential question, "How did baseball help advance the rights of minorities in our country?" required too much scaffolding for the allotted time.

Once the curricular connections were made, the specific standards to be addressed were indicated, and the essential question was determined, I took the lead to begin developing the site-based-inquiry learning experience. Identifying the roles of each unique member of our teaching team was essential. For this unit, the teachers strictly focused on designing the reading and writing units that would prepare the students with the background knowledge they would need for the site-based-inquiry learning experience. I was tasked with leading the delivery of the inquiry to the students, with support from the teachers, while we collaboratively tackled the management of the learning experience.

The management of the learning experience required establishing a connection with *The Baseball Hall of Fame*. This partnership was made easily through their robust website (https://baseballhall.org/discover-more/education/learn). It includes an array of educational programs for classrooms, all of which are aligned with *Common Core State Learning Standards*. Contact was secured with the coordinator of educational programs through a contact form on the website as well. Once the initial contact was established, the coordinator and I partnered on the planning and organizing of a visit that would meet our curricular needs.

Student-centered learning and choice were at the heart of our unit design. While the museum offered many programs, two programs seemed to fit our curricular needs best:

Women's History: Dirt on Their Skirts and *Civil Rights: Before You Could Say "Jackie Robinson."* Students chose one of the programs to attend. We felt this unique program design would provide more relevancy and impact for the students.

Another element associated with the management of the site-based learning experience is the technology. I was responsible for working with the technology department to gather enough iPads for our fifth graders to borrow (they have laptops, not iPads). In addition, I was responsible for selecting the apps that students would use and teaching them how to use them. The teachers and I, together, developed a plan for transporting the iPads in suitcases.

The teachers took on the responsibility of managing administrator approval, student permission slips, transportation, and payment for the trip to the museum. Together we were able to collaboratively support one another in establishing the foundation for a successful learning experience. It was important to have clearly defined roles and responsibilities and ensure that the workload wasn't too heavy for one person.

After establishing a partnership with the museum, addressing some of the necessary management details and determining the components of the inquiry, the inquiry blueprint was finished, and it was now time to deliver the learning experience. In preparation for our site-based learning experience, I spent several days pushing into each of the fifth-grade classrooms. When setting the stage for the unit, I built the students' interest and excitement by telling them that we would be moving our classroom at the end of the week, to the Baseball Hall of Fame. I said that although this will feel like a field trip, it will be a little different. The museum will be our resource for answering the question "What inequalities existed for minorities in baseball?"

Once we introduced the essential question and ultimately the purpose for going to the Baseball Hall of Fame, students began to *wonder*. The students started with basic questions: "What are minorities? "Does inequality mean the opposite of 'equal'?" Once we discussed and addressed these questions as a group, I began to push their thinking and wondering a little further. Students had already been exposed to the topics of segregation and civil rights through literature, but they had not specifically studied this topic. I asked them to identify what they already knew about minorities in baseball, and together students were able to identify the two groups as African Americans and women. Once they were able to identify those groups, I asked them to think about what they already knew about these two groups in history. I had them question whether minorities were treated equal to white American men who played baseball. This activity generated a lot of discussion and questions. After activating the students' curiosity, we referred back to the essential question and had students develop questions that they wanted to find the answers to at the museum. Students recorded these questions on sticky notes and shared them with the class.

Student engagement was at a high, after we developed questions. It was then time to address the value the museum itself would bring to our research. It was critical to let students discover the important role of museums and their rich resources. I began by asking them, "Why do you think we are going to the museum and not simply using the library at school?" This conversation led to important discussion about primary resources, collections, stories, and the invaluable wealth of knowledge museum experts provide. Ultimately we agreed that although we could research and answer the essential question at our school library, we would not be able to have the same experience and gain the insight that the sources at the museum would be able to provide within one day. We recognized that the museum is a warehouse of information and we were lucky to be able to experience it.

The students were excited to visit the museum and knew what their job was at the museum, but they still didn't know their purpose. This was our final unit for the year, and we wanted to use this experience to also assess the students' digital and media literacy skills. Therefore, the final presentation was up to them. After returning from the museum, students would need to create a digital presentation that would answer the essential questions. We shared a rubric (refer to Table 4.3) with the students so they were aware of expectations, but it was up to them, as individuals, to choose the tool they would use to create and share their presentation.

One last thing needed to be addressed before we sent students off to "investigate," and students in all three classes *wondered* this on their own: "How are we going to gather the information?" It was exciting to think that students were anticipating the need for a place to take notes and gather information. Students were excited to learn that we would be bringing iPads to the museum with us. We engaged in rich dialogue about components of digital literacy and the advantages of bringing an iPad versus a pen and paper or even a computer. The app that was introduced to them for note taking was *Notes*. Time was spent sharing the different features that would help them gather evidence: camera, video, sketching, text, and tables.

Once we arrived at the *Baseball Hall of Fame*, the classes were divided into four groups based on the minority that the students chose to study. Each group was provided with an expert tour guide who led them through the museum. The guides stopped at different exhibits to highlight information as we explored the museum and allowed students time to individually explore as well. During this time, students could be found capturing pictures and taking notes to explain how the evidence they captured supported the essential question. The main highlight of the tour was spent in the section of the museum that focused on the minority (women or African Americans) that the students were studying. Each group was able to spend a half hour with the tour guide, diving deep into primary resources and artifacts. Students spent this time engaged, interacting with uniforms, contracts, photographs, and schedules. Inquiring minds were heard asking questions, looking for clarification and drawing conclusions. This experience proved to the teachers and to the students the power of engaging in partnerships with experts and outside resources. As wonderful as our school library is, we do not have the rich resources that *Baseball Hall of Fame* could provide us. In addition, the wealth of knowledge that the tour guides had made it possible for us to gather immediate answers to our many questions. This efficient way of gathering information saved us time and energy.

As we went through the museum, I captured the learning, excitement, and curiosity of our students as they explored and researched. As the champion and advocate for this innovative learning experience, I showcased our experience through the library social media feeds. It is fundamental to our programs that we capitalize on opportunities to reinforce the value we bring to our students' learning and our efforts to support our district's mission, vision, and values.

Upon returning to our district, I pushed into each of the fifth-grade classrooms to accentuate the next step in the inquiry process. We had a great collection of evidence to support our essential question from the museum, but what were we going to do with it? It was our social responsibility as learners to share what we learned and to teach and inform others. Collaboratively, we discussed the need to create knowledge products. This was an opportune time to integrate digital and media literacy skills into instruction. With the help of educational videos from *Media Smarts* and *Companies Committed to Kids* (http://

Table 4.3 Baseball Hall of Fame Project Rubric

	4	3	2	1	
Innovative Constructor	I created a digital knowledge product that included 4 examples of inequalities that existed in baseball, for the minority that I studied, through comparisons.	I created a digital knowledge product that included 3 examples of inequalities that existed in baseball, for the minority that I studied, through comparisons.	I created a digital knowledge product that included 2 examples of inequalities that existed in baseball, for the minority that I studied, through comparisons.	I created a digital knowledge product that included 1 example of an inequality that existed in baseball, for the minority that I studied, through a comparison.	/4
Creative Communicator	I created and presented content to my peers, that included all 4 of the expectations listed below: • Appropriate use of Aesthetics (background, images, audio, font, visuals, transitions) • Accurate and Reliable Information • Primary & Secondary Resources • Citations	I created and presented content to my peers, that included 3 of the expectations listed below: • Appropriate use of Aesthetics (background, images, audio, font, visuals, transitions) • Accurate and Reliable Information • Primary & Secondary Resources • Citations	I created and presented content to my peers, that included 2 of the expectations listed below: • Appropriate use of Aesthetics (background, images, audio, font, visuals, transitions) • Accurate and Reliable Information • Primary & Secondary Resources • Citations	I created and presented content to my peers, that included 1 of the expectations listed below: • Appropriate use of Aesthetics (background, images, audio, font, visuals, transitions) • Accurate and Reliable Information • Primary & Secondary Resources • Citations	/4
Global Citizen & Collaborator	I effectively and collaboratively utilized "local" experts to examine issues of inequalities in baseball by gathering 4 examples in my digital notes that broadened my and my peers understanding and learning.	I effectively and collaboratively utilized "local" experts to examine issues of inequalities in baseball by gathering 3 examples in my digital notes that broadened my and my peers understanding and learning.	I effectively and collaboratively utilized "local" experts to examine issues of inequalities in baseball by gathering 2 examples in my digital notes that broadened my and my peers understanding and learning.	I effectively and collaboratively utilized "local" experts to examine issues of inequalities in baseball by gathering 1 example in my digital notes that broadened my and my peers understanding and learning.	/4
Empowered Learner	I demonstrated the ability to complete 4 of the following expectations: • choose an appropriate medium for my audience. • choose an appropriate medium for my purpose. • effectively constructed a knowledge product with the selected medium. • troubleshooted the selected medium.	I demonstrated the ability to complete 3 of the following expectations: • choose an appropriate medium for my audience. • choose an appropriate medium for my purpose. • effectively constructed a knowledge product with the selected medium. • troubleshooted the selected medium.	I demonstrated the ability to complete 2 of the following expectations: • choose an appropriate medium for my audience. • choose an appropriate medium for my purpose. • effectively constructed a knowledge product with the selected medium. • troubleshooted the selected medium.	I demonstrated the ability to complete 1 of the following expectations: • choose an appropriate medium for my audience. • choose an appropriate medium for my purpose. • effectively constructed a knowledge product with the selected medium. • troubleshooted the selected medium.	/4

mediasmarts.ca/media-literacy-101), which partnered to create short *Media Minute* videos for teaching students to understand key media concepts, I was able to create a Google Slides presentation with embedded videos and activities. This lesson covered vital components to consider when creating a media-based knowledge product: audience, medium, aesthetics, purpose, and deliberate decisions made by the knowledge constructors. This lesson totaled forty-five minutes from start to finish and provided them with the knowledge to become empowered learners and constructors of information.

Before sending students off to synthesize their notes and create knowledge products, we reviewed the expectations for the knowledge product by sharing a project rubric (refer to Table 4.3) with the students. I created the rubric for the students after consulting with the classroom teachers about expectations and reviewing our freshly generated district innovation standards (which I was part of creating). The rubric addressed content along with information, digital, and media literacy skills and was used by teachers to evaluate their work.

Students worked on their projects for three one-hour class periods. All three classes were working at the same time, so I roved between classrooms, providing assistance and coaching students through their thinking. The excitement buzzed as students deliberated over which was the right digital tool for their purpose. Several students began using a tool and quickly reflected on their choice and decided a different tool was necessary. During these moments I recognized and praised them for their ability to analyze and reflect on the usefulness of the tool, which is a strong quality of an empowered learner.

As students dove into synthesizing their notes and constructing their knowledge products, they were each at different levels of understanding. A majority of students quickly developed knowledge products simply showcasing inequalities in baseball. The deeper connection of bridging the "inequality" to a reference point was often overlooked. For example, students stated, "Women had to play baseball in skirts." However, they didn't take the additional step of drawing the comparison to what male American league baseball players wore. This deeper level of thinking both challenged the students and created opportunities for them to grow as communicators. I could be heard saying, "Don't make your audience do the work . . . make the connections for your learners."

There were multiple students who began the task of synthesizing their information and quickly realized that they did not gather enough information during our time at the museum. I would then highlight the inquiry wheel (refer to Figure 1.3, p. 10) and ask these students to identify where they were in the learning process. Students would acknowledge that they were *synthesizing* and that the next step would either be to *express* or revisit the initial step of *wonder*. Through discussion and reflection of their learning, most would discover that they needed to go back through the inquiry process: determining what information they still needed to know; locating where they would find that information (databases and websites); and gathering the necessary information to include in their knowledge product. These opportunities were most valuable to the learner, as they were able to act on my feedback (learner standard I.C.3.) to implement a plan to fill the gaps in their knowledge (learner standard I.B.2.).

Reflection, analysis, and perseverance over the three days of synthesizing positively impacted learner growth and the development of robust knowledge products. This led to the meaningful showcasing of their work to their teachers and peers through a museum walk. All three classes were divided and dispersed among the three classrooms, and students explored and engaged with the knowledge products on display, leaving feedback for their peers on *sticky notes*. This left our learners feeling proud of their work and their personal learning experience.

Suggested Modifications
- Being that not everyone can visit the *Baseball Hall of Fame*, seek out local and state museums that are relevant to your social studies or science curriculum.
- Use the buildings in your community as a springboard for site-based inquiries, by having students answer the essential question "If these buildings could whisper secrets of their past, what would they say?"
- If iPads are limited, try to collect a small number to bring on the site-based learning experience. Students can be broken into groups, and one iPad can be provided per group.
- If your schedule doesn't allow you to push into classrooms, collaborate with classroom teachers on developing a learning experience where part of the instruction will take place within the classroom and the other part during library (class).
- If working at the junior-high or high-school level and teachers and classes aren't able to work with you, consider working with your administration to develop a required research class for each of the grade levels. Then, you can build the site-based learning experience into your curriculum.

Resources

Digital Resources, Tools, and Links
Baseball Hall of Fame Contact: education@baseballhall.org
Checklist Generator: http://pblchecklist.4teachers.org/
Rubric Generator: http://rubistar.4teachers.org

GROW

Grow your library program by . . .

1. Selecting a curriculum area to build an integrated site-based learning experience that addresses *AASL Standards* and, when possible, the meaningful integration of technology standards and district goals.
2. Coconstructing an innovative and authentic site-based learning experience with a combination of instructional partner(s) within your school and an external partner(s) within your community.
3. Delivering and showcasing a site-based learning experience where locations and resources within the community act as a host for learning.

ACTION PLAN

Setting the Stage
Approach this learning experience by determining the following criteria for your work (refer to Table 4.4):

Establishing the Partnership
Use the bullets featured in each section of Table 4.5 to guide you in your actions toward developing a site-based partnership.

Table 4.4

Setting the Stage		
Goals	*Key Players*	*Groundwork*
• What AASL Standards are you planning to address? • What Future Ready Principles are you planning to address? • What content standards are you planning to address? • What are you hoping the host site will be able to provide (expert knowledge, resources, platform for inquiry, etc.)?	• Who will be your instructional partners within the building? • Who are the potential partners associated with the host site of interest? • Will you need to seek approval from building leaders? • Are there people who can help you make connections with potential host sites?	• What content areas are going to be supported through the partnership? • How much time do you have to work with students to prepare them for the visit, carry out the visit, and continue learning post visit? • What technology will be needed, and how will it be managed? • What skills and knowledge do the students need prior to the learning experience? • What skills and knowledge are you responsible for teaching versus your instructional partner(s) and the site-based partner(s)? • What is the desired student learning outcome?

Table 4.5

Who	• Determine who the contact people are at the host site where you are looking to host your experience. • Determine who on your instructional team is going to contact potential partners.
What	• Determine the responsibilities, in relation to the site-based experience, of the partner, your instructional team, and the students before, during, and after the learning experience, and communicate those to the site-based partner.
How	• Seek contact information for potential partners through the host site's website, when possible. • When possible, contact host site first by phone to clearly communicate your goals for the learning experience, and discuss possibilities for learning experience. Follow-up communication can then be carried out through email or less formal means of communication.
Where	• Determine where at the host location specific learning opportunities will take place.
When	• Collaborate with the potential partner to set up a day and time for the learning experience that fits at the appropriate time in the learning process. • When reaching out to potential partners with days and times for learning experiences, offer several options upfront to limit unnecessary multiple back-and-forth responses.

Delivering the Learning Experience

Use the information in Table 4.6 to guide you in your actions toward developing a site-based learning experience with the support of a community partnership.

Table 4.6

Steps to Developing Site-Based Learning Experiences
1. Utilize professional learning networks, conferences across disciplines, and join committees, classes, and webinars to get an understanding of curricular standards and best practices across content areas.
2. Seek opportunities where a curricular need can be met through the integration of *AASL Standards*, with content and technology standards.
3. Collaborate with teachers to develop a unit with a site-based partnership.
4. Assign roles and responsibilities for successful rollout and implementation of the learning experience (establishing partnership, travel permissions and expenses, management of technology, etc.).
5. Capture and showcase the learning experience to stakeholders and beyond.

5

Mobile Reading Partnerships

LEARN

What Are Mobile Reading Partnerships?

Taking learning on the road through mobile reading partnerships requires the librarian to find creative ways to extend reading through travel. Extending reading can mean extending access to books or reading opportunities. These partnerships provide rich learning experiences that touch on *AASL Standards* and several core areas of the *Future Ready Librarian™ Framework*, while promoting a love of reading.

Partnerships for mobile learning are formed by connecting with a physical location or person. Through this connection learners are engrossed in a reading-based experience. Each partnership is uniquely defined by the learners' needs and community-based resources that are available.

Why Do They Matter?

Providing equal access to books and developing strong reading habits for learners are critical roles of librarians. We must commit ourselves to developing innovative lessons, units, programs, and learning experiences that foster students' passion for reading. We need to do everything we can to support students in their efforts to be passionate readers, and it is through our efforts and actions that we can empower students to be avid readers who desire a thirst for books. Mobile reading partnerships are a great place to start. They provide extended access to books and provoke good reading habits.

Our libraries are filled with books that are waiting to be read, but we must not stop there when it comes to providing access to literature. It's time to embrace the innovator within us and create new and improved opportunities that are relevant to our students' needs. We can start by thinking about their needs. What is happening when learners aren't in our buildings? Can they readily access books? Do they know where they can access books? Do they feel comfortable to branch beyond the familiar walls of our libraries? Do they have good role models at home who are promoting reading? These are important questions to consider. Through mobile reading partnerships, we can answer yes to each one of these questions.

Unfortunately, we do not have unlimited access to our students, and they do not have unlimited access to books. *Mobile reading partnerships* afford opportunities beyond the school day by transporting books to students within the community, bringing students to books within the community, or sparking a passion for reading through interactive activities. These experiences allow us to cultivate a lifestyle of reading, where learners feel passionate about engaging with books and eagerly seek access to literature.

It is our job to prepare our students for the future by fostering the skills and passion for continuous learning. A well-suited lifelong learner needs to not only know where to access books outside of school; they also need to feel comfortable doing it. The more we can expose our students to accessing books through various venues, the more comfortable they are going to feel accessing books on their own. Equally so, the more we showcase our reading habits and celebrate reading in all its capacities, the more likely learners are going to champion the same lifestyle.

The beauty of *mobile reading partnerships* is in the innovation. Avid and reluctant readers love these experiences because they are exciting, engaging, and fresh. They embody authentic learner-centered experiences that solely provide for the students and demand nothing in return. These reasons alone make these types of partnerships worthy of implementation.

How Do You Make Them Happen?

When initially designing these partnerships, attention needs to be placed on both the needs of the learner and the amount of time you have to invest. Once this is determined, it will be easier to decide what type of mobile learning partnership is best for you and your students. The three mobile partnerships that will be showcased in the "Leap" section of this chapter each require varying degrees of time and fill different needs. Refer to Table 5.1 to help determine the mobile partnership that best fits your needs.

Once you have selected a *mobile reading partnership* that best suits the needs of you and your students, ease into the development of the learning experience by outlining a basic

Table 5.1

Partnership	Mobile Experience	Need	Time
Sites and coordinators within the local community	Bookmobile	Provides students access to books beyond school hours.	• Requires a large amount of preparatory work. • Requires extended hours beyond the traditional school day for operation.
Sites beyond the local community	"Where in the world are you reading?"	Provides students with an awareness that books can be read and enjoyed anywhere.	• Requires a generous amount of preparatory work. • Requires a minimal amount of work beyond the school day for operation.
Local bookstore	Bookstore visit	Provides students with exposure to bookstores and gives them a sense of comfort for utilizing one. Places value on extending reading outside of school.	• Basic preparatory work is required. • Requires a one-time extended work commitment.

plan. This plan should not place constraints on the final learning experience. The intentional use of the plan is to activate thinking and help create a vision for moving forward. Being cautious not to develop a full-blown plan at this point can save you a lot of unnecessary work in the end. It would be counterproductive to develop a plan only to find out that your administrator will not approve it. This can feel like a *balancing act* at times. The Learning Experience Planning Form found later in Table 5.2 can be a helpful tool to get started with planning.

At the start of any plan, it is valuable to identify your goal for the learning experience. Next ensure your goal aligns to the mission and goals of the school and the library. If it doesn't align, you must assess the value of the learning experience to determine its worth. After establishing your goal, determine whom your audience will be, the dates and times you anticipate to offer the learning experience, whom your potential community partners will be, and a general idea of what activities will take place during the learning.

Table 5.2 Sample Bookmobile Planning Form

Bookmobile Learning Experience Planning Form		
Goal: Design and execute innovative ways to increase access to books over the summer break.		
Mission Statement/District Goal Connections: Increase student proficiency in all academic areas.		
Audience: LGES students, particularly students at our community summer youth programs.	**Date(s) & Times:** July 11–August 29; 11:30–1:00	
	Resources: Vehicle, books, storage units	
Community Partnership(s)	**Contact Information**	**Notes:**
Youth Directors	Mrs. K Mrs. O	Meet with Mrs. O to discuss schedule and specific locations.
School Partnerships	**Contact Information**	**Notes:**
Teachers, staff, administrators, technology specialists	N/A	Elicit volunteer guest passengers. Create a Google Form to share. Seek hotspots for book checkout.
Tasks:	**Actions:**	
Schedule a meeting with Mrs. K or Mrs. O.	Explain bookmobile; establish locations and times. • PEP: 11:45 @ Caldwell Presbyterian Church • Youth Program: 12:15 @ LG High School • Youth Program: 1:15 @ Shepard's Park	
Storage	Book carts • Purchase with *Scholastic Dollars*. • Three total (one for each of the side doors and one for the trunk).	
Vehicle	School van	
Schedule	Wednesdays after open library hours (11:30–1:00). July 11–August 29	
Checkout	One book each week. Provide a basket for returns each week. Use personal/school mobile hotspot and have paper checkout for backup plan.	

(*Continued*)

Table 5.2 (Continued)

Bookmobile Learning Experience Planning Form	
Motivational Incentives	Popsicles Giveaways (bookmarks, stickers, reading bracelets, etc.) Music Guest Passagers (teachers & staff) Hula-Hoops
Google Form	Create a Google Form for teachers to sign up to be guest passangers.
Purchases	Window chalk Magnet for vehicle Popsicles
Marketing Strategies	**Planning and Delivery**
Informational Flyers	Design a flyer to go home with students.
Posters	Use Canva to make poster that will be hung in hallways and on bathroom doors.
Social Media	Post all information on Twitter, Facebook, and Instagram. During the summer months of operation, I will post reminders of the schedule prior to Wednesday's adventure and post images after each week's travel.
Rollout	**Planning and Delivery**
Launch Party	During the second to last week of school, have a launch party in the library. One-hour session where students discover information about all three summer programs (bookmobile, Summer Reading Circles, and Book & Pajamas Virtual Book Club). Reveal the design of the magnet, and solicit student help in decorating and stocking the bookmobile.

Learning Experience:
Each Wednesday from July 11 to August 29, the bookmobile will visit Caldwell Presbyterian Church, the LG High School, and Shepard's Park. The bookmobile will be stocked with three carts full of books. Each cart will target a specific grade range (K–2, 3–4, 5–6). The top shelves will be supplied with fiction books, while the bottom shelves will be supplied with nonfiction books. The students will be able to check out one book each week and can return books the following week in a designated return basket. The bookmobile will be decorated and partially restocked each week by students from 11:00 a.m. to 11:30 a.m. We will depart the school at 11:30 with a guest passenger, computer, scanner, backup checkout sheets, portable table, portable speaker with playlist, safety cones, Hula-Hoops, and step stool. The first stop will be Caldwell Presbyterian Church at 11:45, followed by LG High School at 12:15, and a final stop at Shepard's Park at 12:45. At each stop the two side doors and trunk will be opened for students to access books. A table will be stationed in the parking lot and used as a circulation desk for book checkout. All return books will be placed in the return basket next to the portable circulation desk. A basket will be taken out of the vehicle with giveaways. A cooler full of popsicles will also be removed from the vehicle and placed next to the circulation desk for students to access. Safety cones will be strategically placed around the perimeter of the vehicle, giving room for students to freely access books without the concern of other vehicles. The guest passenger will help students select books and keep the children safe, while I check out books to students.

Celebrating Success:
At the conclusion of each week's travels, I will post images to social media.

This basic information will help support a productive conversation with your administration or school leaders. The detailed action steps, marketing strategies, and rollout can be addressed after approval is granted.

When seeking approval from administrators and school leaders, the most powerful conversations you can have are conversations where you are able to use your school's mission statement and goals to support the proposed learning experience. Rightfully so, administrators want to see that the work within your program is supporting the work of the entire building. Being prepared with these connections not only showcases the value your program brings to the school; it also makes it easier for you to gain approval.

After approval is granted, you can then begin putting your plan into action. Start by identifying the tasks that lie ahead and the actions that need to be taken. One important task that should not be overlooked is how you plan to market your learning experience. With each of the learning experiences that I showcase in the "Leap" section of the chapter, I focused on two audiences when marketing. I focused on the students and the parents.

When marketing external learning experiences, you need to create energy and a ripple of excitement. The best way to do this is to be innovative. Decide what it is that the students love, and use it to motivate them. Do they love competition? If so, include a friendly competitive component to the learning experience? Are there people whom they love? If so, be sure to find a way to build them into the experience. Do they like rewards and treats? If so, think outside of the box, and find a fun incentive that will motivate them to participate. It is always helpful, when trying to engage students in external learning experiences, to think about the students' world and what motivates them outside of school. When reading about the learning experiences that I created at my school (refer to "Experience Summary"), you will see many unique ways for doing this.

Once you have developed ideas for engaging participants, the next challenge is to determine how you are going to teach the students about the learning experience. I always find it to be most useful to treat this as a grand rollout event, meaning that I have teachers and grade levels coordinate special times with me where I can introduce students to the latest and greatest opportunity being offered through our library program. Most often I host this in the library. After the rollout, I also continue to market the learning experience through school mail, the school bulletin, and posters that I place on the back of each bathroom door and throughout the hallways.

As mentioned, I also need to market these learning experiences to parents and guardians as well. Sending a flyer home in the mail is a great way to reach all families. However, I find that the best way to reach parents is through social media. I simply share all the information for the learning experience on the library website and then post information to *Facebook*, *Twitter*, *and Instagram*. Additionally, I ask teachers to share the information on any of the digital platforms (*Dojo* Classroom and *Seesaw* are two of the favorites at my school) they use for communication.

Once you have shared information with your students and families, it will be important to continue to communicate with families. As you begin to approach the start date to the experience, continue to build excitement, and remind families of the upcoming learning experience. A powerful tool for librarians to use is the *Remind* application, which allows you to share reminders through text messages without you or the recipient receiving each other's contact information. This is a free application that makes communication easy for all parties.

Finally, during the learning experience, be sure to capture all the learning and student engagement. Remember the old saying "A picture is worth a thousand words." Capturing and sharing photographs and videos of students is a form of marketing that speaks volumes. Brag away! These experiences are monumental in their impact on students, and if you don't showcase what you are doing, who will? Take the time to celebrate successful learning.

LEAP

Leap (step) forward by . . .

1. Analyzing the opportunities that exist for students to access books outside of the school day.
2. Analyzing the existing opportunities that exist for students to engage in activities where teachers and leaders are modeling good reading habits.
3. Choosing a learner need to focus on improving, through the use of a mobile reading partnership.

MOBILE READING LEARNING EXPERIENCE #1

Named Learning Experience
Bookmobile

Partnership
Community Locations, Families, Librarian, Youth Commission Directors

Future Ready Framework (refer to Figure 5.1)

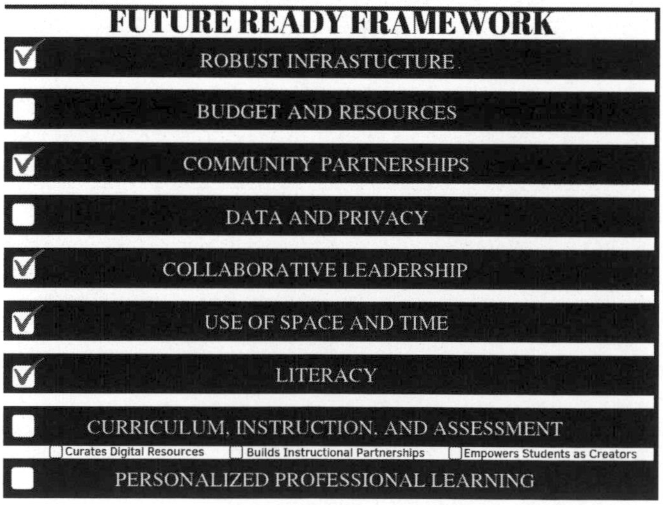

FUTURE READY FRAMEWORK

- ☑ ROBUST INFRASTUCTURE
- ☐ BUDGET AND RESOURCES
- ☑ COMMUNITY PARTNERSHIPS
- ☐ DATA AND PRIVACY
- ☑ COLLABORATIVE LEADERSHIP
- ☑ USE OF SPACE AND TIME
- ☑ LITERACY
- ☐ CURRICULUM, INSTRUCTION, AND ASSESSMENT
  - ☐ Curates Digital Resources ☐ Builds Instructional Partnerships ☐ Empowers Students as Creators
- ☐ PERSONALIZED PROFESSIONAL LEARNING

Figure 5.1

AASL Standards
AASL Standards for School Librarians: III.B.1
AASL School Standards for School Libraries: II.B.2., II.C.1., II.D.2., II.D.3., III.B.1., III.C.1., IV.B.5., IV.C.3., IV.D., V.B.2., V.B.3., V.C.1., V.C.2., V.C.3., V.D.2., V.D.3.

Experience Summary
Each student leaves our building for the summer with a different path. Some will be joining camps, others will be attending childcare services, some will stay at home, and the varying list goes on and on. Just as there is not a unified plan for each student during the day, there also is never a unified plan for reading.

Each year, I wrestle with how to keep books in the hands of our students over the summer and how to ensure that they continue to read for pleasure.

During my time as a librarian, I have had success getting students to read over the summer, by continually working to develop innovative ways to connect readers with books. One of my favorite experiences that I created to improve access to books over the summer is a school bookmobile. This was an idea that I carried with me for several years, before finally deciding to *leap* forward and put it into action.

For some reason, as excited as I was about the idea of offering this experience for our students, every time I thought about it, I felt overwhelmed. I was reluctant to start a conversation with my administration, because there were so many unknowns that I didn't have the answer to. My vision wasn't clear. Eventually, my desire to have a bookmobile trumped my reservation. I knew it would not only fill a need for our students but also bring excitement and energy to reading and the library program.

The first step I took toward action was reflecting on the need for the bookmobile. I wanted to increase the amount of time students spent reading over the summer months, which meant that I needed to create conditions where students would have expanded access to books. I already held open library hours one day a week during the summer, which was well attended, but consistently by the same students and their families. The patrons who came were the students whose parents and guardians were home with them over the summer. They were also the families that prioritized and placed value on continued reading over the summer. I needed to reach those families and students who weren't coming to the library already. I began evaluating where students spent their time during the summer months. I quickly realized, after receiving input from leaders within my building, that a large majority of our students attended local camps in our village during the summer months.

Our local *Recreation Department* provides full-day summer camps for both our younger and older students. These camps are housed at two separate locations within our community. These camps generated the perfect opportunity to reach my target audience. My paradigm instantly changed. My initial vision of a bookmobile had been to travel through neighborhoods throughout our district, with set destinations for delivery. This shift in vision created an opportunity to make my work more manageable. It gave me a target and a focus to move forward with my planning.

Although my focus became clearer, my head was still swirling with a plethora of unanswered questions. Where was I going to get a vehicle? Was I going to have to purchase books? How would I store the books in the vehicle? When would I deliver the books? How would I check the books out? Whom did I need to partner with to organize and launch the bookmobile? How would I market and communicate the bookmobile to families? Similar to other programs and learning experiences, I found it challenging to know where to start. I knew that before I became thoroughly invested, I needed to develop a "loose" plan to present to my administrator for approval. I had to be cautious! I didn't want to get deeply immersed in the process only to find out that my administration wouldn't approve of my idea, but I also didn't want to go to my administrator without a vision.

I began by using the Learning Experience Planning Form. At this point, I didn't take any action. I simply identified the key components within my plan for action to present to my principal. Developing a compelling justification for the mobile reading partnership was easy to do, because I focused on our school's newly designed strategic plan (refer to Figure 5.2). Broadly stated, one of our district goals was to increase student proficiency

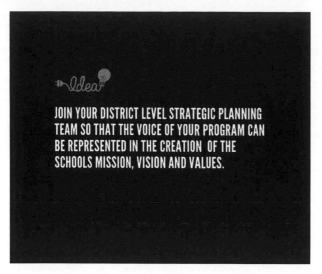

JOIN YOUR DISTRICT LEVEL STRATEGIC PLANNING TEAM SO THAT THE VOICE OF YOUR PROGRAM CAN BE REPRESENTED IN THE CREATION OF THE SCHOOLS MISSION, VISION AND VALUES.

Figure 5.2

levels in all academic areas. The *bookmobile* undeniably provided a mode of action for reaching our target goal. By providing increased access to books, students would be more likely to engage in reading during the summer months, and it will hopefully help to prevent them from sliding backward with their academic progression.

Making the connection to our school's strategic plan was easy, and it was certainly critical in the process. However, I could not go to my administrator with this information alone. Surely, I knew he would have many follow-up questions. I needed to prepare the best I could for any anticipated questions. Most, if not all, administrators' time is sacred; therefore, it was advantageous for me to limit my meeting to one session. This accelerated the process and also indicated to my administrator that I was primed to launch a quality experience, increasing my chances for approval. As a side note, if you continually seek this prepared and efficient approach, you will start to develop merit that will be lucrative for approval with future learning experiences.

Prior to meeting with my administrator, I also needed to put thought into several other details. I began by identifying the partnerships that I would need to form, which, in this case, were with the directors of our *Youth Commission* programs. Then I generated potential modes for transporting the books, which included a school van and an old school bus. The vehicle was a component that I knew would require deeper conversation with my administrator, but I wanted to be sure to have some ideas for talking points, so I equipped myself with ideas and pro and cons for each. I made the decision that for the first year, I would use the books in our library to fill the bookmobile, and hopefully in future years, I would be able to use *book fair* earnings to stock our bookmobile. At this point, I didn't have a clear vision for how the books would be stored as I was not sure what type of vehicle I would be using, yet I came prepared with ideas for both.

I had hoped to start small with everything, including scheduling. I knew that it would be imperative to keep the schedule consistent so that students could prepare each week for the arrival of the bookmobile. I decided to keep the schedule aligned to my current library hours, suggesting to my principal that when my morning hours were finished, I would *head out on the road* with the bookmobile. The final concern would be marketing. Again, I did not need a full-blown plan at this stage in the process, yet I did feel it would be beneficial to make aware to my principal of my intention to host a large-scale event where I would build hype for the launch of our first-ever *LGES Bookmobile*. This insight gave opportunity to voice any concerns or ideas he might have with my future action plans.

Once I presented this plan (refer to Table 5.2 for a sample planning form) to my administrator, he was instantly on board. He enthusiastically began sharing ideas and approaches that he thought would be best. My "loose" plan allowed for me to engage in decisions where

I could hold true to my vision, while also being open and accepting to suggestions that would lead to a successful learning experience for our students. If I did not have a plan going in, it would have been difficult to challenge some of his ideas that weren't aligned with my desires. Instead, I was able to use my plan to support my decisions and engage in a productive discussion that led to the creation of an innovative learning experience. He was able to support my ideas by immediately contacting our bus garage and establishing the approval of a school minivan for our bookmobile. This again reinforced the importance of having a loose plan. Since I was prepared for our meeting, I was able to make quick decisions that led to immediate action and ultimately accelerated the process of implementation.

Once I had approval, it was time to think more deeply about my plan. Fortunately, my conversation was lucrative with my principal. I was able to solidify several decisions, such as audience, time, and vehicle. My biggest concerns moving forward were how I was going to store the books in the bookmobile, where specifically I was going to drive the bookmobile, and how I was going to market and inform students and families. I chose to start with establishing key partnerships within the community. I reached out to the directors of the *Youth Commission Program* and identified times and locations that would be conducive and favorable for both of our programs. I was able to have a sit-down meeting with one of the directors. It was then that we decided for the younger students, it would be advantageous to bring the bookmobile to our community church where the program was located in our village. We felt that dismissal would be an opportune time for the arrival of the bookmobile as parents and caregivers would be there to help students select books and knowingly or unknowingly model the importance of reading. For the older students, who were housed at a separate location in our community, we decided that lunch time would be the perfect opportunity to visit them with the bookmobile. Students would be transitioning between activities and would have a break to stop and enjoy the bookmobile.

The next step was to address how I was going to store the books. I began researching bookmobiles and also asked for advice through my personal learning networks. Unfortunately, I wasn't able to find anything that was ideal for my circumstance. Eventually, I decided to purchase book carts with my *Scholastic Dollars* from my *Book Fair Rewards*. I ordered a total of three carts with the vision of filling the carts and rolling them out of the bookmobile for students to browse through. This vision was eventually presented with a challenge because once the carts were filled, it was much too difficult to maneuver onto the vehicle by myself. Fortunately, the three carts proved to be perfect when left inside the vehicle. I placed one cart in front of each of the side doors and one in front of the trunk, allowing easy access for kids standing outside the vehicle.

As I began piecing together all the details, each decision became a little easier. I was laying a foundation that made all other decisions more logical. The three carts proved to be ideal for organizing the books, allowing me to loosely organize the books into three age bands. I decided to fill the top shelf of each cart with fiction books and the bottom shelves with nonfiction books. I also took into consideration that the younger kids would have difficulty reaching the top shelf of the cart, so I equipped the bookmobile with a step stool as well.

After developing a plan for organizing the books, I reached out to the information technology specialists in my building and asked them about possible ways I could get internet connection while driving off campus. They began looking into options, one of which was a mobile hotspot pack. We used a mobile device called *Kajeet* and had great success. I was able to scan books in and out using my laptop!

Before I was ready to launch this new learning experience to the students and families, I needed to put thought into what would motivationally charge my students to get excited about the bookmobile. I instantly reflected on the success of an ice cream truck and tried to pull out key components that I could mimic. The obvious was the motivation of ice cream that led to the decision of having popsicles on board. Then I thought about how ice cream trucks have music. That led to my decision to add a Bluetooth portable wireless speaker on board with an upbeat playlist of popular tunes. The last motivational element that I added to the bookmobile was a guest passenger. I generated a digital form for teachers, staff, and administrators to sign up to be a guest passenger. Students love seeing their teachers outside of school, and I knew this would get them excited to visit the bookmobile each week. Consequently, the guest passenger also proved to be beneficial in helping with book selection and crowd control.

Finally, it was time to start thinking about how I would share the information with the students and families. Program rollouts cannot be undervalued. If you don't pique your students' interests and hook them from the start, the success rate of the learning experience will diminish instantly. Marketing in the library is no different than marketing anywhere else; it is what captivates the audience's attention and generates chatter. It is the fuel that ignites your success.

The timing of the rollout needed to be strategic. It was the end of the year, and students were disengaged and continually being bombarded with informational flyers that filled their backpacks and eventually recycling bins at home. I knew I needed to be physically present when I revealed the bookmobile to them. I also had two other summer programs that I wanted to package along with this delivery. It was clear that I would need a large *chunk of time* when the students were in the library actively engaged in discovering the new summer learning opportunities that would be available to them. Subsequently, teachers needed a large *chunk of time* in their classrooms to accomplish end-of-the-year business. These needs allowed me to support teachers and students simultaneously. I created a one-hour summer-program rollout party in the library for each grade level where teachers could work in their classrooms while students engaged in active learning fun in the library.

During the summer program rollout, I split the classes into two groups and elicited the help of the instructional technology director to lead one group. Her role is further discussed in Chapter 7. The groups rotated between each of our stations, learning about each of the three summer programs that were being offered through our library. Within my group, I shared two experiences, one of which was the *bookmobile*. I delivered the bookmobile information differently depending on the age of the students. With the younger students, I read *Miss Dorothy and Her Bookmobile* by Gloria Houston and elicited conversation where students could imagine what it would be like to have our own bookmobile. As students' discussions led to energized conversations about a "fictional" bookmobile, I told them I had a surprise for them. It was then that I revealed a large magnet that I had designed using the online digital tool *Buncee*, to stick on the doors of our bookmobile (refer to Figure 5.3).

Figure 5.3

They all looked at me with puzzled anticipation, creating the perfect opportunity to reveal the *LGES Bookmobile*. The room instantly buzzed with excitement each time I announced the bookmobile and the key features of music, guest passengers, locations, and popsicles. I was peppered with questions of wonder about precise details, such as how many books could they checkout, how would they get the books back to me, could they request books, would their favorite books be on the bookmobile, could their younger siblings borrow books, etc. The energy was electric and better than I could have anticipated.

The older kids required a different delivery. Although they still enjoyed a good picture book, they needed a different motive for engagement. As students get older, they are typically driven by a desire to feel important or helpful. They love when they can be trusted and called upon to carry out "adult" roles. Therefore, when I revealed the bookmobile to them, I used a different approach. I told them about my idea for the bookmobile and all the key features, but I built upon their love of being involved and asked for their help. I expressed to them that I needed their creativity and ideas. Quickly the bookmobile grew to be much better than I had ever imagined as students showered me with ideas for decorating, book selection, and activities at each stop. It resulted in students volunteering to decorate the windows of the bookmobile and student volunteers who wanted to stock the carts with their favorite book selections each week. This small shift in delivery proved to be effective. By making this learning experience student centered, they felt ownership of the bookmobile and valued it as a resource.

The student launch party was a success. Now it was time to share this learning experience with parents and guardians. I created posters using *Canva*, hung them around the building, and shared them through social media (refer to Figure 5.4). I also sent students home with informational flyers in their backpacks. The poster included dates, times, and location, while the informational flyers included additional information about guest passengers and pertinent details about bookmobile times and locations (refer to Figure 5.5).

As word started to spread about the bookmobile, the excitement *snowballed*. It began popping up in *Board of Education* slideshows, district newsletters, and conversations throughout the building. My marketing efforts paid off! I had set my program up for success; I had a captive audience; I had the support of my district, families, and the community; and I had a car full of books ready to be checked out and read.

Figure 5.4

Dear Families,

This summer Mrs. Crossman will be putting the library on wheels and rolling into the community! She will be driving the *LGES Bookmobile* each Wednesday starting July 11th and ending August 29th. The *Bookmobile* will be stopping at three select locations: Caldwell Presbyterian Church, LG High School (under walking overpass), and Shepard's Park (Amherst Street Entrance). We encourage families and students to visit the bookmobile weekly at one of the select locations.

The bookmobile we be filled with a large selection of books that students will be able to borrow a book from each week. Students can return their book the following week and get a new book to read. We can't wait to see our students and families at the Bookmobile this summer!

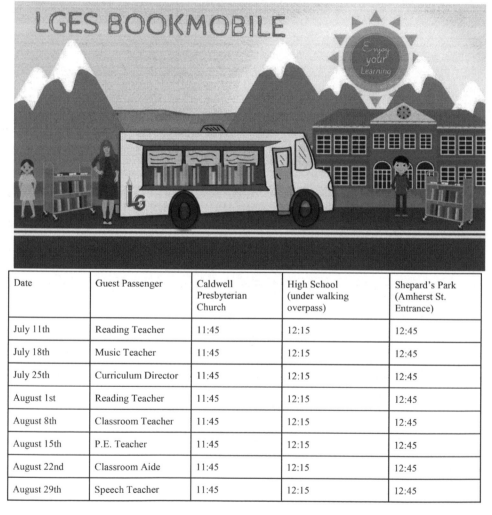

Date	Guest Passenger	Caldwell Presbyterian Church	High School (under walking overpass)	Shepard's Park (Amherst St. Entrance)
July 11th	Reading Teacher	11:45	12:15	12:45
July 18th	Music Teacher	11:45	12:15	12:45
July 25th	Curriculum Director	11:45	12:15	12:45
August 1st	Reading Teacher	11:45	12:15	12:45
August 8th	Classroom Teacher	11:45	12:15	12:45
August 15th	P.E. Teacher	11:45	12:15	12:45
August 22nd	Classroom Aide	11:45	12:15	12:45
August 29th	Speech Teacher	11:45	12:15	12:45

Figure 5.5 Sample Informational Flyer

Before rolling out on my first adventure, I took some time to think about last-minute details. I bought window chalk for the kids to decorate the windows, I had my daughter create a playlist (in hindsight, I should have asked a student to do this), I created backup paper forms for checking out books in case I could not get an internet connection and a paper form for book requests (refer to Tables 5.3 and 5.4), and I made a basket for book

Table 5.3 Book Request Form

Book Requests		
Name	*Book Title*	*Bookmobile Location*

Table 5.4 Book Checkout Form

Book Checkout			
Name	*Book Title*	*Barcode*	*Date*

returns. I also added safety cones from the gymnasium to put around the perimeter of the bookmobile; a small collapsible table to put my computer on for checkout; and some fun giveaway bookmarks, bracelets, and stickers. As a last-minute idea, one of the teacher guest passengers suggested adding some Hula-Hoops for students to use once they had checked out a book. This simple detail added a perfect touch to the learning experience, generating an element of additional fun.

The bookmobile was a huge hit all summer long, delivering books for eight weeks to students and their families. It not only got students reading; it also validated yet another reason our library is so pertinent to our district. A new parent in our school intentionally pulled me aside to say "The library alone, if for no other reason, is worth someone moving to the district." It is words like these that solidify the value in our work and continue to drive us to develop innovative and impactful learning experience for our students.

Suggested Modifications

Each bookmobile will be unique if it truly is meant to fill a learning need. However, the success of the bookmobile will require you to actively seek and engage in conversations with members of your learning community. The process of creating a bookmobile taught me, more than any other experience, to have an open mind and be a good a listener. Our bookmobile was successful because I took the time to synergize with community partners, my administrator, teachers, and students. To me, this step is nonnegotiable. There are, however, many negotiables in the process of development that I have highlighted here. Hopefully these suggestions will give you different perspectives and ideas for your potential bookmobile.

- **Vehicle.** School vans are a great starting place because they are usually easily accessible and require very little expense for your school district. However, they certainly aren't ideal. In searching for something larger and a little more suitable to your needs, you might consider an old school bus that can no longer transport students. Often these are put up for bid at a very cheap cost. Another great option is to seek out online postings at garage sale sites, where used food trucks and other optimal vehicles can be found at a fair price. To cover the costs of these items, consider using *Donors Choose* (Donorschoose.org) or other online fundraising sites to gather funds for your purchase.
- **Route.** Although my route was to set locations where my students were already gathered, you may want to consider analyzing data to determine your route. It would be beneficial to speak with your literacy specialists, classroom teachers, and school social workers to determine key students who could benefit from increased access to books. Once these students are identified, you can work with the transportation department to identify where they live and build a route that reaches each of these students.

    Other great locations to consider are community parks and beaches, youth bureaus, shopping centers, and recreational facilities. It is also advantageous to consider making an appearance at events within your community, such as sporting events, farmers markets, parades, carnivals, and festivals.
- **Partnerships.** Your partners are going to vary depending on your anticipated route. It will be beneficial to look for key locations that students and families utilize within your community

and work with the leaders or directors of those locations to establish that location as a stop along your route.

Partnering with significant community members, who are also parents in the building, could be a great starting point. Try and brainstorm a list of parents who work in community service positions and begin by reaching out to them with your idea. I am certain they will be able to foster connections and ideas that will lead to a successful learning experience.

- **Books.** I chose to pull books off the shelf of my library to stock the bookmobile. However, this isn't necessarily the most ideal means for supplying your bookmobile. You may want to consider building a permanent library on your bookmobile. In the long run, this will alleviate time and ease in the management of tracking books. Please refer to Table 5.5 for a list of ideas to consider when trying to stock you bookmobile.

Table 5.5   Resources for Building a Library of Books

Scholastic Book Fair Rewards	If you host a *Scholastic Book Fair*, you earn rewards for each dollar spent. You can chose to receive your rewards in the form of books. These books can then be used to stock your bookmobile.
Book Drive	You can host a book drive where families donate used and new books to stock the bookmobile.
Donors Choose	*Donorschoose.org* is a website designed for educators to raise funds for school materials and programs. The recipients are provided with a link that can be shared digitally so others can contribute to your cause.
Parent-Teacher Organizations	Most schools have a parent-teacher organization that provides minigrants or funds to support programs and needs within the school. Consider approaching these organizations for funds.
Community-Based Organizations	Communities typically have organizations that support the financial stability of educational causes and beyond. Consider seeking out organizations that exist in your community, such as *The United Way*.

- **Storage.** Arranging the books within your vehicle will vary tremendously depending on the size of your vehicle. When trying to arrange your space, it might make the perfect authentic learning experience for a particular course or classroom to engage in an inquiry where they develop a blueprint for storing and organizing the books on the bookmobile. If you do not have the means to collaborate with a classroom on the design, you could develop a club that would be charged with designing the space within the vehicle during after-school hours.
- **Checkout.** Checking out books on the road can be a challenge, and not everyone has access or even wants to use personal hotspots. You can consider using a mobile hotspot to be purchased by your school. If you choose to go that route, seek the input of other schools that are using successful products in your area. Schools are starting to look into options for placing hotspots on school buses, and it would beneficial to see what products they are using successfully.

Depending on how many checkouts you plan to receive, creating a paper checkout (refer to Table 5.4), where you can record the student's name and barcode, might be the most practical route. It might even be logical to use old-fashioned index cards to track checkouts. Think practical when trying to establish the system that best works for your situation.
- **Hours.** Time is a tricky element to a bookmobile. It is plausible that you will be required to work out of contract hours. If you have the support of your building leaders and have worked

to anchor your efforts on supporting the school's mission, vision, and values, you might be able to seek approval for a stipend. Do not be afraid to ask for compensation for your work. What you do is valuable and is skilled work that should be viewed not as an extra but as an essential part of student learning.

- **Motivational Incentive.** You know your students best. What motivates them? Some students love to be part of designing programs; others like when events are hyped up with parties, games, and incentives. I always find that digital tools and games captivate an audience and hold their attention. Finding ways to use *Breakout EDU Kits* or interactive games like *Kahoot* to introduce your bookmobile are additional and innovative ways to motivate students and get them energized for the bookmobile.

- **Marketing.** Once your program has been launched, you must be prepared to broadcast your program. If you choose to make flyers, as I did, you don't need to utilize *Canva*. There are other free digital poster-creation tools, such as *Smore* and *Adobe Spark*, that will allow you to make beautiful designs that can be downloaded for free to share on websites and social media.

- **Rollout.** When designing a rollout, it might be challenging to have time with all the students, as I did. Perhaps if you are not in an elementary school, you could visit homerooms in junior and senior high-school classrooms and share your information. If that isn't conducive, consider creating a trailer for the bookmobile using *I-movie* or *Animoto* to grab the attention of your audience. Another option could be to host a launch party in the library during lunch, with music, treats, and information on the bookmobile.

Resources

Digital Resources, Tools, and Links

Adobe Spark: https://spark.adobe.com/
Animoto: https://animoto.com/
Bookmobile Book Request Form: http://bit.ly/BookmobileRequestForm
Bookmobile Checkout Tracking Form: http://bit.ly/BookmobileCheckoutForm
Bookmobile Informational Flyer: http://bit.ly/BookmobileInfoFlyer
Buncee: https://app.edu.buncee.com/
Canva: https://www.canva.com/
Donors Choose: https://www.donorschoose.org/
Facebook: https://www.facebook.com
I-Movie: https://itunes.apple.com/us/app/imovie/id377298193?mt=8
Kahoot: https://kahoot.com/
Kajeet: https://www.kajeet.net/
Learning Experience Planning Form: http://bit.ly/LearningExpPlanningForm
Remind: https://www.remind.com/
Seesaw: https://web.seesaw.me
Smore: https://www.smore.com/
Twitter: https://www.twitter.com

Books

Houston, Gloria, and Susan Condie Lamb. *Miss Dorothy and Her Bookmobile*. New York: Harper, 2011.

MOBILE READING LEARNING EXPERIENCE #2

Named Learning Experience
Where in the World is Mrs. Crossman Reading?

Partnership
Community Locations, Students, Librarian, Instructional Technology Team

Future Ready Framework (refer to Figure 5.6)

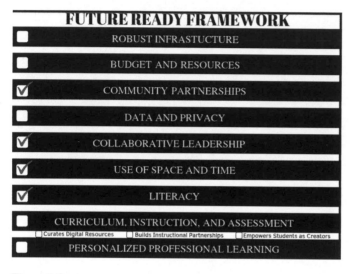

Figure 5.6

AASL Standards

AASL Standards for School Librarians: III.B.1.

AASL School Standards for School Libraries: II.D.2., II.D.3., III.B.1., III.C.1., IV.C.1., IV.C.2., IV.C.3., IV.D.2., IV.D.3.

Experience Summary

Many of our students are not fortunate enough to be able to attend open library hours over the summer or visit our bookmobile. I recognize the fact that some students truly cannot attend, while others have little interest in attending. Nevertheless, I hold myself and my program to a high standard and choose to never give up on persistently growing our programs to reach and impact as many students as possible. This mindset allows me to continually develop learning experiences, such as mobile reading partnerships, that engage and work to increase the amount of students participating in literary learning experiences during the summer months.

Where in the World is Mrs. Crossman Reading? is a learning experience that I designed to engage readers from the convenience of their own homes. This unique opportunity allows me to model a *readerly life*, where students are able to witness me enjoying literature in various locations around the world. This high-interest program is appealing to students because of the interactive game component that is required for participation. Students wait in anticipation each week to view a picture of me reading and then use their best research skills to try and determine where I am reading. Once they have decided where I am reading, they digitally submit their vote to me. If they are correct, they receive a digital badge. Each digital badge earned gets them closer to a personal prize and a collaboratively earned group prize.

Students who were invested in this activity were focused on the gaming component and are unknowingly being influenced by the images. Each image was a powerful representation of reading at its finest, showcasing that reading can take place anywhere.

In addition to this message, students were also utilizing higher level thinking skills to research where my location was. This led to yet another powerful, but hidden, impact on their learning.

When developing this learning experience, I used the Learning Experience Planning Form (refer to Table 5.11). Although this learning experience did not require administrator approval, the planning form gave me the structure and focus I needed to plan a successful learning experience. Every learning experience that I design originates from a need, typically a direct learner need, but sometimes the need originates specifically from the needs of the school. For this learning experience, my goal was to address the need to improve summer literary experiences for an expanded audience of students.

Where in the World is Mrs. Crossman Reading? requires a unique partnership. This mobile reading partnership does not require me to connect with a physical person, but with physical locations. This alleviated a lot of work upfront, but it still required the establishment of set locations to capture my *readerly life*. I had planned to travel over the summer, visiting the national parks on the West Coast, which provided ample medium for my partnerships. It was important that I planned out these locations ahead of time to guarantee that I would have an image for each week. Due to the preplanning of my partnerships, I was able to alleviate potential problems that I may have otherwise overlooked. Many of the locations that I visited during my travels were in the same week, meaning that I would need to capture more than one photo in a week and save the additional photos to spread out over the weeks ahead. If I had not planned for this, there is a good chance that I would have missed out on capturing needed photographs along the way.

When outlining the required tasks in the development of the mobile learning experience, I had one clear vision. I envisioned having a logo for my program that I would include on each of the pictures of me reading. This would not only brand my program; it would also distinguish the photograph of me reading from the many other photos I share on a daily basis. The need for a logo created the perfect opportunity for student involvement. I reached out to one of my sixth-grade students, Olivia LaPoint, who loved to draw and asked her if she would design a logo for the learning experience. She eagerly developed an incredibly detailed drawing with me standing among a scene of books and fictional characters (refer to Figure 5.7). Her work also provided the ability to detach the illustration of me from the scene of books and characters and add it to each of the weekly pictures I would take of me reading. It was brilliant.

As the image was being designed, I simultaneously addressed my instructional technology team about digital badging programs that existed for education. One particular specialist on the team jumped at the opportunity to design a program that would be created specifically for this learning experience. I shared with him my vision for the tool: (1) I wanted students to be able to receive digital badges for each correct guess they made, (2) I wanted students to be able to track their guesses, (3) I wanted students to be able to monitor both their individual success among other participating students in school, and (4) I wanted students to be able to track the collaborative success of everyone in the school working toward a school-wide goal. The specialist went to work and designed a program that was ideal for our needs.

As amazing as the digital badge tool was, it was limited in its functionality. This presented me with my first real challenge. The tool did not provide a unified platform where I could post my picture, allow students to submit guesses, and have the functionality to

Figure 5.7

present them with a badge. I needed to streamline the process as much as I could for students. I knew if I didn't, I would lose half my audience from the start. This led to my decision to utilize the library website as the main platform. The website was ideal as students were already familiar with how to access it, and it would create a perpetual weekly habit for them to visit the site. Each week I would post a picture of me reading to the website. I used the built-in *form* feature on *Weebly* (website generator tool) to present multiple choice options for guessing my location. I also included a link to the leaderboard so that students could easily access their digital badges. Once students submitted their guesses on the website, *Weebly* would notify me that a student has placed a vote. I would then log in to the leaderboard and administer a digital badge to each student for each correct guess.

I was excited by my idea to use the library website. It would be suitable for housing all the information that was pertinent for the student. However, I needed to also think deeply about the information I was going to put on the website. The three things that I needed to include were the image, the feature to vote, and the link for the leaderboard. For the image, it was important to capture me reading in a place each week that would be easy enough for our kindergartners to figure out, but not easy enough that our sixth graders would be bored and not participate. The students needed to be able to look at the image and recognize something familiar, but yet uncertain as to exactly where I was. Strategically, I wanted to be able to help them by providing them with clues through multiple choice options. Through the use of the clues, they would be able to narrow down my location to at least two choices. This would force them to conduct a search to quickly determine where I was. The final feature needed on the website was access to the leaderboard that housed the digital badges. This was easily provided by adding a button with a link.

The management of this learning experience may seem overwhelming. But, in fact, it is quite simple if you set a systematic routine in place upon initiation. Refer to Table 5.6 to view the steps I took each week while leading this learning experience. The routine

Table 5.6

Steps	Activity
Take a photograph of myself reading once each week.	I choose a location with an identifiable feature that when captured in a photograph would be recognizable in a basic search of that location.
Create a *PicCollage* with my image.	I imported my image into *PicCollage* and set the picture of me reading as the background. I then added an image of my logo on top of the background. Once I finished the creation, I saved it to my photo library.
On Monday (each week), I updated the library website with a new round of *Where in the World Is Mrs. Crossman Reading?*	I uploaded my *PicCollage* image from the photo library to the library website. Then I created a *Form* on *Weebly* using the *Toolbar* to generate multiple choice options. I ensured that if my students were to research the locations listed in the multiple choice options, they would be able to find images with the features that I captured in my photograph.
On Monday, I also posted the image of me reading on all my library social media feeds.	I posted the image to *Facebook* and *Twitter* with a link to the library website. I also included #whereRUreading to each of my posts.
On each of the nights that followed, I would check my email notifications for form submissions.	For each student who submitted a correct guess, I would access the leaderboard and administer the student a digital badge.

I set in place consisted of capturing a picture each week, branding the image with the program logo, and posting a picture each Monday. On each of the evenings that followed the posting, I would check my notifications and administer a digital badge to each student who made the correct guess. In addition to posting the featured picture of me reading on the website, I would also post the picture to my social media feeds with a link to my website and the hashtag #whereRUreading. This created a reminder for families and also highlighted to a larger audience the valuable work that was being carried out through the library over the summer.

Having motivational elements or incentives built into learning experiences entices a larger participating audience. I deliberately built this learning experience around the concept of digital badging and competition. Students at our school are extremely motivated by both of these, and by pairing them with the ability to participate from the convenience of their own homes, I was able to break down the barriers for reluctant participants. Initially, I deliberated over how I was going to use the badging. I liked the idea of competition, but I feared that if there became a clear leader that others would not continue to participate. Eventually, I arrived at the idea of creating a collaborative competition, where the entire school would work toward a set number of correct guesses. If the school reached their goal, I would have a dessert party in the library at the start of the new school year for everyone who participated. This coupled with the individual winner prize of *Scholastic Dollars* to spend at the school book fair, made this an enticing learning experience.

The final element to this learning experience was the rollout. It is worth repeating that the key to a successful program or learning experience is in the rollout. The energy you create will set the stage for success; therefore, be sure to take the time to develop a memorable experience for your students. I chose to deliver the launch of this experience with

Where in the World is Mrs. Crossman Reading?

I will be found reading all over the country this summer! My goal is simple... get kids excited about reading by showing them that reading can be done anywhere. Through a fun, engaging activity of guessing my location, I hope to place value on reading during the summer months. Please encourage your children to follow my journey and participate in guessing my location.

Each Monday starting June 25th, I will post an image of myself reading at a well-known location. Students will visit the library webpage (www.lkgeorge.org) to view the image and guess where I am reading. If students guess my location correctly, they will be rewarded with a digital badge. Each student is working to gain as many personal digital badges as possible, but also working towards reaching a school goal of 200 badges. If we reach our school goal by the end of the summer, students will earn a dessert party in the library! The student who collects the most digital badges will get Scholastic Dollars to spend at the Fall Book Fair!

This exciting learning opportunity would not be possible without the incredible talents of 6th grader Olivia LaPoint who created the logo for this program. In addition, I would like to recognize the extreme talents of Dane Davis (IT Director at Lake George) who created our digital badging system for this program. Thank you Lake George Leaders!

Please don't forget to visit the library website each week to view the latest reading destination!

Happy Summer Reading! ~ Mrs. Crossman

Figure 5.8   Where in the World is Mrs. Crossman Reading? Flyer

the launch of the *Bookmobile* (discussed earlier in this chapter) and the *Books and Pajamas Virtual Book Club* (discussed in Chapter 7). The combination of these three experiences created an energetic *buzz* throughout the library, where students excitedly shared with their peers the learning experiences they were planning to join. When debuting the information for this particular learning experience, I started by asking the students if they had any travel plans for the summer and then shared with them that I had a few travel plans of my own. I told them that as much as I love to travel, I always miss them and sharing books with them while I am gone. Then I revealed that I wanted to take them on my journey this summer, so I developed a way to do that through an interactive learning experience called *Where in the World is Mrs. Crossman Reading?* They were beyond excited and instantly wanted to know how to get started.

Prior to the launch, I had set up a practice example for them with a sample photo of me reading at a local ice cream shop. The students were eager to participate in this experience, so I explained the steps of accessing the website, viewing the photo, voting, and then checking the leaderboard. They quickly learned the steps and tried for themselves. It was fun watching as the students engaged in the activity and saw their digital badges for the first time. I had them hooked from the start.

Once I had the students excited, it was important to share information with teachers and families. I created an informational flyer (refer to Figure 5.8) to be sent home with families and shared information with teachers and staff at strategic committee meetings. Additionally, I touted the learning experience during a presentation to the Board of Education. Each of these avenues granted me the ability to market the learning experience to a wider audience who would surely help market the experience as well.

The program was a huge success over the summer. Parents and teachers even placed guesses. Subsequently, it ended up becoming a great conversation starter and helped me to form some additional relationships that will no doubt benefit the future success of the students and the library. This unintentional effect led me to imagine the possibilities that could grow from this simple concept. If this simple yet powerful experience could create connections locally, I have no doubt it could generate connections for readers and libraries around the world. I can only dream that you will help me grow this idea by establishing this learning experience at your schools and sharing it to the wider world of readers with the hashtag *whereRUreading* (#whereRUreading). Together we could be modeling and celebrating a love of reading across the globe, reinforcing that reading is something that connects us all.

Suggested Modifications

- **Digital Badging.** I was fortunate enough to have a technology department that could develop a badging program for me. If you are not in the same situation, consider getting creative with digital classroom community tools, such as *ClassDojo*, which allows you to award trackable points to your students.
- **Platform.** If your website generator tool is limited in its capabilities, you might consider using *ClassDojo* at the lower elementary levels to manage this learning experience from one platform. If you are working with upper grades, consider using *Google Classroom*, which allows for you to embed questionnaire forms where students can submit their guesses using a *Google Form*.
- **Timing.** I strategically chose to do this over the summer, but that doesn't mean you couldn't offer this over the course of a year. This could make a great school-wide activity during the school year. You could then share your pictures on bulletin boards in the building or in digital announcements, making it fun for classrooms and individual students to participate weekly.

- **Rollout.** If you don't have the ability to meet with each of your classes for a launch party, consider creating an alluring video that will captivate and motivate your students to visit the library for further information on the learning experience. This video can be shared at homerooms or within each individual classroom, depending on the level. Additionally, you could plaster the walls and doors of the school building with informational posters that encourage students to seek additional information at the library.

- **Marketing.** If you are feeling really motivated to challenge your marketing skills, perhaps you could use your logo to get kids curious and questioning what the logo is for. Place your logo around the building, perhaps on lockers or cubbies, in the lunchline, or on the school bus, and get students talking. Then place a question in the morning bulletin, asking if anyone has seen the logo. Ask all curious students to visit the library to learn what the logo is all about. Using your logo in this way can be a great way to market. It creates a need within the students for information, which provides you with an interested audience.

- **Reading Locations.** Generating new locations for photographs can be a challenge each week. To help alleviate this stress, work on building a stockpile of images throughout the year. Each time you go to a new location, whether it be a day trip to a neighboring town or a flight to a faraway location, bring a book and your camera, and save your picture to use during the course of your program.

- **Logo.** If you do not have a student who can generate a logo, consider seeking input from classroom teachers or specialists, such as the art teacher. Another great option would be to hold a contest within your school where you collect proposals and the student body votes on the winning design.

Resources

Digital Resources, Tools, and Links
ClassDojo: https://www.classdojo.com
Google Classroom: https://classroom.google.com
Google Form: https://www.google.com/forms/about
Learning Experience Planning Form: http://bit.ly/LearningExpPlanningForm
PicCollage: https://pic-collage.com
Weebly: https://www.weebly.com
Where in the World Is Mrs. Crossman Reading? Informational Flyer: http://bit.ly/WhereRUreading Flyer

MOBILE READING LEARNING EXPERIENCE #3

Named Learning Experience
Bookstore Visit

Partnership
Local Bookstore, Students, Librarian

Future Ready Framework (refer to Figure 5.9)

AASL Standards
AASL Standards for School Librarians: V.C.1.
AASL School Standards for School Libraries: II.D.3., III.B.1., III.C.1., V.A.2.,V.B.2., V.B.3., V.C.1, V.C.3., V.D.2., V.D.3.

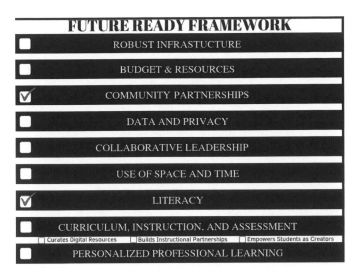

Figure 5.9

Experience Summary

How many of your students visit bookstores? This was a question I often wondered to myself. It occurred to me that children may never have the luxury of visiting a bookstore. This alarming reality drove me toward action. If students were being deprived of this experience, I needed to ensure that they had the opportunity to take part in this cherished experience. I felt the responsibility to develop students' love and comfort with exploring a bookstore. These needs resulted in a magical field trip to a local bookstore, where students participated in authentic learning that prepared them with skills for lifelong learning.

Through a dynamic mobile reading partnership with a neighboring community bookstore, I generated an innovative learning experience that left a footprint on my journey as a librarian and a lasting memory in the minds and hearts of our young readers. Like all successful learning experiences, this experience took planning and vision. I began by using the Learning Experience Planning Form to help me create a clear vision with tentative details and action steps (refer to Table 5.7). The goal for my work was clear; I wanted to provide students with the opportunity to visit a bookstore. This goal aligned with the district goal of *cultivating community partnerships that actively support the district's initiatives.* I knew this connection alone would help conjure the support I needed for approval by my administrator.

When planning, I needed to consider my audience. Inviting the entire school to participate would be the pinnacle experience; however, I feared that the reality of managing an extensively sized audience would hinder the success of the experience. I began focusing on a target group where I could provide this experience to students who could benefit most from it. Originally I considered partnering with the reading specialists and bringing the students that they serviced to the bookstore on a field trip during the day. We would visit the bookstore with the intention of seeking out recommendations for books that we could all read over the summer. I would then purchase that title for each of the students who attended. Luckily, I did not invest more than a vision into this element of the plan, because my administrator did not favor this idea for valid reasons.

Fortunately, my principal was willing to work with me on brainstorming further possible audiences. Instead of focusing on a specifically targeted group of students for the mobile experience, my principal preferred that I focused on a range of grade levels and offered the opportunity for each student in those grades. He recommended that I provide this experience as an after-school field trip, making it an extended learning experience.

Table 5.7 Bookstore Learning Experience Planning Form

Goal: Provide students with the opportunity to visit a bookstore.		
Mission Statement/District Goal Connections: *Cultivating community partnerships that actively support the district's initiatives.*		
Audience: Third- sixth-grade students *Maximum number of students fifty.	**Date(s) & Times:** June 13th; 2:00–4:30	
	Resources: N/A	
Community Partnership(s)	**Contact Information**	**Notes:**
Northshire Bookstore	Mrs. L	Will lead the behind-the-scenes tour.
Building Partnerships	**Contact Information**	**Notes:**
Carol & Heidi	*omitted	Assign a volunteer to each group.
Tasks:	**Actions:**	
Meet with administration for approval.	Meet on May 22 to seek approval. Determine dates, times, and audience. • Potential date: June 13th • After-school field trip • Select grade bands	
Contact Northshire Bookstore	Share vision with Mrs. L for a connected partnership. Share desire to have book talks and time to explore the store. • Three stages: behind the scenes, book talk, exploring.	
Field trip details	Consult with bus garage about size of bus and times. • Departure from school: 2:00, arrival to store: 2:45, departure from store: 3:45, arrival at school: 4:30. • Submit field trip request by June 1.	
Build permission slip	Use *Print Shop* to create flyer. Deliver on June 4 and collect by June 11.	
Put information in bulletin	Put information for field trip reminder in the bulletin beginning June 11.	
Information tracking	• Create a spreadsheet with student/parent contact information. • Separate students into three groups, and assign a volunteer to each group.	
Consult the school nurse	Once the student list is completed, consult with the nurse to review medical needs.	
Marketing Strategies	**Planning and Delivery**	
Bulletin Social Media	• Share information in daily bulletin. • Post countdown updates on social media for parents, students, and community members.	
Rollout	**Planning and Delivery**	
Informational flyers	Place flyers in mailbox on June 4.	
Learning Experience: Visit Northshire on June 13 with 50 students in grades 3–6. Depart at 2:00, and arrive back at 4:30. Students will visit the bookstore for one hour, participating in three different activities: behind-the-scenes tour, book talks, and exploring.		
Celebrating Success: Create an *Adobe Spark* video of the experience. Share on social media, and embed on website.		

Living in a rural community, our closest bookstore is a forty-minute drive away, making my choice for a community partner an obvious one. I couldn't think of a more suitable partnership than a privately owned successful bookstore with an exquisite children's department. After my principal gave his support to move forward with planning, I reached out to the head of the Children's Department. Together we collaborated on building a well-balanced experience for the students. Students who visited the store would be broken into three groups, which I grouped prior to the visit, and cycle through three stages. The three stages entailed a behind-the-scenes tour of the bookstore, a book talk session on *hot summer reads*, and time to explore the store and purchase books. The learning experience would include one hour of jam-packed fun.

The partnerships for this experience required more than a community partnership. Additional partnerships needed to be formed within my building. The large number of students participating combined with the three structured activities provoked a need for additional support. A brief review of the list of participants revealed that there were two students attending who also had parents who worked in the building. Without hesitation, I approached these parents and solidified them as volunteer partners in this learning experience.

For this experience, I did not have a grand rollout, mainly because the bookstore had asked that we limit our first trip to forty students and I didn't want to generate a large interest to only disappoint students. My goal was to put information in the bulletin and also send each student home with an informational flyer in grades 3–6. If I hadn't filled all the spots at that point, then I would visit each classroom and highlight the incredible opportunity. My suspicion proved to be correct. The morning after I had distributed the flyer, my mailbox was full with permission slips, and we were overfull after the first day. Luckily, the bookstore was accommodating and let us tag on several additional students to the original number.

Since the program enrollment was a success right from the start, marketing took on a different role. I didn't need to market the event for participation, but I did need to market the success of the event to our school community and beyond. This type of marketing reinforces the important role that our library plays in the education of our learners. As a result I posted countdowns to the event on social media and used the digital tool *Adobe Spark* to create a celebration video of our event.

Prior to the field trip, there were several key tasks that needed action. The main task was to develop an informational flyer with an attached permission slip. The information in the flyer not only required a description of the event but also included the fine details that would be pertinent for parents. One of the major decisions that I had to make, and you will too, is if students would be allowed to purchase books while at the bookstore. This is something that I wrestled with and eventually settled on the decision to allow them to purchase books. I included this information in the flyer along with other significant details. Refer to Figure 5.10 for a model of what to include in your informational letter.

This experience was a powerful one that broadened our students' worlds through active engagement with books. It is an experience that should be part of every school curriculum and not one that is an extra opportunity for a select few. I am currently working to grow this opportunity within my building and make it an established experience for all.

We have partnered with Northshire Bookstore to give your child a unique learning experieince. Mrs. Crossman will be facilitating an after-school field trip on June 13th, 2019 to the bookstore in Saratoga. Students in grades 3-6 are invited to join us on this exciting learning experieince. During our visit students will receive: a behind the scenes look at the store, an engaging presentation of the summers "must read" books, and an opportunity to explore the store with the option of purchasing their own book (with their own money). The bus will be leaving the elementary school at 2:15 pm and returning to school at 4:30 pm. This trip is limited to the first 40 students to return their permission slips to the library. Please see Mrs. Crossman with any further questions. We are looking forward to an amazing trip!

Mrs. Crossman

Please return this form to Mrs. Crossman by June 11th!

My child _____ has my permission to attend an after-school field trip to Northshire Bookstore on June 13th, 2019. I will pick them up at the school at 4:30 pm.

Signature:_____ Date:_____

Medical concerns:_____Phone #:_____

____ I will be sending my child with money to purchase a book.
____ I would like my child to explore the bookstore and hear about "must reads" for the summer, but he/she will not be purchasing a book at this time.

Figure 5.10   Bookstore Field Trip Informational Letter

Suggested Modifications

- **Audience and Activity.** There are many potential audiences for this learning experience. Choosing the appropriate audience will be contingent upon the needs of the learners and the school. The following are some alternate suggestions:
  - A potential audience could be a student book advisory club, and students can go to the bookstore with the task of selecting books to purchase for the school library.
  - A local bookstore could be hosting an author, and classes who have read his or her work can take a field trip to the event.
  - A high-school course focusing on careers could collaborate with you to build a learning experience with the bookstore, where they are taught about the many unique career opportunities with a successful bookstore.
- **Schedule.** The schedule you create for your experience will be impacted by the goal of your experience. Some schedule options worth considering that might fit your circumstances are as follows:
  - Offer the learning experience on a weekend, when families and community members could meet you there.
  - Stagger multiple visits to the bookstore throughout the day, allowing you to accommodate several classes at the same grade level.
  - Host a summer field trip for families to join you on a trip to the bookstore.
- **Activity.** If planning stations is overwhelming, consider arranging time for students to explore the store. Give them time to develop curiosity and wonder. Then arrange a guided tour of the store where students' questions and curiosities can be addressed.
- **Partnership.** If you do not have a neighboring bookstore, consider visiting a public library.

Resources

Digital Resources, Tools, and Links

Adobe Spark: https://spark.adobe.com/about/video
Learning Experience Planning Form: http://bit.ly/LearningExpPlanningForm

GROW

Grow your library program by . . .

1. Reviewing your school district's mission and goals and identifying mobile learning experiences and partnerships that could support them.
2. Generating a learning experience plan for a mobile reading partnership.
3. Approaching your administrators with your plan and unleashing your new experience.

ACTION PLAN

Setting the Stage

Approach this learning experience by determining the following criteria for your work (refer to Table 5.8):

Establishing the Partnership

Use the bullets featured in each section of Table 5.9 to guide you in your actions toward developing a mobile partnership.

Table 5.8

Setting the Stage		
Goals	*Key Players*	*Groundwork*
• What needs exist in your building that can be met through a mobile reading learning experience? • How can you use mobile reading partnerships and learning experiences to support the progression of your district's mission and goals? • What content standards are you hoping to address? • What AASL Standards are you hoping to address? • What Future Ready Principles are you trying to address?	• What locations exist in your community to support mobile reading partnerships? • Will you need to form partnerships within your building to support this learning experience? • Will this community partnership–based learning experience require the approval of your building leaders or administrators? • Who is your audience?	• What type of mobile reading partnership do you hope to provide? • What time frame best suits your needs and the students' needs when creating, designing, and launching the learning experience? • What resources will you need, and are they available?

Table 5.9

Who	• Determine locations and individuals within the community who will be most conducive to supporting the needs of your mobile learning experience. • Determine if there are individuals within your building who can help make connections for partnerships or help in supporting the community partnership. • Ensure that the partnership is engaging and appealing to students.
What	• Determine what it is that you need the partnership to be able to provide (an area for activities to occur, Wi-Fi, physical features, books, etc.). • Consider what it is that you will need to contribute to the partnership (camera, vehicle, books, students, etc.).
How	• When partnerships are with a physical location, determine if permission is needed for use of that location. • When selecting community locations as partners, choose locations that are convenient for you. • When seeking to establish physical partners at locations, reach out through telephone, mail, or email, and share your vision and goals for the learning experiences.
Where	• Determine practical and suitable locations that fit the needs of the learners and you.
When	• Ensure that the timing of the connected partnership is aligned with the needs of the learning experience. • When applicable, consider continual management of activities with connected partnerships, and build a feasible structure and system.

Delivering the Learning Experience

Use the information in Table 5.10 to guide you in your actions toward developing a mobile learning experience with the support of community partnerships.

Table 5.10

Steps to Developing Mobile Reading Learning Experiences
1. Identify needs of the learners and the district.
2. Identify the time available to commit to a learning experience.

3. Develop a learning experience plan with an unconstrained outline.
  • Determine a goal.
  • Draw a connection to the school district's mission, vision, values, and goals.
  • Identify potential audience.
  • Identify potential dates and times.
  • Identify potential partnerships.
  • Identify potential activities.

4. Put the plan into action.
5. Design and carry out motivational incentives when applicable.
6. Design and carry out a dynamic rollout of the learning experience when applicable.
7. Market learning experience to students, parents, and community when applicable.
8. Have detailed and continual communication prior, during, and after the learning experience with students, parents, and the community, when applicable.
9. Celebrate the learning experience successes.

Table 5.11

"Where in the World is Mrs. Crossman Reading?" Learning Experience Planning Form		
Goal: Provide students with the ability to participate in literary experiences over the summer break.		
Mission Statement/ District Goal Connections: Increase student proficiency in all academic areas.		
Audience: Students K-6	**Date/s & Times:** 1 x per week.	
	Resources: Ipad, logo, *PicCollage*, Digital Badging Program	
Community Partnership/s	**Contact Information**	**Notes:**
Recognizable locations around the USA	N/A	Potential locations: California, Zion National Park Bryce Canyon National Park, Liberty Bell, Saratoga Race Track, Crandall Library
School Partnerships	**Contact Information**	**Notes:**
N/A	N/A	N/A
Tasks:	**Actions:**	
Logo	Seek student to draw logo. Logo must have ability to be added to a photograph.	

Digital Badging Program	Contact technology department about potential badging programs with abilities to administer badges, track badges and take part in a group competition.
	  • They will create one
	     ° Send logo once created.	

(Continued)

Table 5.11 (Continued)

"Where in the World is Mrs. Crossman Reading?" Learning Experience Planning Form	
Platform	Need a platform for sharing images each week that has a tool for submitting guesses. • Website • ~~Google Forms~~ • Forms on Weebly
Management	Structure for weekly activity: • Take picture • Add picture to background of *PicCollage* and place logo on top. • Post picture on Monday to website with multiple choice options for guessing. • Share link to website and image for the week on Social Media. Hashtag posts with #whereRUreading. • Each following evening administer digital badges to each student who guesses correctly.
Locations	Take photographs in 11 different locations. • June 25th: Wrigley Field • July 2nd: Crandall Library • July 9th: Six Flags Great Escape • July 16th: Liberty Bell • July 23rd: Lake Placid • July 30th: Zion National Park • August 6th: Bryce Canyon • August 13th: Grand Canyon • August 20th: Northshire Bookstore • August 27th: Washington County Fair • September 3rd: Saratoga Race Track
Motivational Incentives	Individual competition for correct guesses • Scholastic Dollars to spend at Book Fair Collaborative goal • Dessert Party
Marketing Strategies	**Planning and Delivery**
Information Sharing	Share information with families through informational flyers. Social Media Board of Education Presentation
Rollout	**Planning and Delivery**
Launch Party	An hour long interactive event in the library, combined with the rollout of Summer Reading Circles, the bookmobile, and the *Books and Pajamas* virtual book club. Have students practice guessing and logging in to leaderboard. Use a sample picture with *Martha's Ice Cream Shop* as my location.

Learning Experience:
Each Monday starting June 25th post a photo to the library website of me reading in a different location. Students will guess my location by placing their vote using the form on the library website. Once students have placed their votes, they will check the leaderboard the following day to see if they were awarded a digital badge. They can also track how well they are doing compared to other students in the class. Additionally, they can track the progress of our team goal of reaching 200 correct guesses. If students collaboratively make 200 correct guesses there will be a dessert party in the library. The student with the most correct guesses will receive *Scholastic Dollars* to spend at the Book Fair.

Celebrating Success:
Reward students with a dessert party and recognize students who participated in the school bulletin.

6

Personal Learning Partnerships

LEARN

What Are Personal Learning Partnerships?

Personal learning partnerships are derived from students' individualized personal learning experiences. These partnerships are between the learner and a critical resource—be it a person, location, or organization. The personal learning experience and partnerships are learner driven and determined by the learners' interests. They can matriculate through a classroom assignment, be initiated independently by learners, or developed by identifying and matching needs within a community to the interests and skills of the learner. While the work throughout the learning experience is student led, the learner's work is supported by the librarian and often the classroom teacher. Together they help facilitate connections and guide the learning through an inquiry-based learning process.

Personal learning experiences connect learners with authentic learning opportunities and partnerships. They often lead to impactful work that can provide a service, solve a problem, meet a need, leverage learning, or enhance a community or program. Librarians have the ability to create an environment where personal learning experiences and partnerships can be generated collaboratively or independently within school curriculum, programs, or initiatives.

Depending on each unique situation, some learning experiences are individual, while others are collaborative. Regardless, learners take part in sustained inquiries where they exercise the skills and learning processes necessary for acquiring knowledge and making real-world connections. Consequently, learning experiences both impact personal learning growth and support the work of their community partner.

Why Do They Matter?

Creating skilled, empathetic, informed, and empowered citizens is an important responsibility of librarians and all educators. Luckily, when these responsibilities are coupled with the fortunate job of fostering learners' personal interests and outfitting students for success in the global world, we get the opportunity to create dynamic learning experiences. We are tasked with empowering learners by equipping them with lifelong learning skills and processes necessary to solve problems and address challenges. By creating meaningful personalized learning experiences where students transfer the skills learned within the classroom to the real world, we are changing the impact of learning for both the learner and the world we live in.

Librarians are masterful at seamlessly embedding skills into content area curriculum. Although this is an important first step, it is not enough. So what if a learner can utilize skills in *fictitious* content-driven situations in the classroom? Sure, they are practicing valuable skills when they are presented with a content-specific inquiry, but does it really matter to them? I often think about an essential question that I once cocreated and deemed as great: "If you were a colonist, would you have become a loyalist or a patriot?"

Yes, this essential question allowed for student choice and led students through the inquiry process where they developed a knowledge product, which was undoubtedly valuable. However, in the end, it was a pretend assignment that lacked a real-world connection, and it certainly wasn't relevant to the students. I once heard Dayna Laur and David Ross say at a conference that we need to alter our learning experiences from "pretend to practical." This shift provides extended opportunities for impactful learning that will stay with the students when they leave our buildings. For further information on creating these types of learning experiences, visit Project Arc (http://www.proj-arc.com/).

When pondering why personal learning partnerships matter, it is equally as important to recognize the universal student gripes that are echoed from the walls of our school buildings—the gripes where students challenge teachers as to "why" they need to learn a particular content. There is little urgency for learners when they are continually placed in insignificant learning experiences. However, once learners are challenged with personal learning experiences, where they are required to participate in an authentic learning partnership, learning becomes relevant, interesting, and fun!

The sad reality is that students walk in and out of schools each day rarely being challenged to think about the skills and learning processes that they are being taught. Once learning becomes relevant for the learner, skills and learning processes start to matter. Personal learning partnerships yield prime opportunities for learners to identify, develop, and reflect on skills and processes necessary to empower their learning. Librarians specialize in skill building and inquiry-based learning processes, but we also need to evaluate whether we are taking time to specifically discuss the skills and the stages of learning with our learners. If you asked students to list the skills needed to complete a task, would they be able to identify those skills? Would they be able to tell you the stages of learning they go through when acquiring new knowledge? Why do we keep these a secret? How are learners going to know what tools they need from their personal toolbox, if they don't even know what tools are in there? We need to fuel our students with the ability to recognize and utilize these skills and processes by deliberately identifying these skills and building discussion into innovative personal learning experiences. Only then will they truly be able to hone these skills and mindfully apply them toward growth in and outside of the classroom.

How Do You Make Them Happen?

It is exciting to think about the endless possibilities that exist for students to transfer their skills to their own personal learning experiences. When designing opportunities for personal learning experiences, it is imperative that this is manageable for the librarian, the learner, and any potential instructional partners. Starting with a small group or a specific student who has a passion is an excellent way to begin. It can also be valuable to collaborate with teachers, faculty, or administration when searching for existing small group opportunities. This can be done through individual conversations, emails, monthly newsletters, faculty meetings, committee meetings, or embedded time in curricular professional development.

If you are looking to jump right in and immerse yourself in providing a full-blown personalized learning experience to a group of learners or even an entire class, challenge-based learning is a great option. This approach allows students to create personal challenges and solutions, calling upon skills and a structured learning process. Challenge-based learning can take a week or an entire year and can be structured to meet the needs of any learning experience.

Challenge-based learning is impactful, but you don't need to tackle challenge-based learning to provide meaningful personalized learning experiences. Oftentimes, opportunities present themselves; you simply need to be tuned into the wants and needs of the students, school, community, and beyond. The number one way I discover opportunities for partnerships is through engagement. Knowing your students, their passions, and their skill sets can help you to establish partnerships that will leverage student learning and potentially impact the community. It is also advantageous to partake in building-level decision-making committees and community-based networks with shared information so you can be aware of potential connections. If engagement is not a priority of yours, you should consider making it one.

It is our job to support our students in their personal learning experiences. Helping students to identify and develop critical partnerships within their learning process is crucial. These partnerships help guide students toward their goals and are synergetic in nature. A true partnership is made when there is a benefit for both members of the partnership. Typically, partnerships are formed in one of two ways. Either there is a community need the student is interested in helping with or the student has an interest and would like to apply it to a need. As specialists we work to make powerful connections by understanding the needs of both the learner and their potential partner to help create a symbiotic partnership.

Developing partnerships can be a daunting task. When it comes to making connections and developing partnerships, keep it simple. There is no need to focus on trying to establish each partnership individually. Consider your professional learning networks and professional social media groups. We are globally connected through technology, and we should capitalize on digital platforms to solicit connections and establish authentic partnerships. When seeking to establish partnerships, you might consider the recommendations in Table 6.1 or consider partnerships that exist among friends, colleagues, and the community around you.

It is vital, as the librarian, that you are supporting and facilitating the learning process, yet not driving it. Utilizing a structured inquiry process will be imperative to the success of the work. There are many effective inquiry models, such as Barbara Stripling's *Stripling Model of Inquiry*, that can be employed at your school. At our school, we adapted the WSWHE (Washington, Saratoga, Warren, Hamilton, Essex) BOCES *WISE Model of Inquiry*, which has proven to be extremely successful (see Figure 1.3, p. 10).

As students work through the stages of the inquiry model, conversations with learners should be structured through the lens of a "coach" and not a "player," meaning you are not actually the one on the field making the *game-time decisions* and doing the work, the students are. Additionally, within the inquiry-based learning process, it is imperative that an environment is created where learners feel safe to fail. In my library we have a sign that says *Welcome to the Library, where we are learning, failing and growing.* It is this mindset that allows students to take risks and persevere through challenges in their work.

Seeing yourself as a learner and embracing a growth mindset, when taking this journey with learners, will be extremely valuable. In some cases the personal learning experience

Table 6.1   Professional Social Media Learning Networks

Facebook Professional Groups	Future Ready Librarians
	Learning Librarians
	American Association of School Librarians
	ISTE Librarians Network
Twitter Groups	#futurereadylibs
	#tlchat
	#istelib
	#librariansofinstagram
	#Skype2Learn
	#edchat
Classroom Management Platforms	Class Dojo
	Seesaw
	Google Classroom
	Edmodo

Table 6.2   Guide to a Successful Personal Learning Experience

What it is. . .	What it is not. . .
Based on student interest and skills	Based strictly on content
Inquiry-based learning process	Linear learning process
Student directed	Teacher directed
Authentic audience	Fictitious audience
Relevant experience	Assigned experience
Active learning	Passive learning
Requires partnerships	Functions without a partnership
Relies on building skills and a knowledge base	Relies on existing knowledge
Student does the thinking (student = player; teacher = coach)	Teacher does the thinking
Contingent upon a growth mindset	Compliant with a fixed mindset
Knowledge product is multidimensional	Knowledge product is one dimensional (e.g., test)
Transfer of skills to an authentic task	Using skills in isolation
Applying critical-thinking skills	Applying passive-thinking skills
Seeing learning as social responsibility	Learning for the purpose of strictly knowing

may not come to fruition, but there will be valuable learning in the process, and growth will be in the reflection learned from the failures. It is well worth the risk of deviating from your current learning experiences to explore the implementation of personal learning experiences in your curriculum. When creating these experiences, use Table 6.2 to keep your work on track and true to a successful personal learning experience.

LEAP

Leap (step) forward by . . .

1. Looking for potential opportunities to create personal learning partnerships with a small group (via conversations, emails, newsletters, faculty meetings, committee meetings, professional development sessions, etc.).
2. Identifying students with a passion or skill that you could help foster through a personal learning experience.
3. Researching challenge-based learning to gain an understanding of the framework.

PERSONAL LEARNING EXPERIENCE #1

Named Learning Experience
Challenge-Based Personal Learning Experience

Partnership
Student, Librarian, Community Partner Specific to Student Challenge

Future Ready Framework (refer to Figure 6.1)

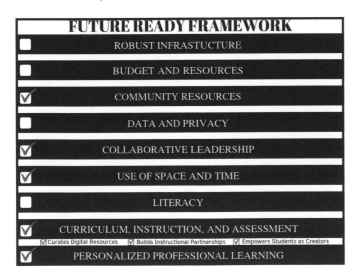

AASL Standards

AASL Standards for Learners:
I.A.1., I.A.2., I.B.1., I.B.2., I.B.3., I.C.1., I.C.2., I.D.1., I.D.2., I.D.3., II.A.3., II.D.1., II.D.3., III.A.1., III.A.3., III.B.1., III.B.2., III.C.1., III.C.2., III.D.1., III.D.2., IV.A.1., IV.A.2., IV.A.3., IV.B.1., IV.B.4., IV.D.3., V.A.3., V.B.1., V.C.1., V.C.2., V.C.3., V.D.1., V.D.2., V.D.3., VI.A.1., VI.A.2., VI.B.2., VI.C.2, VI.D.1.

AASL Standards for School Librarians: I.A.1., I.A.2., I.B.1., I.B.2., I.B.3., I.C.1., I.C.2., I.D.1., I.D.2., I.D.3., II.A.3.,

Figure 6.1

II.D.1., II.D.3., III.A.1., III.A.3., III.B.1., III.B.2., III.C.1., III.C.2., III.D.1., III.D.2., IV.A.1., IV.A.2., IV.A.3., IV.B.1., IV.B.4., IV.D.3., V.A.3., V.B.1., V.C.1, V.C.2., V.C.3., V.D.1., V.D.2., V.D.3., VI.A.1., VI.A.2., VI.B.2., VI.C.2., VI.D.1.

AASL School Standards for School Libraries: I.A.1., I.A.2., I.B.1., I.B.2., I.C.1., I.C.2., I.D.1., I.D.2., II.A.1., II.A.2., II.A.3., II.B.1., II.B.2., II.D.1., II.D.2., III.A.1., III.A.2., III.B.2., III.C.1., IV.A.1., IV.A.2., IV.A.3., IV.B.1., V.A.1., V.A.2., V.B.1., V.B.2., V.B.3., V.C.1., V.C.2., V.D.1., V.D.3., VI.A.2., VI.A.3., VI.B.2., VI.C.1., VI.D.2.

Experience Summary

When creating a personal learning experience through a challenge-based learning model of instruction, it was important that I became familiar with the framework and developed methods for integrating our school's inquiry-based learning process within the structure. Like all good librarians, I immersed myself in research and settled on two resources found in the *I-books* library: *Challenge Based Learning Guide* (Nichols, M., Cator, K., & Torres, M. 2016) and *Write to Change the World: Challenge Based Learning for Persuasive Writing* (Morrow 2014). From these resources I was able to acquire a solid framework and understanding of how to structure the learning experience for my students that was true to the framework and allowed for learners to work through the stages of inquiry-based learning.

I began by looking at my goals and objectives for this learning experience. I knew I wanted to provide an opportunity for students to transfer the skills and knowledge they learned in the classroom to an authentic and meaningful task, but I wasn't sure what that would look like or who my audience would be. After analyzing the amount of time, resources, curricular needs, and potential instructional partners, I settled on a small group of sixth-grade students.

Together, the classroom teacher and I spent several brief sessions coplanning a challenge-based learning experience. When designing the unit, we determined the *Big Idea* and *Essential Question*. The *Big Idea* was the broad theme of the student work, and the *Essential Question* was what the students were trying to answer through their work. These can be provided for the students, or the students can develop and define these (for potential challenge-based learning experience ideas, see Table 6.3.)

Table 6.3

Big Idea	Essential Questions	Challenge
Potential Challenge-Based Personal Learning Experiences		
Impact	How can you use knowledge, skills, and interests to impact _____ (a **specific audience**: community preschool, senior citizens, boys and girls club, etc.)	Teach _____ how to _____.
Global participation	How can you use knowledge, skills, and interests to teach others outside our classroom?	Teach _____ to a global audience.
Technology	How does technology change learning?	Teach a skill to learners in the community through a digital platform.

Due to the limited amount of time and the goals of our work, we decided to define the *Big Idea* and the *Essential Question* for the learners (Table 6.4). The goal of the learning experience was to help our students recognize they acquired skills, knowledge, resources, and a framework for learning during their time at the elementary school. Now they can

Table 6.4

Big Idea	Impact
Essential Question	How can you use your knowledge, skills, and interests to impact the school, community, or world?

Preassessment Library Survey

1. What are the skills that you have learned during your time at the elementary school?
2. How likely do you think you are to use the skills you have learned at the elementary school when you are outside of school?
   - Very likely
   - Likely
   - Unlikely
   - Very unlikely
3. What are the steps/stages in the learning model we use here at the elementary school?
4. How likely do you think you will be to use this model of learning outside of school?
   - Very likely
   - Likely
   - Unlikely
   - Very unlikely
5. What are the digital resources and tools that you have acquired at the elementary school?
6. How likely do you think you will be to use these digital resources and tools outside of school?
   - Very likely
   - Likely
   - Unlikely
   - Very unlikely
7. Please check all that apply:
   - I can make an impact in my school using the skills that I learned in elementary school.
   - I can make an impact in my community using the skills I learned in the elementary school.
   - I can make an impact in the world using the skills that I learned in the elementary school.
   - I will make an impact in the school, community, or world with the skills I learned in the elementary school.
   - I do not agree with any of the above statements.
8. Please check all that apply:
   - I can make an impact in my school using the learning model I was taught in the elementary school.
   - I can make an impact in my community using the learning model I was taught in the elementary school.
   - I can make an impact in the world using the learning model I was taught in the elementary school.
   - I will make an impact in the school, community, or world using the learning model I was taught in the elementary school.
   - I do not agree with any of the above statements.
9. Please check all that apply:
   - I can make an impact in my school using the digital resources and tools I used at the elementary school.
   - I can make an impact in my community using the digital resources and tools I used at the elementary school.
   - I can make an impact in my world using the digital resources and tools I used in the elementary school.
   - I will make an impact in the school, community, or world using the digital resources and tools I learned in the elementary school.
   - I do not agree with any of the above statements.

Figure 6.2   Preassessment Survey

use those skills and knowledge to impact others in and outside of school. This led us to settle on the theme of "Impact" for our *Big Idea* and an *Essential Question* of "How can you use your knowledge, skills, and interests to impact the school, community, or world?"

Prior to introducing the unit to the students, we conducted a brief survey (refer to Figure 6.2) to determine a baseline assessment of what skills and knowledge the students thought they obtained and whether they thought they could use those skills and knowledge to make an impact. This survey was delivered to them through the learning platform *Google Classroom*. We established a "class" for this specific learning experience and shared the survey that I created in *Google Forms*. I chose to create our survey in a *Google Form*, but other free tools such as *SurveyMonkey* and *TypeForm* are also effective (Table 6.5). Once the students submitted their surveys, I evaluated their responses and recorded them on an individual record sheet I used to track student growth (refer to Table 6.6).

Table 6.5   Digital Survey Tools

Google Forms
SurveyMonkey
TypeForm

We spent the first two sessions of the personal learning experience activating interest in the project and analyzing the essential question. We explored both their interests and their skills using *Padlet* as our platform. At first, students created sticky notes on *Padlet* with topic areas that they were interested in impacting. Then, they listed skills that they thought could help them in that impact area. As a learning community, we discussed the skills that all students thought they would need for this experience. This deliberate discussion forced our students to identify skills they previously hadn't thought of as skills (Figure 6.3). This allowed students to recognize the value of these skills and what these skills would bring to their work.

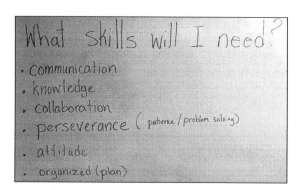

Figure 6.3   Sample of Skills Identified by Students

After our brainstorming session, it was time to create our own personal *challenge statements*. These statements would turn our essential question into an actionable solution. When creating a challenge statement, students were required to start their challenge statement with a verb. As showcased in Figure 6.4, students needed to identify what it was they were going to do that would answer the essential question and address our *Big Idea*. Proper time was necessary for students to create challenges that were meaningful to them. Although we spent class time doing some of this

Figure 6.4   Example Student Challenge Statement

Table 6.6   Survey Reflection and Analysis Form

Challenge-Based Personal Learning Experience Survey Reflection and Analysis		
Question	*Preassessment*	*Postassessment*
Name: Student #1		
What are the skills I have learned at the elementary school?	Shot put, shooting a basketball	Collaborating, listening to others, using my tools on my computer, etc.
How likely are you to use these skills outside of school?	3	4
What are the steps/stages in the learning model used in the elementary school?	*Wasn't able to identify any	Wonder, investigate, synthesize, express
How likely are you to use this learning model outside of school?	2	4
What are the digital resources and tools that you have learned during your time at the elementary school?	NoodleTools, Pixabay, Google Classroom	Google Slides, NoodleTools, Code.org, Library Media Center, etc.
How likely are you to use these tools and resources outside of school?	4	3
Impact of skills	All	All
Impact of learning model	All	All
Impact of digital resources and tools	All	All

Reflection Notes
I was happy to see that she recognized:

- skills that were utilized throughout the challenge-based learning project
- the learning model throughout the process
- that the learning model was useful outside school
- that she could use the skills, resources, and learning model to impact the school, community, and world.

The area I was most surprised about was that after the assignment she didn't feel as likely to use the digital tools outside of school. She also didn't list many of the digital tools she used during the process, such as email.

I am proud of her in that she really struggled in the beginning of this process. She had a grand idea, but she didn't even have an idea for a course of action. She also didn't even recognize the work that needed to be done in order for this experience to take place. She was not able to carry out her experience yet, because the group she chose to work with will not be available until September. But she has already reached out to partners in the community to carry out her work, and Mrs. O will continue to support her learning in the fall.

work, students were asked to go home and think about a challenge that would be meaningful to them. If the students did not feel connected to their challenges, then all future work would lack engagement. In fact, a couple of students didn't take the proper time and later switched to a more meaningful challenge.

Excited and motivated by our challenge statements, students began to *wonder* what it is that they needed to learn or know before they could develop an informed solution.

Students then spent an extensive amount of time turning their ideas into a list of *guiding questions* that would lead them to their solution. During this time the classroom teacher and I worked as coaches supporting in the development of students' questions and challenging them to push their thinking. As coaches it was important to be cautious not to do the thinking for them and strategically guide them from the sideline.

Once the students developed a comprehensive list of *guiding questions*, the students were tasked with categorizing their questions. They used multiple colored highlighters to group similar questions together, then prioritized their questions by numbers. Once questions were ranked, they began to investigate each question in sequence. This organizational step helped students feel a little less anxious and a little more comfortable with starting their challenge. Refer to Figure 6.5 for a sample guiding questions notecard.

Figure 6.5   Sample Guiding Questions Notecard

Figure 6.6

Before students were ready to jump into "investigating," we spent time discussing the different resources and activities they might consider utilizing in their research. We discussed the typical research options of using databases, websites, and books for research. We also helped them to discover that there might be more practical ways to gather the information for their specific questions. Together, we explored different approaches such as conducting interviews, consulting experts, engaging in experiments, and creating surveys (refer to Figure 6.6 for sample student work). We also emphasized the need for learners to follow ethical and legal guidelines for gathering information. Students then spent time revisiting the guiding questions on their notecards and indicating which activity or resources they were going to employ for each of their specific questions.

We were almost ready to set the students free and watch them apply the skills, knowledge, and learning framework to their own personal challenge. However, we needed one more *practice day*, where we reviewed our plan before the *big game*. They needed to choose a digital tool where they would manage their work plan and share it with us. We did not select the tool for them because we wanted them to choose a tool that met their personal

Planning Requirements

- ☐ **AUDIENCE**
- ☐ **DATES/ TIMELINE**
- ☐ **LEARNING PROCESS ACTIVITIES**
- ☐ **COSTS**
- ☐ **QUESTIONS/ ANSWERS**
- ☐ **SKILLS**
- ☐ **WORK NEEDED**
- ☐ **PARTNERSHIPS**
- ☐ **ANTICIPATED DIFFICULTIES**

Figure 6.7

Table 6.7

Digital Tools Students Chose First
Padlet
Google Docs
Google Slides

needs. We did however have a collaborative discussion on what information we thought would be valuable to include in their digital work plan (refer to Figure 6.7).

As instructors it was powerful to see the collaboration tools that the students chose to use. During whole group discussion, they were able to identify what they needed the tool to do for them, but when it came time to select a digital tool, they didn't always select a tool that was capable of meeting all their needs (refer to Table 6.7). Building in unplanned time for reflection became imperative. As they started to work and they needed to share with us all the information outlined in the *planning requirements*, some students began to discover that the tool they chose wasn't necessarily the best match for their needs. At this point, students reflected on what the best tool would actually be and selected a more appropriate digital tool.

After students developed and shared their plans, they began *investigating* the answers to their questions through the various activities and resources they had indicated in their plan (refer to Table 6.8). They spent six remaining work sessions *investigating, synthesizing* (building and creating), and working their way through the inquiry process over and over again.

Table 6.8

Students' Personal Challenges	
Challenge	*Activities and Resources*
Teach foster children about parrots.	Researched local foster care placement centers to determine where she could potentially be put in touch with the audience she wanted to reach.
Teach others how to make crepes.	Watched *YouTube* videos where experts taught how to make crepes. Emailed an outside local expert for advice on teaching others to make crepes. Experimented with making crepes.
Help my younger brother with school.	Emailed his brother's teacher to find out what areas his brother needed support in. Researched digital programs that would be useful in helping his brother practice the skills he needed to work on.

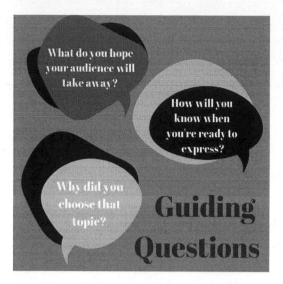

Figure 6.8

As learners worked through these stages, the classroom teacher and I met with students individually and consulted with them. Our goal was to guide the students in the process, by assessing where they were and the work that they had ahead of them. It was extremely important that we did not project our ideas on them, but we simply asked guiding questions (sample questions shown in Figure 6.8) that would lead them in their work. It was difficult at times to watch the learners go down a path that we knew wasn't going to be successful for them, but it was important for us to remember that there is potential for tremendous growth in failure. Equally as important was our job of helping them to recognize their failures and grow from them, ultimately guiding them toward *failing forward.*

We moved around the room, essentially interviewing each of the students and asking them to pause and reflect on their learning up to their current stage in the learning process (refer to Table 6.9 for Progress Monitoring Record Sheet). Giving the learners time to reflect allowed them to identify the skills and stages of the learning process they had put into practice already. Identifying these skills and stages allowed them to recognize the value the skills played in helping them be successful in their work. It also gave us, as coaches, a chance to measure each individual's growth toward the standards and competencies. Additionally, we took time to provide the learner with constructive feedback and support.

During our consultation, we allotted time to discover how we could be a resource to the learners. Learners would typically ask us to help them with the *when, where,* and *who*:

- When can I do this?
- Where can I do this?
- Whom can I partner with?

This is where, as the librarian, I helped our learners explore potential partnerships within the community, sometimes the community being our school community and sometimes the community being the community outside our school walls. Through dialogue we would collectively settle on an adequate partnership that was meaningful to their work. The student would then engage in communication to establish a partnership. A majority of the communication was carried out through email, but in some cases, the students had in-person conversations.

Learners delivered the work of their challenges at different times and locations. Many of the experiences were carried out outside of school time. Although the culminating projects where students *expressed* their work were important, the most powerful lesson was in the reflection. The postassessment reflection was designed to measure the learners' understanding of the standards and competencies. However, it was also used as a time for learner reflection that would help guide them toward continually applying and improving

Table 6.9 Sample of Challenge-Based Learning; Progress Monitoring Record Sheet

				Challenge-Based Learning: Progress Monitoring			
Student Name	What is your challenge?	What skills have you utilized?	What stages have you gone through in the learning process?	What digital tools have you used and do you plan to use?	What research have you done, and do you still need to do?	What are some challenges that you encountered, and what challenges do you foresee?	What are you looking for in a potential partner? How can we help support that connection?
Student 1	To present about birds to kids at the teen center in the fall. *Original audience was children in foster care.	Speaking Communication Research Organization	Wonder Investigate Synthesize	Email (communication) Google Slides (presentation)	Foster Homes Parents	Getting a bird Finding an audience (Originally the student wanted to present to foster children, but there was a privacy issue, and we couldn't find a home. After conversation the student was going to approach teen center. Time is going to be an issue because the teen center isn't open in the summer.)	Seeking a place where kids are looking to connect. Note: Potential connection with teen center. Connect her with Mrs. O who knows the director of the teen center.
Student 2	Teach others how to make crepes. *Original goal was to collaborate with student #1.	Listening Synergy Teamwork Perseverance Planning Communication	Wonder Investigate Synthesize Wonder (again)	Padlet Google docs (project management tool) Google drawing (flyers) Google Slides Email (communication)	How to make crepes How to teach making crepes (YouTube) Ingredients	Finding an audience Time	Kids Note: It would be great to create an external partnership, but for the limited time and need, have him establish partnership here at school. Perhaps look for external partnership opportunity over summer.

their skills and utilizing the learning process as a means to impact others. In an exit interview, I briefly asked students to answer a series of questions (refer to Table 6.10). These questions, once again, required them to revisit the skills they brought to the learning experience and articulate how they were capable of transferring them to a real-world experience. By placing an emphasis on their abilities and successes, they could see the value in what they learned in the classroom and why what they learn matters.

The exit interview was instrumental in my future instructional work as a librarian. It gave me a true assessment of where the students were and the extensive work that lay ahead for me. It showcased that students had indeed developed critical skills that would equip them for lifelong learning; however, they needed more work in identifying these skills and recognizing the inquiry-based process that they used to apply those skills. My future instructional goals, professional learning, and cocurricular conversations were contingent upon this postassessment evaluation, which shifted my focus moving forward. Reflection is key to growth, for both the learner and the instructor. Without time for reflection, I fear that learning will become static and growth will become limited for both the student and the instructor.

At the end of the challenge, the students were administered the same survey they were given before the challenge started. Although the survey may have reassured the students that they do have a skill set and that they use a process of learning that can help them design experiences that impact others, the results of the survey were more informative for me and the classroom teacher. These results provided us with data that would inform our work moving forward.

Not all the students were successful in their challenges, not all the students were able to identify their skills, and not all students found value in their impact on the community. In most cases unsuccessful students recognized that they set out to accomplish a challenge that they didn't have enough time to follow through with. Several students also acknowledged that they picked a challenge upfront that wasn't necessarily meaningful to them, which proved to be a challenge. Ultimately, this resulted in them feeling

Table 6.10   Reflection Questions

Explain the learning process you went through to meet your challenge.
What was the most challenging stage in the learning process, and why?
What skills were utilized throughout this process? What skills do you think you improved upon? What skills do you think you still need to develop most?
Did you discover that you had skills that you hadn't considered before? If so, what were the skills?
Explain your final authentic experience. Was it what you had envisioned in the beginning?
Describe your experience with your community partnership(s)? How was your communication? How did you help one another?
What would you do different if you were to go through this entire process again? Why?
Would you be willing to take on another challenge like this again? Explain.
How did technology and digital skills help you?
What are you most proud of?
What was your big takeaway from these experiences?
Complete the following statement: "When I started this challenge, I thought _____ about my impact in the global learning community. Now I think _____."

unsuccessful and lacking the ability to make an impact. This is where our work lies. This research informed us of the need to build in additional time so that students can successfully carry out their work and go through the inquiry cycle multiple times before fully completing their challenge.

Suggested Modifications

The beauty of personal challenge-based learning experiences is that they can be adaptable to any library program. Being creative and flexible is the key to being successful. When developing a personal learning experience through challenge-based learning, consider some of the following options that might be more conducive to your program:

- Personal challenge-based inquiries can vary in length and time. Consider narrowing the goal of the work to adjust to your allotted time frame by focusing on one standard or competency. If the schedule allows for you to expand your time, consider offering this experience over the course of an entire year.
- If your library runs on a fixed schedule, be creative with your schedule. Start by introducing the challenge during class time in the library. Then through instructional collaboration, coordinate with the classroom teacher for meaningful work time for the students outside the classroom. This may mean that the classroom teacher will provide work sessions without you there, but that is okay. Instruction and guidance can still occur between each scheduled library class, through digital learning platforms such as *Google Classroom*, *Seesaw*, and *Edmodo*.
- Another option would be to consider scheduling a *Hangouts on Air with YouTube Live*. Through this free tool, you can schedule a live Google Hangout with an unlimited amount of guests, which can be archived for later access. This digital tool would allow for you to either teach live without actually being present or provide on-demand instruction that can be viewed in the classroom at a time that works best for the classroom schedule. If your school does not have access to *YouTube*, consider recording your lesson using your preferred video tool, to be viewed at a time deemed most appropriate to the classroom schedule.
- Having students engage within the community can be challenging. It can prove to be especially difficult when you need to establish multiple locations that students need to be present at. Instead, a partnership can be built around a specific location, where the entire class could visit at one time. Think about challenges that could be built around the local park, community library, soup kitchen, or nursing home. The options are endless and can still be personalized.
- Sometimes finding instructional partners within a traditional classroom can prove to be difficult because of strict curricular programs and pacing calendars. Seeking partners among special area teachers can prove to create a dynamic relationship that lends itself to meaningful personalized learning experiences.

Resources

To gain a complete understanding of the work that was being carried out through these challenge-based personal learning experiences, you can access two bonus extended experience summaries. These extended experience summaries are to provide you with an understanding of what this looked like through the lens of the students' work.

- Challenge-Based Personal Learning Experience #1: http://bit.ly/personalexp1
- Challenge-Based Personal Learning Experience #2: http://bit.ly/personalexp2

Challenge-Based Learning Unit

In addition, use the sample challenge-based learning unit outlined in Table 6.11 to help structure a similar personal learning partnership through your library program.

Table 6.11 Sixth-Grade Challenge-Based Learning Unit

Instructional Partner(s): Mr. Smith	Curricular Objectives: Students will transfer skills and knowledge learned in the classroom to an authentic learning environment.	Standards: *Inquire:* I.A.1., I.A.2, I.B.1., I.B.2., I.B.3., I.C.3., I.C.4., I.D.1., I.D.2., I.D.3, I.D.4.
Grade: 6		*Include:* II.A.3., II.D.3., *Collaborate:* III.A.1., III.A.3., III.B.1., III.B.2., III.C.1., III.C.2., III.D.1., III.D.2.
Curricular Content Area: WIN		*Curate:* IV.A.1., IV.A.2., IV.B.1., IV.B.4., IV.D.3. *Explore:* V.A.3., V.B.1., V.B.2., V.C.1., V.C.2., V.C.3., V.D.1., V.D.2., V.D.3 *Engage:* VI.A.1., VI.A.2., VI.B.1., VI.B.2., VI.C.1., VI.C.2., VI.D.1.

Stage 1: Engagement

Preassessment: Students will take a brief survey to assess their knowledge of skills, learning process, and their view on the impact of these skills and learning process.

Big Idea: Impact	Essential Question: How can you use your knowledge, skills, and interests to impact the school, community, or world?
Date: 5/14	**Date:** 5/15
Time Allotted: 30 minutes	**Time Allotted:** 30 minutes
Engagement Activity: Watch Kid President video: How to Change the World. Think about "How you can be awesome?" All of you have talents and interests that can be used to impact the world. Introduce Big Idea. Use Padlet to build collaborative conversation about student interest and areas of impact. Students will record Big Idea on individual notecards.	**Activity:** Introduce EQ and record on front of notecards. Discuss hard versus soft skills and how they are both valuable. Revisit areas of interest/impact on Padlet. We know the areas that we are interested in, but do we know what skills and knowledge we have that will help us have an impact in that area? Looking at your area of interest, what skills and knowledge will you need to have an impact in those areas? List on your sticky note. Model with Promoting Reading: Creativity, knowledge of books, communication, empathy, etc. Collaboratively discuss skills listed, and build a class list of skills that everyone will need. *Next year consider having students develop their own EQ after watching the Kid President video.
Date: 5/16 **Time Allotted:** 25 minutes	**Challenge Statement Activity:** Students will use the Big Idea, EQ, and information on Padlet to develop their own challenge statements. Model challenge statement and criteria. Challenge statements need to start with a verb and be actionable, something you are interested in, and not too broad or too narrow. E.g.: Build a bookmobile program for LG students. Students will record challenge statements on notecards.

Formative Assessment:
Use collaborative digital work, discussion, and individual notecards to measure progress with standards: I.A.2., II.A.1., III.A.2., III.A.3., III.B.1., III.D.1., V.C.1., VI.D.1.

Stage 2: Inquiry		
Wonder		
Date: 5/21 **Time Allotted:** 30 minutes	***Wonder*** **(Guiding Questions [GQs]) Activity:** Revisit challenge statements: "What needs to be learned to develop an informed solution?" Students will list GQs on the back of notecards.	
Planning *Investigation*		
Date: 5/22	**Date:** 5/23	**Date:** 5/24
Time Allotted: 20 minutes	**Time Allotted:** 30 minutes	**Time Allotted:** 30 minutes
Categorizing and Prioritizing GQs Activity: Provide each student with different colored highlighters to categorize GQs. • Highlight GQs that are similar (merge together) with the same color. Prioritize GQs • Number GQs, placing a #1 next to the questions that you should address first, etc.	**Activities and Resources for Gathering Information:** Students will revisit GQs on notecards. Pose question: "How can I gather information to answer my GQs?" Discuss traditional versus nontraditional ways of researching. Share visual with different types of activities and resources for gathering info. • Students will indicate their planned means for gathering info next to each GQ.	**Research Planning Act:** Create a collaborative digital organization and management tool. This tool will be used for them to track and manage work and for instructors to help support them in their work. Share requirements with them: research planning requirements visual. Let them choose preferred digital tool and get their tool set up with required information. Students must share tool with instructors before end of class period.
Formative Assessment: Use work done on notecards as a formative assessment for standards: I.A.1., I.B.2., III.A.3., III.B.1., IV.A.1., IV.A.2., IV.B.4., IV.D.3., V.C.2.		
Investigate and Synthesize		
Work Session: Students will begin working on GQs starting with their #1 item: • Utilizing predetermined activities and resources indicated on notecards. • Continually updating digital organization and management tool. • Consider potential partnerships.	**Coach Role:** Consult with students whose work plans seemed a little shaky. Help provide them with direction by asking probing questions. Engage in conversation about potential partnerships.	
	Date: 5/30	
	Time Allotted: 30 minutes	
Work Session: Students will continue working on GQs: • Utilizing predetermined activities and resources indicated on notecards. • Continually updating digital organization and management tool.	**Coach Role:** Consult with students whom we haven't yet met with. Help provide them with direction by asking probing questions. Engage in conversation about potential partnerships.	
	Date: 5/31	

(*Continued*)

Table 6.11 (Continued)

Investigate and Synthesize	
Work Session: Students will continue working on GQs: • Utilizing predetermined activities and resources indicated on notecards. ○ Establish connection with partners. • Continually updating digital organization and management tool.	**Coach Role:** *Consult with students using Progress Monitoring Record Sheet. • Help keep students on track by assessing what work has already been done and what needs to be done moving forward. • Have deliberate conversations about skills and stages of the learning process (wonder, investigate, synthesize, express, reflect) that they have utilized. • Create a plan for connecting partners and fostering partnerships. • Ask probing questions to guide work. *Formative Assessment
	Date(s): 6/1, 6/7, 6/8, 6/9, 6/11
	Time Allotted: 30 minutes per session

Formative Assessment:
Formative Assessment: Progress monitoring form used for formative assessment of standards: I.B.1., I.B.2., I.D.2., I.D.4., III.A.1., III.B.2., III.C.2., V.A.3., V.B.1., V.D.2., V.D.3., VI.A.1., VI.A.2.

Stage 3: Delivery		
Express		
Implementation of Challenge: Students will independently implement challenge: • Where applicable instructors will be present. • Challenges can be videoed and shared.	**Delivery Dates:** vary	**Completion Dates:** *6/18 *Some partnerships might not allow for this completion date, and appropriate accommodations will be made.
Reflection		
Assessment and Reflection Activity: Students will complete exit interview. The interview and delivery of challenge will be used to assess the following standards: I.C.4., I.D.2., I.D.3., II.A.3., III.B.2., III.C.1., III.D.2., V.A.3., V.B.1., V.C.3., V.D.2., VI.B.1., VI.B.2., VI.C.1., VI.C.2. • Explain the learning process you went through to meet your challenge. • What was the most challenging stage in the learning process, and why?	**Date:** 6/18–6/20	

Reflection	
• What skills were utilized throughout this process? • Did you discover that you had skills that you hadn't considered before? If so, what were the skills? • Explain your final authentic experience. Was it what you had envisioned in the beginning? Explain. • Describe your experience with your community partnership(s)? How was your communication? How did you help one another? • What would you do different if you were to go through this entire process again? • Would you be willing to take on another challenge like this again? Explain. • How did technology and digital skills help you? • What are you most proud of? • What was your big takeaway from this experience? • Complete the following statement: "When I started this challenge, I thought _____ about my impact in the global learning community. Now I think _____."	
Post Survey: Readminister survey.	Date: 6/18

Challenge-Based Learning: Big Idea Notecard

The notecard template in Figure 6.9 can be used as a resource for students during challenge-based learning units.

Challenge-Based Learning Reflection and Analysis Form

The reflection and analysis template shown in Table 6.12 can be used for a pre- and post-experience reflection tool.

Digital Resources, Tools, and Links

Challenge-Based Learning Notecards: http://bit.ly/CBLnotecards
Challenge-Based Learning Planning Form: http://bit.ly/CBLformPL
Challenge-Based Learning Progress Monitoring Record Sheet: http://bit.ly/CBLtable
Challenge-Based Learning Reflection and Analysis Form: http://bit.ly/CBLreflectionform
Challenge-Based Learning Sixth Grade Unit: http://bit.ly/CBLSampleUnit
Postassessment Survey Link: https://goo.gl/forms/qGG2tUj22FMGKuKJ2
Preassessment Survey Link: https://goo.gl/forms/yoC1KYYunT2QlxoC3
Project Arc: http://www.proj-arc.com/

PERSONAL LEARNING EXPERIENCE #2

Named Learning Experience
Independent Personal Learning Experience

Partnership
Active Members of the Military, Veterans of the Military, Spouses of Military Members

Name:_____

Big
Ideas:_____

Essential
Question:_____

_____

_____

Challenge:_____

_____

Guiding Questions:
_____

_____

_____

_____

_____

_____

_____

_____

Figure 6.9   Challenge-Based Learning: Big Idea Notecard

Table 6.12 Challenge-Based Learning Reflection and Analysis Form

Challenge-Based Personal Learning Experience Survey Reflection and Analysis		
Question	*Preassessment*	*Postassessment*
Name: Student #1		
What are the skills I have learned at the elementary school?		
How likely are you to use these skills outside of school?		
What are the steps/stages in the learning model used in the elementary school?		
How likely are you to use this learning model outside of school?		
What are the digital resources and tools that you have learned during your time at the elementary school?		
How likely are you to use these tools and resources outside of school?		
Impact of skills		
Impact of learning model		
Impact of digital resources and tools		
Instructor Reflection Notes:		

Future Ready Framework (refer to Figure 6.10)

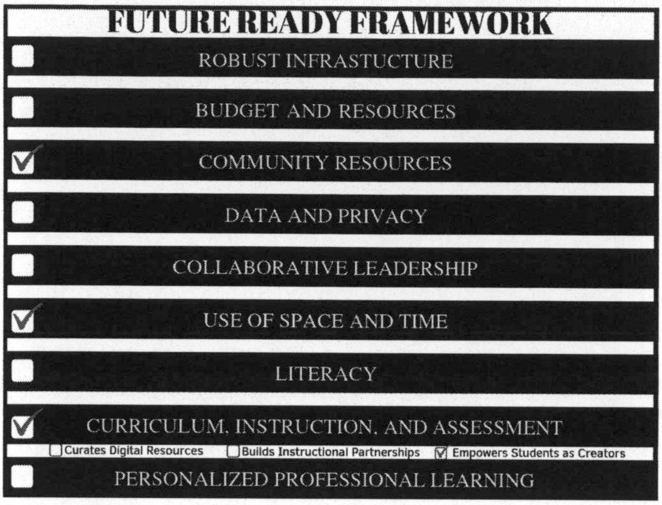

Figure 6.10

AASL Standards

AASL Standards for Learners: I.A.1., I.A.2., I.B.1., I.B.2., I.B.3., I.C.4., I.D.2., I.D.3., II.A.1., II.B.1., II.B.3., II.D.1., II.D.2., III.A.1., III.A.2., III.B.1., III.B.2., III.C.2., III.D.1., IV.A.1., IV.A.2., IV.A.3., IV.B.2., IV.D.1., V.A.3., V.C.1., V.C.2., V.C.3., VI.A.1., VI.A.2., VI.C.1., VI.C.2., VI.D.1.

AASL Standards for Librarians: I.A.1., I.A.2., I.B.1., I.B.2., I.B.3., I.C.2., I.D.1., I.D.2., I.D.3., II.A.1., II.B.1., II.B.3., II.D.1., II.D.2., III.A.1., III.A.2., III.A.3., III.B.1., III.B.2., III.C.2., III.D.1., IV.A.1., IV.A.2., IV.A.3., IV.B.2., IV.D.1., V.A.3., V.C.1., V.C.2., V.C.3., VI.A.1., VI.A.2., VI.C.1., VI.C.2., VI.D.1.

AASL Standards for Libraries: I.A.1., I.B.1., I.B.2., I.C.1., I.C.2., I.D.1., I.D.2., II.A.1., II.A.2., II.B.2., II.B.3., II.C.3., II.D.2., III.A.2., III.C.1., III.D.1., IV.A.1., IV.A.3., IV.B.2., IV.B.5., V.A.1., V.A.2., V.B.1., V.B.2., V.B.3., V.C.1., V.C.2., V.D.2., V.D.3., VI.A.1., VI.A.2., VI.C.1., VI.C.2., VI.D.2.

Experience Summary

Some of the most meaningful personal learning experiences happen *independent* of structured class time. As librarians we have the unique perspective of understanding learners through their book selection choices. We know the students who are animal lovers, war experts, athletes, and science buffs. Couple that knowledge with the knowledge gained from collaborative work on committees, discussions with administration, involvement in program design and initiatives, and we are given the ultimate view of the school as a whole. This panoramic view puts us in the prime position to connect the most compatible learners with the needs of the school, district, and community, allowing us to foster powerful partnerships that leverage student learning in significant ways.

Veterans Day was often a holiday that was celebrated among individual classrooms to varying degrees at our school. As the curriculum leader of our social studies committee, I was able to lead discussions among our committee about different ways we could recognize Veterans Day at our school. Our discussions led to the idea of having our students, who were interested in the military, plan our school-wide recognition of Veterans Day. This decision presented a wonderful opportunity to help extend learning beyond the classroom and support personal learning opportunities through connected partnerships.

When initiating this experience for the first time, it was easy to locate students who would relish this learning opportunity. I reached out to all my avid readers who had read every book in the military science shelves; the response I received from the learners was a resounding *yes*. Wanting to extend this learning opportunity beyond this specific cohort, I invited others to join through an open invitation announcement in the daily school bulletin.

The final planning committee encompassed a range of motivated learners from grades K through 6. Having a flexible schedule allowed me to meet with students during their lunch and recess periods. In addition, I collaborated with another member of the social studies committee to work with students after school. Many of the students also worked independently outside of school. In the beginning, we met after school as a whole group to establish the goals of our work, and during the following sessions, students met in small groups during their assigned lunch periods.

We approached our work like we approach many learning experiences at our school, through inquiry. We began in the *wonder* stage and developed questions that would guide our work. Students quickly determined that our work would rely heavily on partnerships with current or past members of the military, with the goal of sharing their unique perspective on Veterans Day. Together we investigated some of our options. Many of our learners knew of a veteran or current member of the military whom they wished to interview, but they weren't always sure how to connect with those partners. My instructional partners and I were able to foster and facilitate many of the connections for our learners by gathering a deep understanding of each student's unique situation. I began this process through a broad discussion with all the learners in which we collaboratively determined their needs and shared best ways to meet those needs. During those conversations I needed to address the following three questions:

- Do you have a partner?
- Do you have a means to connect with your partner outside of school?
- Do you need resources (place, technology, an extra set of hands, etc.) to connect with your partner?

After our group discussion, we were excited about the large number of students who had identified a partner and developed a plan for connecting with their partners outside of school. We were equally excited about facilitating connections for learners who either didn't have a partnership in mind or had a partnership in mind but didn't have a means of connecting with their partner. When searching for partnerships for learners who were in need, we began by asking staff members who were veterans if they would be willing to work with one of our students. Then I turned to my digital platforms such as the library *Facebook* page and the *Remind* app to see if I could make any further connections. Through these approaches a partnership was established for each of our learners.

Each of the personal learning experiences looked different as they fit the individual needs of the learners and their partnerships. This learning experience could be seen as both an internal and external learning experience because *a handful* of the connections made with the partners happened in the library. However, the majority of them happened outside of the school.

The internal learning experiences that happened within the library took on two different formats. Some of the students conducted traditional interviews with their partner and relied on me to help video their work. Other connections were made through virtual video chats. One student interviewed his uncle who was actively serving at the Al Udeid Air

Force Base in Qatar. Through coordination with the student's classroom teacher and his uncle, I was able to find a time where the two of them could connect for a video interview using *Skype*.

Students who were able to connect with their partners for an external learning experience outside of school connected in a variety of ways. Several students hosted interviews through *FaceTime* conversations. Other students had their partners answer a series of questions in an independently recorded video, and some students held face-to-face interviews in their homes or at community venues. In all cases students recorded their interviews that would later be used to create a collaborative *knowledge product*.

The students used each of the videos to create an *I-Movie*, showcasing *What Veterans Day Means to Us* through the eyes of those who had served, those who were currently serving in a branch of the military, and spouses of members serving in the active military. Several days were spent during the *synthesize* stage of the inquiry process, creating an *I-Movie* with clips from each interview. The final video was broadcasted (*express* stage of inquiry) during lunch on a big-screen television and embedded on the library website for viewing. In addition, it was featured in our school district newsletter and shared through the library social media feeds (*Facebook* and *Twitter*).

Suggested Modifications

- Holidays and school events create opportunities for independent personal learning experiences. You don't need to create a new program or event; simply explore current programs that are offered within your school to see how they could be enhanced through a learner-led partnership with an outside resource.
- These learning experiences also do not need to be large group experiences. They can be individual experiences tailored to the interest of one passionate learner. Continually stay tuned-in to the interest of the students who walk through the library doors, and look for opportunities to connect a motivated learner with a powerful partnership that will meet the needs of both partners.
- Realizing that not all libraries, especially not elementary libraries, run on a flexible schedule, coordinating time to work with students can be challenging. In these cases consider the following options:
    - Host an initial after-school whole group session to establish the goal and the future work plan. Follow this up with a field trip to a local organization such as Veterans of Foreign Wars (VFW) and Auxiliary, Rotary Club, where students can connect with partners and conduct interviews. The remaining work can mostly be done independently.
    - Start an after-school club that would run through the course of the event. Together, generate potential partnership opportunities, and then arrange for partnership connections outside or inside school hours.
    - Seek out instructional partners, such as teachers, school counselors, committee members, and parents, to help share the responsibilities of meeting times.

If you work in a high-school setting,

- select strong student leaders who can lead group activities and help facilitate the work;
- host work groups during study halls and during lunch periods; and
- use an online platform such as Google Hangouts or Google Hangouts on Air with YouTube Live to host group discussions.

Resources

Parent Letter (see Table 6.13)

Table 6.13   Parent Letter

Dear Parent/Guardian,

In recognition of Veteran's Day, we have had student leaders volunteer to help us create a visual display to honor our veterans. Your child was one of several students who volunteered to help plan and create our production. This video will be showcased during lunch and will feature veterans, active members of the current military, and members of our school community. It is our hope that the video will capture "What Veterans Day means to each of us."

As a student leader, many of the students have determined someone they have in mind to interview and have also developed questions they would like to ask the person. Listed below are helpful guidelines for this project. We hope that this will make the process easier for everyone who is partaking in the creation of the video.

- Students can interview a current or past member of the military or their spouse.
  *Please ask if the interviewee would be willing to wear their uniform during the interview.
- Videos should be no longer than sixty seconds and can be shorter.
- Possible interview questions could include the following:
  - "What does Veterans Day mean to you?"
  - "What branch of the military did you serve or do you currently serve?"
  - "How does it feel to be a member of the military/a veteran?"
- If students do not have anyone to interview, please see Mrs. Crossman to help arrange a partnership.
- All videos can be shared with Mrs. Crossman through email: crossmanb@lkgeorge.org.
- If you have pictures of veterans or active military members that you would be willing to share, please send your images to Mrs. Crossman (crossmanb@lkgeorge.org), and include the name of the person featured in the image.

We are both thankful and proud of your student for their leadership. They should be proud of all the work they have done to help organize this important event at our school. It is exciting to watch the students design and deliver an authentic experience such as this for LGES. If you have any questions about this process, please do not hesitate to contact Mrs. Crossman.

Sincerely,

Bridget Crossman
Librarian

Digital Resources, Tools, and Links
Veterans Day Parent Letter: http://bit.ly/LearningExpVet

GROW

Grow your library program by doing the following:

1. Creating a personalized learning opportunity for students.
   a. Challenge-based learning opportunity (or)
   b. Independent learning opportunity
2. Establishing a learner or group of learners to work with.
3. Utilizing professional learning networks to connect learners to authentic learning partnerships.

ACTION PLAN

Setting the Stage

Approach this learning experience by determining the following criteria for your work (refer to Table 6.14):

Table 6.14

Setting the Stage		
Goals	*Key Players*	*Groundwork*
• What content standards are you hoping to address? • What AASL Standards are you hoping to address? • What Future Ready Principles are you trying to address? • What needs are you hoping to meet? • What type of experience are you hoping to provide: challenge based or independent? • What method of delivery do you plan to use to deliver the learning experience?	• Who is your audience: a classroom, small group, or individual student(s)? • Will you have an instructional partner(s)? If so, who?	• How will you connect with potential instructional partner(s)? • How do you plan to connect with learners? • What time frame do you have available for the learning experience? • What structure do you plan to use when designing and delivering the learning experience?

Establishing the Partnership

Creating partnerships can be tricky for personal learning experiences because the learner is at the center of the learning experience and the partnership is most often determined by their unique needs. However, for each partnership, the *who, what, when, where,* and *how* need to be determined. Use the following chart to assist with each of these elements of the partnership. Select only the bulleted suggestions that are appropriate to the learning experience.

Table 6.15

Who	• Locate a person or a resource in the community that can directly meet the needs of the learner and the standards, competencies, and skills that you are trying to cover. • Acknowledge that the partner must have a meaningful connection to the work of the learner. • Capture the interest and skill sets of learners, and seek opportunities to match them with relevant needs within the school, district, community, and beyond. • Identify a need in the community, and match that need with the interests and needs of a student.
What	• Identify what it is that you need to do to help support the connection of the partnership. • Be explicit when communicating with potential partners, and ensure that they understand the criteria, expectations, and the roles within the partnership. • Determine what needs, if any, the personal learning partner or the student needs from you.
How	• Use professional learning networks to seek potential partnerships. • Post partnership opportunities on social media, classroom digital learning platforms, and digital communication apps, such as *Remind* and *ClassDojo*. • Seek out possible partnerships by directly contacting partners who specifically match the needs of the learner. • Communicate partnership needs through newsletters, announcements, and other means of communication with parents and guardians. • Collaborate with teachers and administrators in committee meetings, faculty meetings, professional development sessions and planning times to generate a list of potential partners.
When	• Establish connections with potential partners prior to the learner to see if they can help meet needs. Then provide contact to the student. • Set timelines for students to establish partnerships that are in conjunction with the correct stage of the learning process. • Establish a specific time for all learners to connect with partners at the same location. This can be much like a field trip.
Where	• Determine the most beneficial location for partnerships based on the needs of both the learner and the partner. • Be flexible and creative when partners are encountering difficulty connecting. • Connections don't always need to happen in physical spaces.

Use the bullets featured in each section of Table 6.15 to guide you in your actions toward developing a personal partnership.

Delivering the Learning Experience

Use the information in Tables 6.16 and 6.17 to guide you in your actions toward developing challenge-based personal and independent learning experiences with the support of community partnerships.

Following an outlined plan for delivery will be helpful once you have set the stage for the learning experience. Although these plans will not always be linear, it will be a useful (advantageous) tool for developing and administering the learning experiences.

Table 6.16

Challenge-Based Learning Plan for Personal Learning Experiences
1. Identify opportunities for alignment of your curricular needs with those of an instructional classroom.
2. Seek and establish instructional partners.
3. Identify a predetermined challenge-based framework and learning process that will be used.
4. Coplan learning experience, building in intervals for instructional reflection.
5. Develop preassessment measure and administer to learners.
6. Introduce the learning experience to learners, following a structured framework that supports student learning through an inquiry-based process.
7. Carry out the learning experience in collaboration with the instructional partner, acting as a coach by using *probing questions. *Refer to *RX for the Common Core: Toolkit for Implementing Inquiry Learning* by Mary Boyd Ratzer and Paige Jaegar as a resource for probing questions.
8. Consult with learners using a structured progress monitoring form, utilized to assist in student reflection, guide learning, identify needs of learners, and assess growth in standards and competencies.
9. Seek potential personal learning partnerships by utilizing professional learning networks and personal connections.
10. Provide learners with authentic partnership contacts when applicable, and establish connections when deemed appropriate.
11. Support students' success by providing them with resources to administer their challenge (i.e., physical space or location, supplies, technology access, etc.).
12. Provide learners with flexible time to deliver personal learning experiences.
13. Deliver a preplanned postassessment reflection tailored to measure standards and competencies, and provide discussion that leads to personal learning growth.
14. Administer a postassessment survey.
15. Build in time to reflect with instructional partners so you can adjust and improve the learning experience for future delivery.

Table 6.17

Independent Personalized Learning Experience Plan
1. Discover the need (i.e., learner, curricular, school, district, community).
2. Engage learner(s).
3. Establish meeting time for all interested learners.
4. Set goals, and determine *wonder* questions that will guide work.
5. Establish a work plan with roles and responsibilities. When appropriate, communicate plan expectations and incremental deadlines with parents, faculty, administrators, and others.
6. Determine the needs of each learner via conversation or questionnaire. Refer to the "Experience Summary" of independent personal learning.
7. Begin seeking personal learning partnerships through professional learning networks and personal connections.
8. Create partnerships, and foster connections through most applicable means.
9. Assist in developing and planning a timeline with suggested timelines.
10. Continually support student work, progress, and growth by coaching students during scheduled and unscheduled consultations and providing access to resources and technology.
11. Facilitate in the coordination of the authentic learning experience (final knowledge product).
12. Celebrate and showcase learning and final knowledge product when applicable.

7

Parent Partnerships

LEARN

What Are Parent Partnerships?

Parent partnerships go beyond seeing and using parents as an extra set of hands. Parents can be beneficial partners when they are actively engaged learners for the benefit of their child and oftentimes themselves. This innovative approach requires parents to participate as students of the learning experience. In some cases, the learning experience that is created through the partnership is exclusive to parents and the librarian, while, at other times, the students are involved as well, learning side-by-side with their parents. In both cases, the ultimate purpose of the partnership is to support student learning.

Why Do They Matter?

Parent partnerships allow librarians to seize innovative opportunities for student learning. Parents are most often the first line of academic support for their children outside of school. When we take the time to build strong partnerships with parents, they become a resource for both you and their child, bridging the learning from school to home. Capitalizing on parents as a resource through new and improved (innovative) approaches has the potential to impact students in ways that other approaches may have fallen short.

Students benefit tremendously when support at home echoes that which they receive at school. We need to find ways to partner with parents and educate them on the beneficial resources that are available for their child. Additionally, we need to create opportunities where parents experience learning alongside their child. It is these experiences that not only enlighten the parents but also unconsciously portray the importance of the learning onto the child. Parents are role models for their children; if they are invested in the learning, then their children are more likely to be invested as well.

Parents have a richer appreciation and understanding for both the learning experience and its impact on their child when they become students or learners themselves. By being active participants of the learning, parents invest valuable time toward developing knowledge to support their children. As a result, we are able to strengthen and expand the students' circle of support and build their team of champions.

How Do You Make Them Happen?

As a general rule, when building partnerships with parents, much like with students, the partnership needs to be relevant and meaningful to the parent; they must understand the value in the partnership and be motivated by its beneficial value. You can create this value by determining what it is that parents need. Listening for consistent patterns of need provides the perfect opportunity to build authentic parent learning experiences.

Once you have recognized a need, it is important to meet parents and families where they are at. Families are overloaded; we must take any extra burden away from them and be their support by respectfully adhering to their needs. There are a couple of ways to do this. One way is to build a flexibly scheduled learning experience where parents can participate at their own pace. Other experiences require everyone to be present at the same time and require more attentive planning. To enhance the experience and show your appreciation for their time and support, consider providing small giveaways or gifts.

It is imperative to seek parent input when planning experiences. The question becomes "How do you gather this information?" Questionnaires can help gather an understanding of *how*, *when*, and *where* you can deliver a learning experience that accommodates the needs of the majority of parent learners. By accommodating parents' needs, they will be more inclined to invest in a partnership. However, keep in mind that you should keep your needs in check as well. You will want to determine parameters in which you can ensure will work before offering specific options in your questionnaire. Think about time, location, and duration of the experience prior to giving parents an option. Refer to Table 7.1.

If you are in a situation where it is more difficult to seek parent partners, think about what it is that you can offer parents that would make them more inclined to participate. When you can provide them something that is of value outside of the intended purpose of the learning experience, they might see a hidden value in the partnership. Free childcare, food, and a favorable location are all great starting points when considering how to encourage reluctant parents.

The means in which you execute the learning experience through the *parent partnership* are wide open for possibilities. Remember this is an *external learning experience*, meaning that it happens outside of the school building. Most often we think about hosting the learning experience at a physical space, which is effective when it meets the needs and

Table 7.1

Details	Questions to Ask Yourself
Time	What time of the day? What time of the year?
Location	How far am I willing to drive? What size location will be most conducive? What do I need the location to have (tables, Wi-Fi, a screen, etc.)? Is there a place where I can use the space for free? What places are inviting or appealing and set a positive tone? Is it possible to host this experience virtually?
Duration	Will this be a one-time learning experience? Will there be multiple sessions? How much time will I need to invest for each session?

interests of the learners. Other times it is more effective to host a virtual learning experience, where parents (sometimes alongside their child) can engage in learning without having to be physically present. In this case you could connect with partners through platforms such as blogs, collaborative web tools, classroom learning management systems, and video discussion tools. Refer to Table 7.2 for examples of digital tools that can be effective in connecting virtually with parents.

After determining the means and needs of the learning experience, it is now time to actively seek interested partners. As mentioned throughout this book, marketing learning experiences through social media is useful. In this case, it is more than useful; it is imperative. You don't have the luxury of vast amounts of parents filing into your libraries every day to learn about your programs and experiences. If you want to teach them about your experiences, you need to *meet them where they are*, and where they typically are is online. Unlike with the other experiences that you market on social media, for this experience, you will not be able to simply post a blurb with a catchy phrase to build excitement; you will need to inform parents about the details of the event. This can be tricky because you need to make it brief, effective, and intriguing. Videos, digital posters, and digital newsletters can be extremely useful in sharing elaborate information on social media and will most likely be the most successful tools in this case.

Social media is a highly effective approach; consider using other means of sharing information as well. Other options to consider are attending monthly parent organization meetings, such as *Parent Teacher School Organizations* (*PTSO*) meetings, to speak to parents directly, informational letters sent home in student backpacks, shared information on your library website, and classroom communication tools and apps, such as *ClassDojo* and *Remind.*

These partnerships are certainly unique and require creativity on your part, but they don't require a large amount of continual effort. In many cases they are brief in nature, and the benefits are worth the time invested. Your efforts will undoubtedly support student learning and showcase your desires to help and support all individuals in your work toward student growth. As mentioned throughout this book, it is important to showcase the success of these partnerships to school stakeholders. Consider having parents join you at a board meeting so stakeholders can hear the excitement from another perspective.

Prior to the launch and throughout the learning experience continue to use social media and your library website to share information and build interest and excitement. Parents will welcome the continual reminders with information about time, location, and expectations, while onlookers will grow appreciation for your efforts and dedication. Using images on social media to reflect the success of the experience after it is finished will also have a lasting impact on the positive mindset of parent partners and potential future partners.

Table 7.2

Type of Platforms	Tool
Blogs and vlogs	WordPress, Edublogs, YouTube Channel
Collaborative web tools	Google Sites, Padlet, Seesaw (parents as students)
Learning management systems	Google Classroom, Schoology, Edmodo
Video discussion tools	Google Hangouts, Flipgrid, VoiceThread

LEAP

Leap (step) forward by . . .

1. Listening to parent needs and determining areas where you could help support parents through a parent partnership.
2. Brainstorming potential parent partnership–based learning experiences that would be beneficial for parents to be involved in, absent of their children.
3. Brainstorming potential parent partnership–based learning experiences that would be beneficial for parents and students to participate in together.

PARENT LEARNING EXPERIENCE #1

Named Learning Experience
Coffee Click

Partnership
Parents, Local Café Venue, Librarians

Future Ready Framework (refer to Figure 7.1)

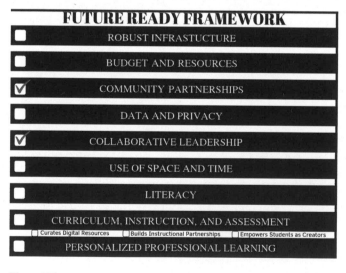

Figure 7.1

AASL Standards
AASL Standards for School Librarians: III.B.1., IV.A.2.
AASL School Standards for School Libraries: I.B.1., II.A.1., II.A.2., II.A.3., II.D.2., II.D.3., III.A.1., III.C.1., III.C.3., IV.B.1., IV.B.2., IV.D.1., V.B.1., V.C.2., V.C.3., VI.D.1., VI.D.2.

Experience Summary
Have you ever had an idea come to you that is so obvious that you wonder why you had never thought of it before? The *Coffee Click* was that idea for me. We spend vast amounts of time supporting our students and giving them the tools and resources to independently seek and acquire knowledge. As with any other teacher, we hope that our students will apply what we taught them when they leave our libraries and especially our school buildings each night. We want them to go home and use the databases to support them in their studies, access our digital books for reading assignments, and apply all the critical skills we taught them for using those

resource. Do they? I know that there are many students who do, but there are many students who could certainly use reminders and support at home. The problem is that unlike with other subjects, parents didn't grow up using the digital resources and tools that students have today, and typically they have no knowledge of them or how to use them. This is where the obvious hit me *square on*; we need to educate parents by teaching them the tools and resources and how to use them.

Educating parents was a whole new challenge for me and something I knew I wanted a collaborative partner for. I am more creative when I can collectively work with a partner who shares my beliefs and visions. I found a partner in the high-school librarian. This learning experiences fell in line with our vision of building a kindergarten to twelfth grade aligned library program, making her the perfect partner for this work. Together we tackled this challenge by planning and coordinating a learning opportunity that placed the parent as the learner.

Obviously, having parents as your learner presents a whole new set of challenges that differ from that of a typical student, one being students are required to sit in your classrooms, whereas parents are invited, making it more crucial to give them a reason to attend. This quickly became the driving factor for many of our decisions when trying to plan a successful learning experience. We needed to put ourselves in the role of the parent and consider their needs: (1) Where could we host this event that would be most convenient and appealing to them? (2) What time of the day would work best for parents? (3) When in the year would parents be less busy and available to attend? Each of these questions helped us generate a list of possibilities and options, but ultimately, we knew we would need the parents' input if we wanted to design an event that was truly catered to their needs.

Creating a digital survey using *Google Forms* to share with parents seemed to be the most suitable option as it would allow us to distribute the survey to a large number of parents through the use of a shareable link. There were many steps that would need to take place prior to preparing a survey. Before we could share a survey that asked parents of their preference of time and location, among other things, we needed to create viable options for them.

The high-school teacher-librarian and I initially began our search to find a community partner who would be willing to support this parent partnership. We wanted this experience to have a relaxed and inviting feel. Knowing that parents enjoyed our local coffee shop, we felt it would be the ideal location. Parents feel at home there and would be motivated to come and spend additional time in that environment. We also felt it was a good location because it is positioned between our two buildings (elementary and high school) that are set a few miles apart. As excited as we were about this option, we needed to first seek the approval of our administrator, followed by the owner of the coffee shop. Once we received both of their approvals, it still was not a guarantee until we got the "thumbs-up" from our parents. Through a survey, we offered parents three options to consider for where the learning experience should be offered: the local coffee shop or one of the district's school libraries where we would provide coffee and treats from the local coffee shop. Our survey had options of time and days of the week that interested parent learners would most likely attend. This gave us a basis for selecting a date that would be most conducive to our schedules and the learners' schedule. The final and most important information that we needed to collect from the survey was the content that they thought would be most valuable for us to teach. We provided several options with a rating scale that indicated their interest level. The options we presented were as follows: (1) Would you be interested in learning strategies for navigating media, organizing and accessing online reading, and identifying credible information? (2) Would you be interested in learning tips and tools for digital reading? or (3) Would you be interested in exploring social responsibility in a digital world? We also included a short answer response where they could indicate if they had another content option they would like to be considered. Refer to Figure 7.2 to view the survey.

The survey was easy to create, but the difficulty lay in how we were going to share it. We knew we could share it digitally, but it needed an explanation that we didn't feel we could effectively offer through a social media post. We began brainstorming opportunities to share with a captive audience. This led to the decision to present the survey at our *Parent Teacher Student Organizations* (PTSO) monthly meeting. At that meeting we also encouraged members to share the survey with their friends. This method, although not perfect, gave us an adequate amount of responses to build a learning experience that would successfully appeal to our parent audience.

We were excited that the local coffee shop was selected as the location of choice. This allowed us to be present in the community and give back to our local business for supporting us. The café had agreed to open their doors in the evening and serve coffee, tea, and pastries to our learners while they were actively engaged in a one-hour hands-on learning session. This made for a relaxed and social learning environment where parents felt comfortable and eager to partake in learning.

The results of the survey also revealed the parents' desire to explore *Organizing and Accessing Online Reading*, which proved to be a perfect topic. It lent itself to great resources that are beneficial to both the elementary and high-school audience. The tools we chose to teach were *Overdrive, Feedly* (feed reader), and *Flipboard* (news aggregator). These tools would not only help them support their child in their online reading but also support them as consumers of digital reading.

It was fun to develop and create a beneficial learning experience that would not only improve parents' understanding and ease of online reading tools but also improve their child's. The next challenge in the process was to determine how we were going to share information about the *Coffee Click* with the parents. This experience would require an explanation, which would be difficult to deliver in a concise and appealing method. We struggled to think of one specific means that we felt would be effective. As a result, we settled on more than one! We made digital flyers using *Smore* that we shared on our social media feeds and printed to send home with our elementary students. We also displayed the flyer in our buildings (refer to Figure 7.3).

Next I created a screencast using *QuickTime Player* that recorded both my voice and my computer screen as I shared information about the first *Coffee Click*. In the screencast I shared information about why *Coffee Click* would be beneficial and the digital tools we would be exploring during our time together. The video was then shared on both our library websites and through social media. In addition, we spread the word through conversations with parents and presented information at a *PTSO* meeting and Board of Education subcommittee meeting.

We wanted the night of the event to not only be worthwhile but also be memorable. Our ultimate goal was to host a *Coffee Click* quarterly. That being the case, we needed to focus on the details. It is the details that excite your audience and create that warm feeling of joy and

Coffee Click

Our school librarians are interested in creating a community partnership. We would love to help connect you with your child's learning and perhaps provide you with tools and resources that can help you personally. This form is strictly to collect information from you that will help us plan the most beneficial experience possible.

1. What is your email address?
2. Would you be interested in attending a personal learning opportunity provided by our school librarians?
   - Yes
   - No
   - Maybe
3. Would you be interested in learning strategies for navigating media and identifying credible information?
   - Extremely interested
   - Very interested
   - Somewhat interested
   - Not so interested
   - Not at all interested
4. Would you be interested in learning tips and tools for digital reading?
   - Extremely interested
   - Very interested
   - Somewhat interested
   - Not so interested
   - Not at all interested
5. Would you be interested in exploring social responsibility in a digital world?
   - Extremely interested
   - Very interested
   - Somewhat interested
   - Not so interested
   - Not at all interested
6. Would you be interested in exploring tools for organizing and accessing online reading?
   - Extremely interested
   - Very interested
   - Somewhat interested
   - Not so interested
   - Not at all interested
7. Is there something that you would like us to consider giving instruction on?
8. Where would you prefer that we offer the "Coffee Click"?
   - Elementary library
   - High-school library
   - Outside location (coffee shop, etc.)
9. What time of day is best for you?
   - Morning
   - Afternoon
   - Evening
10. Which day(s) of the week work best for you?
    - Monday
    - Tuesday
    - Wednesday
    - Thursday
    - Friday

Figure 7.2

Join the "Coffee Click"

Hosted by Lake George School Librarians

Organizing and Accessing Online Reading

Join Sarah Olson and Bridget Crossman as they help parents access, organize and explore a variety of online reading tools. Parents will learn about free digital book resources, blogs, and articles, while also discovering ways to organize and manage their reading in one place.

This friendly workshop style program will meet the needs of all levels of digital users. Participants will be introduced to a tool and then be provided time to explore the tool, ask questions and establish set-up.

What will you need?

- Your own device (phone, laptop, ipad, e-reader, etc.)
- Coffee & pastries will be available for those that are interested.

Caffe Vero

When

Monday, April 30th, 6:30pm

Where

253 Canada Street Lake George, NY

Get Directions

RSVP

Although it is not necessary to RSVP, we encourage parents to respond at the following link: https://goo.gl/forms/AbncBQtPJ1daqz2k1 or by contacting Sarah or Bridget directly.

Figure 7.3

Figure 7.4

happiness that we want them to associate with their experience. We not only created an intimate learning space in the corner of the café but also brought in a small projection screen for the presentation. To add to the experience, we made coffee sleeves with our library logo on them (see Figure 7.4 for a sample of our library logo) and raffled off a coffee mug with our logo. In the spirit of ensuring that our parent learners would be set up for success, we prepared screencasts of each of the tools shared and uploaded them to *YouTube*, with an explanation of how to access and use them. Every detail counts when creating these experiences. You only get one opportunity to make a first impression; be sure to make it a good one.

It's easy to get wrapped up in the many details of the event. The best advice is to keep it simple and stay focused on the learners' needs. It can be easy to overplan, but for many learners it can be overwhelming and cause them to shut down. For each of the tools that we choose to present, thirty minutes was allotted. A half hour allowed enough time to teach the tool, get it set up on their device, and provide ample time for them to explore. Another strategy that was advantageous for us was creating and administering a survey ahead of time to determine who would be attending and the type of device they would be using. This allowed us to prepare instruction and support for each particular device and ensured we had enough instructional support (teachers) to meet the needs of all the learners. By focusing on the needs of our audience, we were able to set ourselves and our learners up for success.

The event was a success. We had Board of Education members and parents attend. Each of them praised the event and encouraged us to offer more *Coffee Click* experiences. At the conclusion of the event, we provided our community partner, the owner of the café, with a gift and recognized her for her wholehearted support. We plastered social media, our library websites, and the scrolling slideshows in our libraries with images of the event and praise for the café. This simple act not only markets the successful experiences that you provide but also intrigues curious minds to acquire about the learning experience and perhaps be our next students.

Suggested Modifications
- **Instructional Partners.** I chose to collaborate with the high-school teacher-librarian on developing and executing this learning experience. You may consider partnering with other instructional partners within your school. Depending on the nature of the content, some colleagues will be more fitting than others. However, when trying to educate parents on content that deals with filling the generation gap in digital instruction, consider collaborating with your district or building technology specialists.
- **Community Partnerships and Location.** Community partner and location go hand-in-hand. Seeking the right community partner is dependent on the needs of both the parent learner and

you as the instructor. Seek partners who provide access to resources that are both familiar and appealing to the parent learner but also conducive to your needs (space, technology, distance). A local library, indoor arena, or open community venue are all great starting points to consider in your quest.

- **Time.** The time of the year and the time of the day you offer the learning experience can make or break the success. Asking parents for their preference is of course helpful but may not always be practical. If this is the case, brainstorm a list of events currently happening at your school. Consider where parents drop off their kids and then return to pick them up a short while later. School play practice, athletic practices, and rehearsals might be the perfect window of opportunity for you to offer your learning experience.

Table 7.3

Survey Tools	Screen-Recording Tools
SurveyMonkey	Screencastify
Poll Everywhere	QuickTime Player (Apple product)
Google Forms	iOS 11 Screen Recording

- **Digital Tools.** Two of the digital tools I used during the creation of this learning experience were *Google Forms*, to create a survey, and *Quicktime Player*, to make a screencast. Alternate options for these tools would be as follows (refer to Table 7.3).

- **Sharing Information.** When considering where to market your event and share information, think about where large audiences will be. Open house, book fairs, and conferences are great opportunities to reach an audience. Even if your event isn't at that particular time of the year, you can share information and collect contact information so interested participants can be contacted as the event draws near.

- **Details.** The little details are so important. Take time to think about what you provide your learner. You want the experience to be as enjoyable and hassle free as possible. Some of the things to possibly consider are as follows:
  - Providing food
  - Childcare accommodations
  - Giveaways
  - Follow-up support

Resources

Digital Resources, Tools, and Links
Coffee Click Planning Survey: https://goo.gl/forms/mktnhiyHXqIxTC3o2
Coffee Click Participating Learner Survey: https://goo.gl/forms/dNclXgO7bUibzuWs2
Coffee Click Smore Digital Poster: https://www.smore.com/x3ck5

PARENT LEARNING EXPERIENCE #2

Named Learning Experience
Books and Pajamas Virtual Book Club

Partnership
Parents, Librarian

Future Ready Framework (refer to Figure 7.5)

AASL Standards
AASL Standards for Learners: II.B.1., II.C.1., II.C.2., III.A.2., III.B.1., III.B.2., III.D.1., V.A.1., V.D.1., VI.A.2.

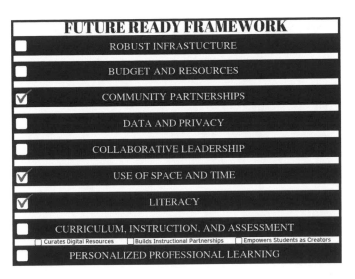

Figure 7.5

AASL Standards for School
Librarians: II.B.1.,
II.C.1., II.C.2., III.B.1.,
III.B.2., III.D.1., V.A.1.,
V.D.1., VI.A.2.

AASL School Standards for
School Libraries: II.A.2.,
II.B.3., II.C.1., II.D.2.,
II.D.3., III.C.1., III.C.3.,
V.B.1., V.B.2.,   V.C.1.,
V.C.2., V.C.3., V.D.2.,
VI.C.1.

Experience Summary

I wanted to engage
readers in a virtual book
group over the summer,
and I recognized the
need for parent support in this learning experience. Instead of seeking parent support
directly, I decided to reverse my marketing strategy and have students unconsciously
elicit support by trying to get as many parents and adults as they could to join our book
club. The idea was that this strategy would draw less attention to their needed support
and more motivation toward building a large group of readers. It worked! The students
built a robust group of diverse readers from parents and grandparents to many other
adult relatives and friends.

Schools do a fantastic job of motivating students to keep reading over the summer
by providing incentive programs that reward them for reading a certain number of
books while on break. These programs are successful and results in a long tally of
books read by students during the summer months. Even with this strong program,
I recognize a need—a need that I know I can support through my library program.
Some students are disciplined enough to independently carry out a sustained reading
goal over the summer months, while others really need support. They need a program
that includes structure, incremental progressions, progress monitoring, motivational
factors, and facilitative support. Through this need, I developed a *Books and Pajamas
Virtual Book Club.*

Books and Pajamas Virtual Book Club was designed to meet the needs of students who
needed a summer reading program with a little extra support, but it was available for all
readers. Prior to activating this learning experience, I went through several critical steps
in the development process: addressing a need, creating an opportunity, and marketing
the program. It was offered to two different age groups (kindergarten to third graders and
fourth to sixth graders) throughout the month of July. I choose a book for each group
(*Mercy Watson: Something Wonky This Way Comes* and *Flora and Ulysses* by Kate DiCa-
millo) and made a calendar of the weekly reading assignments for each book. Using the
digital tool *Flipgrid*, I was able to create a *Grid* for our class to have virtual video discussions about the weekly readings. Each Sunday, I would post a video to the Grid with my
thoughts about the events in the weekly reading and questions I wanted the students to
answer. The students then took the following week to both read the assigned pages for the
week and leave a video response on *FlipGrid* to my post. This tool was indispensable in its

abilities to connect us from distant locations and engage a diverse group of readers in rich literary conversations.

Structure was a necessity to the success of this learning experience. I was not going to have access to the students once they left for summer vacation, so I needed to establish a weekly routine of activities that was both simple to follow and manageable to complete. I recognized that the three things the readers would need to do were

- read a digestible amount of chapters,
- check in weekly, and
- access a tool that allowed for discussion.

As mentioned, *FlipGrid* became my tool of choice. It allowed for discussion but also provided flexibility for the user. Fellow readers did not need to connect at the same time and on the same day, but they could contribute to discussion at a time that was most feasible to them. As accommodating as I wanted the experience to be for the readers, I also recognized that I needed to provide consistency with my role. I consciously chose a specific day of the week to post my video so that readers would be able to establish a routine for checking in and completing incremental tasks. This proved to be extremely effective and valuable to student readers who benefited from progress monitoring.

Both personally and professionally, I recognize the value in making things manageable. We can all appreciate this concept in some fashion. Many marathoners don't focus on the entire 26.2 miles of their race all at once; they focus on one mile at a time. A challenging day is made easier when we don't focus on the twenty tasks we need to complete, but instead choose to focus on one task at a time from a physical to-do list. By choosing to break things down into manageable tasks, once-overwhelming tasks begin to become feasible and oftentimes more enjoyable. We can't leave students to their own devices and expect them to know how to build this manageable structure on their own. We need to model this behavior and help facilitate their success, which was my goal in this learning experience.

Similar to students having difficulty independently managing their workload, students also struggle with staying intrinsically motivated and engaged for a sustained course of time. As a facilitator of *Books and Pajamas*, I was able to maintain a high level of energy and a desire to stay invested through the entirety of the experience. By creating a theme of *Books and Pajamas*, a relaxed tone was established from the initial rollout through the end of the experience. Each week when I set the stage for my video post, I would consciously choose a space that reflected a laid-back nature. I wore fun-spirited pajamas and a shirt that read *Books and Pajamas*. My hair was usually loosely fixed in a bun, while I sipped on a coffee mug imprinted with my branded library logo (refer to Figure 7.4). These small yet meaningful details created an inviting *space* for students to engage in each week. Students were not only intrigued to see me each week outside of the school setting, but they were also excited to engage in a nonthreatening learning space with their friends, parents, and other adults.

Strategy also went into creating a learning experience that would engage our most reluctant readers. I knew that when I employed this learning experience that it needed to be innovative and unique to any other reading experience that they had participated in. We are all intrigued by new experiences, and I recognized the need to use that as motivation. I boosted the first-ever virtual book club, as if it was the *hottest ticket in town*, rallying off a list of motivational incentives, such as rewards for students who could get the most adults to participate, exclusive access to an online group, and the opportunity to see Mrs. Crossman in her pajamas each week. The students went wild over the idea and quickly jumped at the opportunity. Placing posters (refer to Figure 7.6 for a sample poster) throughout the building and marketing the event through social media and informational letters also helped to elicit participants.

To ensure equity of resources, I purchased extra copies of each title with *Scholastic Dollars* earned from our school's annual *Book Fair*. We are fortunate that within our district that all students indicate that they have access to digital devices outside of school, but in the case where a student does not have access, the library is open one day a week over the summer, and students are encouraged to come and use our devices to access *FlipGrid*. Additionally, I worked to accommodate the different needs of the participating parents and adults by creating both a hard copy registration and an online registration form. Each of the many accommodations I offered ensured equal opportunity for all students to succeed.

Of all the learning experiences I have offered, this proved to be the most refreshing. Watching as students and adults of all different ages and walks of life embarked on a collaborative reading adventure was heartwarming. Parent partners turned into student role models who unknowingly shaped the perceptions and understandings of our young readers. Students were able to witness, through virtual book discussions, adults shifting

Figure 7.6   Sample Books and Pajamas Poster

their views toward a book that they initially thought was out of their wheelhouse and grew to love and appreciate it. They were able to witness enjoyable and healthy conversations with different views about characters and events in a story. These experiences were more powerful than any experience I could have offered without a partnership.

At the conclusion of our virtual book group, I wanted to do something special for our participating readers; they had worked hard to participate in an extended learning opportunity, and I wanted to ensure that this experience would have a lasting impression on them as readers. During each Sunday morning video post, I would wear a new fun pair of pajamas and a T-shirt that read *Books and Pajamas*. I thought it would be exciting to send each participating student a *Books and Pajamas* T-shirt, like the one I wore each Sunday morning, in a personally addressed package to their homes. We can all remember that exhilarating feeling when we received mail as a child, and I had hoped that when they received their surprise package, that feeling of pure joy would have a lasting effect on their future perception of reading. Sure enough, it had a positive affect; my inbox filled with photos of smiling faces sporting their new T-shirts. Parents and adult readers sent me notes of praise and extended a note of praise to my principal as well. This small detail had a huge impact on students and families but also on the perception of the library program.

Suggested Modifications

- **Theme.** For the virtual book club, I wanted to set a relaxed and laid back tone, leading me to my decision of a books-and-pajamas theme. You know your audience and their needs best; perhaps one of the options in Table 7.4 might be more fitting for your students' needs.
- **Partners.** I understand that parents of junior-high-school and high-school students might not seem to be motivational factors when encouraging students to read, but if presented correctly, they could be. Parents are often harping on their children to pick up a book and read, and in reality most parents don't have time to read themselves. Use this reality to create a challenge for your readers. Let your readers think that they are in control, and have them be the ones to challenge their parents to participate in the book club. There could be incentives for the students who get their parents and other adults to join.
- **Time of year.** This program addressed a need to support students during summer reading, but it could be used to keep students reading over the course of a semester or school year. Many students are required to read a set number of independent reads outside of the classroom, and this learning experience could help them manage their time and keep them focused on the extended task.
- **Virtual Tool.** *FlipGrid* was a powerful tool that allowed for students to post at various times. Another phenomenal video-response tool is Recap. Recap also works with various platforms such as Google Classroom, Edmodo, Blackboard, Canvas, and Schoology.

Table 7.4

Theme	Activity
Playful	You and students wear sporting jerseys while posting videos.
Vacation mode	You and students post videos from beach chairs or beach towels, wearing sunglasses and sun hats.
Warm and cozy	You and students post videos wrapped up in favorite blankets, sipping on hot cocoa or warm treats.

- **Books.** If you do not host Scholastic Book Fairs but have classroom teachers who place Scholastic Book orders through their book club, consider asking teachers to use their *Scholastic Bonus Points* to help purchase multiple copies of books. Other options for gathering multiple copies of books are to make a request from your school's parent organizations, contact your local bookstore for a donation, contact a local not-for-profit literacy organization, or utilize an online fundraising tool such as *DonorsChoose.org*.
- **Gift.** Although it is not necessary to give a gift as pricey as a T-shirt, simple gestures to recognize their accomplishments in a timely fashion can have a lasting impression. Placing a card or a letter in the mail with a small gift card will give significance to their role in the learning experiences. Oftentimes, ice cream shops, arcades, coffee shops, bookstores, and beyond are happy to donate to such a worthy educational cause.

Resources

Use Figure 7.7 as a model resource for sharing and gathering information with families about the Books and Pajamas Virtual Book Club.

Digital Resources, Tools, and Links

Books and Pajamas Informational Flyer Link: https://bit.ly/2CEzIjp
Books and Pajamas Online Registration Form: https://goo.gl/forms/KXqGw5XpUz1iNjHV2

GROW

Grow your library program by . . .

1. Identifying a student and parent need that you will help support through a parent partnership–based learning experience.
2. Determining the type of parent partnership you will utilize for supporting both learners' needs.
   a. Librarian and parent
   b. Librarian and parent, alongside student
3. Creating a valuable parent partnership–based learning experience that supports the needs of both the student and parent.

ACTION PLAN

Setting the Stage

Approach this learning experience by determining the following criteria for your work (refer to Table 7.5):

Establishing the Partnership

Use the bullets featured in each section of Table 7.6 to guide you in your actions toward developing a parent partnership.

Delivering the Learning Experience

Use the information in Table 7.7 to guide you in your actions toward developing a parent learning experience with the support of a community partnership.

Books and Pajamas Virtual Book Club

Are you up for the challenge? Let's see how many parents, admired adults & kids we can get to join our ***Books and Pajamas*** virtual book club! Students are tasked to find a parent or an admired adult to join in the fun, or if you are a parent you can find a kid/s. We will be holding 2 book groups over the summer. Mrs. Crossman will be using a free digital tool called **Flipgrid** to host an online book discussion. If you are interested in joining us you will need to access Flipgrid online at www.flipgrid.com or download the free app to your device.

We want to have a relaxing summer enjoying books and so does Mrs. Crossman! In fact she will post a discussion to FlipGrid on each of the selected dates in her pajamas. Students and adults will leave a brief video comment in response to Mrs. Crossman's Flipgrid post each week. **Participants do not need to leave a comment to Mrs. Crossman's post on the same day she posts.** Leave a comment anytime that week, but try to comment prior to the next week's post. Everyone is encouraged, but not required, to get comfy in their pajamas and relax while leaving a post on Flipgrid. This is a simple way to make reading a fun community event! I can't wait to see some of the cozy pj's our students (& adults) enjoy reading in!

Grades K-3	Grades 4-6
Mercy Watson: Something Wonky this Way Comes by Kate DiCamillo	*Flora & Ulysses* by Kate DiCamillo
Virtual Discussion Posts: July 1st, July 8th, July 15th, July 22nd	Virtual Discussion Posts: July 1st, July 8th, July 15th, 22nd, & 29th
Flipgrid URL: Code: Password: MercyWatson	Flipgrid URL: Code: Password: Flora&Ulysses
Mrs. Crossman has a select amount of each book title for students and partners to borrow. Please let Mrs. Crossman know if you need a copy of the book. Students and adults, if interested are encouraged to borrow the titles from the public library or order a copy of the book from Amazon or the local bookstore.	

All interested participants must notify Mrs. Crossman prior to June 30th. Entries can be submitted via email, Google Forms (located on the library website: www.lakegeorgelmc.org), or by submitting the attached form to Mrs. Crossman. Please see Mr. Crossman if you have any questions or need help downloading or accessing FlipGrid.

Figure 7.7   Books and Pajamas Virtual Book Club

Books and Pajamas Virtual Book Club

Student Reader_____

Partner Readers	
Name:	Email:

Figure 7.7   (Continued)

Table 7.5

Setting the Stage		
Goals	*Key Players*	*Groundwork*
• How are you going to use parents to support their child in their learning? • What program will this parent partnership–based learning experience support, if any? • What AASL Standards are you hoping to address? • What Future Ready Principles are you trying to address?	• Who will be involved in the learning experience, solely parent partners or parent partners alongside their child? • Will you need to rely on additional community partners for resource support? • Will you need the support of an instructional partner(s), and if so, who?	• What factors will determine when you will you offer the learning experience? • How long will the parent partnership–based learning experience last? • Will you need the support of your administration? • How will you elicit parent partnerships? ○ Will you do it, or will the students do it? • What resources will be needed to make this learning experience possible? • What experiences can you provide to support parents in their efforts to support their child learner? • Where can you host the parent partnership–based learning experience? • What do you need from your parent partner? • How will you communicate with potential parent partners?

Table 7.6

Who	• Identify parents within specific grade levels you plan to target. • Identify which students could use support of parents through parent-based learning partnership.
What	• Identify what learner needs parents can support. • Ensure that parents will be interested in creating a partnership, by helping them to fill a need. • Identify the responsibilities and expectations of the parent partners, and communicate that to them.
How	• Determine the means in which you will solicit parent partners (social media, informational flyers, informational videos, student persuasion, etc.). • Seek opportunities to have face-to-face conversations with parents. • Seek opportunities to share information at parent organizations and public school-associated meetings. • Build a good report with parents, for when you are seeking their support, they can feel comfortable partnering with you.
Where	• Identify inviting and popular spaces that are located in your community when applicable. • When selecting a physical space, ensure that the space meets the needs of you and the learner (Wi-Fi, tables, screen space, outlets, private area for presenting, etc.). • When selecting a digital communication tool, choose a *free* and *easy-to-use* tool that can be used across all devices.
When	• Solicit parent input when selecting a time that they need to be physically present. • Accommodate the needs of parent partners by creating a flexible schedule for posting virtually (when applicable). • When determining the time of the year to build parent partnerships, consider when parents will be available and when students need the most support.

Table 7.7

Steps to Developing Parent Learning Experiences
1. Build relationships with parents to better understand where and how you can support parents in being a resource and champion of their child's learning and growth.
2. Accommodate parents' schedules by building either • flexible learning experiences or • gathering input from parents about *how*, *when*, and *where* they would like to partner.
3. Determine the means or location for partner engagement.
4. Seek interested partners, and market your learning experience.
5. Use digital communication tools to share information and celebrate success.

Glossary

AASL Standards   "standards designed to guide your interactions with learners, educators, and stakeholders, as well as help you to engage in deep, effective professional practice" (AASL 2018, 3).

Adobe Spark Video   A free digital tool for creating videos through selected or personal soundtracks, images, and icons.

Animoto   A digital tool for creating videos.

Big Ideas   The broad themes of the student work during challenge-based learning.

Book Fair   An event for students to purchase new books.

Book Fair Rewards   Rewards earned from *Scholastic* Book Fair profits.

Bookmobile   A vehicle that transports books to readers in the mode of a traveling library.

Breakout Edu Kit   "A unique collection of resettable locks, boxes and items that can be used to play immersive learning games" (The Power of Breakout EDU n.d.).

Buncee   "A creation and presentation tool for students and educators to create interactive classroom content, allowing learners of all ages to visualize concepts and communicate creatively" (Buncee n.d.).

Canva   A free digital tool for designing graphics.

Celebrity Reader   A community member who holds a position or skill that brings them attention or status and agrees to partner with the library to become a reader for *Celebrity Summer Reading Circles*.

Celebrity Summer Reading Circles   A student-centered summer learning experience where students participate in a fun and engaging book-related activity developed around a specific title and carried out by a *Celebrity Reader*.

Challenged-Based Personal Learning Experience   A student-generated personal learning experience that is designed to address a *Big Idea* and an *Essential Question*.

Challenge Statements   Actionable solutions to *Essential Questions* (Nichols, Cator, and Torres 2016).

ClassDojo   "is a communication app for the classroom. It connects teachers, parents, and students who use it to share photos, videos, and messages through the school day" (ClassDojo n.d.).

Coffee Click   A learning opportunity housed at a local coffee shop that places the parent as the learner.

Co-Lead Professional Development A collaborative effort between two or more leaders to educate professionals on a specific topic.

Community Partnership A connection that is made between the learner and an individual, organization, or physical place outside of the school building. This connection is made by the librarian or with potential instructional partners to support student learning.

Community Partnership–Based Learning Experiences Learning experiences provided to student learners through the creation of a connected community partnership.

Curriculum-Based Learning Experiences Inquiry-based learning experiences that utilize community expert partners to support the curricular work of students during one or more stages of the inquiry process.

Curriculum Partnerships Expert community partners who support the curricular work of learners during various stages of the inquiry-based learning process.

Digital Literacy The ability to use information and communication technologies to find, evaluate, create, and communicate information, requiring both cognitive and technical skills (American Library Association Task Force 2011).

DonorsChoose.org "empowers public school teachers from across the country to request much-needed materials and experiences for their students. Right now there are thousands of classroom requests that you can help bring to life with a gift of any amount" (DonorsChoose.org n.d.).

Edmodo "is a global education network that helps connect all learners with the people and resources needed to reach their full potential" (Edmodo n.d.).

Educreations "is a unique interactive whiteboard and screencasting tool that's simple, powerful, and fun to use. Annotate, animate, and narrate nearly any type of content as you explain any concept" (Educreations n.d.).

Empathy The ability to put yourself in another person's position and understand their emotions and experiences.

Essential Question What students are trying to answer through their work in *Personal Learning Experiences.*

Express The final stage of the WISE inquiry process where students share what they have learned to an audience.

External Learning Experiences Learning experiences where the connected learning between community partners and the learner takes place outside of the school building. Oftentimes, student learners travel to connect with the community partner. However, in some cases, the learning is brought to the student when they aren't physically at the school.

FaceTime A video-calling tool that allows users to make audio and video calls on iOS mobile devices and Macintosh computers (Apple n.d.a).

Failing Forward A concept that we can make forward progression toward growth when we learn from our mistakes or failures.

Feedly A digital tool that allows you to curate online articles, blogs, tweets, videos, news, and any site with an RSS feed (Feedly n.d.).

Flipboard A news app that curates stories into a digital magazine (Flipboard n.d.).

FlipGrid A video discussion platform where students can share their voice (Microsoft n.d.).

Future Ready Librarians "is an expansion of the Future Ready Schools' initiative aimed at raising awareness among district and school leaders about the valuable role librarians can play in supporting the Future Ready goals of their school and district" (Alliance for Excellent Education n.d.).

Future Ready Principles   "highlight how school librarians support schools in transitioning to student-centered learning and identify special ways librarians can become future ready" (Alliance for Excellent Education 2018).

Global Awareness   An understanding and appreciation for the diverse perspectives and experiences among people and cultures around the world.

Global Read Aloud   A global project started by Pernille Ripp to connect learners around the world through one book.

GoFundMe   A digital fundraising tool.

Google Classroom   A digital tool designed to ease collaboration, organization, and the sharing of files and assignments between teachers and students (Google n.d.b.).

Google Earth   A digital tool that allows users to view "satellite imagery and 3D terrain of the entire globe and 3D buildings in hundreds of cities around the world" (Google n.d.d.).

Google Expeditions   Google provides students and classrooms with virtual field trips through both augmented and virtual reality (Google n.d.a.).

Google Form   A free tool provided for educators by Google for creating and sharing surveys and collecting data (Google n.d.c).

Growth Mindset   A frame of mind that allows a person to accept that growth in knowledge and understanding can be achieved through hard work.

Guiding Questions   Questions formed by students in *Personal Learning Experience*, to guide them in their work toward answering their *Essential Question*.

Hangouts on Air   A web-based tool that allows users to live-stream Google Hangouts on air through YouTube Live.

Idea Boxes   Text features that provide useful tips for facilitating the learning experience.

I-Movie   Allows iOS and macOS users to create trailers and videos using images, video-clips, and music.

Innovation   The act of creating "something new and better" (Couros 2015, 34).

Inquiry   A learning process that students go through when acquiring new knowledge. It progresses through the stages of Wonder, Investigate, Synthesize, Express, and Reflect in a cyclical and iterative fashion.

Internal Learning Experiences   Learning experiences where the connected learning between community partners and the learner most often take place within a school building. However, there are times when the learning happens in the building but the partner is not physically present.

Investigate   The second stage of the WISE inquiry process where students locate, gather, select, and analyze information that will help them answer their wonder questions.

Kahoot   "is a game-based learning platform" to use on technology devices (Kahoot n.d.).

Kajeet   A platform for educators to manage and connect mobile technology (Kajeet n.d.).

Key Ideas   A Key Component of the New York State Social Framework that is "aligned to the standards and represent enduring understandings that should be the focus of teaching and learning for each grade" (University of the State of New York 2014).

Knowledge Product   The creation of work developed through application of acquired and applied knowledge.

Learner   Information seekers, including, but not limited to, students, teachers, librarians, and administrators.

Lifelong Learning Process   An individual's personal quest for continual knowledge throughout their lifetime.

Literacy Partnership-Based Learning Experience   A learning opportunity that encourages and nourishes a student's love of reading through a connected community partner who provides knowledge and skills, experiences, or a product.

Literacy Partnerships   When community members and the librarian work together to create an inviting literacy-based learning experience.

Media Literacy   Ability to "access, analyze, evaluate and create messages in a variety of forms-from print to video to the Internet. Media literacy builds an understanding of the role of media in society as well as essential skills of inquiry and self-expression necessary for citizens and democracy" (Center for Media Literacy n.d.).

Mobile Reading Learning Experience   Reading opportunities that are provided to learners because of travel.

Mobile Reading Partnerships   A connected relationship between the librarian and a person or location in the community that allows for extended reading opportunities through travel.

Notability   A paid note-taking app that allows for annotation, typing, recording, and sketching on iPads, iPhones, or Macs (Apple n.d.b.).

Notes   A digital note-taking app that allows users to create checklists and drag and drop movies, pictures, links, and files (Apple n.d.c.).

Padlet   "is a software people use to make and share content with others. Somewhere between a doc and a full-fledged website builder, Padlet empowers everyone to make the content they want, whether it's a quick bulletin board, a blog, or a portfolio " (Padlet n.d.).

Parent Partnership   When parents partner with the school librarian to participate as active learners in *Parent Learning Experiences*.

Parent Partnership–Based Learning Experience   Learning opportunities where parents support their child as a learner by becoming the learner themselves. These opportunities can entail parents learning independent of their child or alongside their child.

Personal Learning Experience   An experience that connects learners with authentic learning opportunities and partnerships.

PicCollage   A digital tool used to create photo collages.

Poll Everywhere   A live polling tool for collecting instant information.

Professional Learning   Instruction provided to professionals to help improve classroom practice.

QuickTime Player   "a multimedia framework geared towards digital video" (SOFTONIC INTERNATIONAL S.A., n.d.).

Readerly Life   An individual's lifestyle that encompasses a continuous behavior of reading for both professional and personal knowledge development and pleasure.

Remind   A tool that allows teachers to communicate with students and parents through their device without having to share contact information (Remind n.d.).

SAMR Model   A framework designed by Ruben Puentedura to define four levels of technology use: Substitution, Augmentation, Modification, and Redefinition (Puentedura n.d.).

Scholastic Book Fair Points   Points earned from Scholastic Book Orders that accumulate toward free merchandise.

Scholastic Dollars   Earnings profited from the overall sales of a Scholastic Book Fair. Scholastic Dollars can be used to purchase items from the Scholastic Catalog or items from the Book Fair. Their value is worth double of that of the cash profit option (Scholastic n.d.).

Screencastify   A free chrome extension that allows users to record their screen to make an editable and shareable screencast (Screencastify n.d.).

Seesaw   A classroom digital learning platform that allows for teacher, student, and parent communication.

Shared Foundation   "The highest level of the AASL Standards that describes a core educational concept for learners, school librarians, and programs. The AASL Standards are based on six Shared Foundations: Inquire, Include, Collaborate, Curate, Explore, and Engage" (AASL 2018).

Site-Based Learning Experience   Learning opportunities that take place an outside entity to support learner personal or academic growth.

Site-Based Partnership   Connected relationships between a librarian and an outside entity used to support personal or academic learning growth.

Skype   A digital communication tool that allows users to connect through video, audio, or text.

Smore   A tool for creating shareable digital posters.

SurveyMonkey   A free online survey generator.

Synthesize   The third stage of the WISE inquiry process where students build meaning from their newly gathered information.

TypeForm   A free or paid digital tool that allows users to create surveys, polls, questionnaires, and polls.

Twitter   A free social media and online news tool used to communicate and network through brief sentences, called tweets (Gill n.d.).

Virtual Learning Experience   Learning opportunities where learners are connected virtually with classrooms, people, and places outside of their school through digital means.

Virtual Partnerships   Connected relationships between the librarian and members or resources of the outside community that provide opportunities for students to communicate with classrooms, people, or places outside of your school through digital means.

Weebly   Free blog and website generator.

WISE Model of Inquiry   The iterative stages of learning that take the learner through the process of Wondering, Investigating, Synthesizing, and Expressing.

Wonder   The first stage of the WISE inquiry process where students' thinking is activated and questions are created for investigation.

YouTube Live   Allows users to live-stream events to their audience with audience participation through live chatting.

Works Cited

"About." n.d. The Power of Breakout EDU. Accessed October 9, 2018. https://www .breakoutedu.com/about/.

Alliance for Excellent Education, ed. n.d. "Future Ready Librarians." Future Ready Schools: Preparing Students for Success. Accessed August 24, 2018. https://futureready .org/program-overview/librarians/.

Alliance for Excellent Education. June 2018. "Future Ready Librarians Framework." PDF. Future Ready Librarians. Accessed October 9, 2018. https://1gu04j2l2i9n1b0 wor2zmgua-wpengine.netdna-ssl.com/wp-content/uploads/2017/01/Library_flyer_ download.pdf.

American Association of School Librarians. 2018. *National School Library Standards for Learners, School Librarians, and School Libraries.* Chicago, IL: ALA Editions, an imprint of the American Library Association.

American Library Association Digital Literacy Task Force. 2011. *What Is Digital Literacy.* PDF. Chicago, IL: American Library Association. http://www.dla101.org/wp-content/ uploads/2015/07/what-is-digilit-2.pdf.

Apple. n.d.a. "FaceTime on the Apple Store." App Store. Last modified May 26, 2016. Accessed October 9, 2018. https://itunes.apple.com/us/app/facetime/id1110145091? mt=8.

Apple. n.d.b. "Notability." App Store. Last modified 2018. Accessed October 11, 2018. https://itunes.apple.com/us/app/notability/id360593530?mt=8.

Apple. n.d.c. "Notes for Mac: Notes Overview." Apple Support. Last modified March 30, 2017. Accessed October 11, 2018. https://support.apple.com/kb/PH22608?locale= en_US.

Buncee. n.d. "What Is Buncee." Buncee. Last modified 2018. Accessed October 9, 2018. https://www.edu.buncee.com/what-is-buncee.

Center for Media Literacy. n.d. "Media Literacy: A Definition and More." Accessed August 24, 2018. http://www.medialit.org/media-literacy-definition-and-more/.

ClassDojo. n.d. "About Us." ClassDojo. Last modified 2018. Accessed October 9, 2018. https://www.classdojo.com/about/.

Couros, George. 2015. *The Innovator's Mindset: Empower Learning, Unleash Talent, and Lead a Culture of Creativity.* San Diego, CA: Dave Burgess Consulting.

C3 Teachers. 2018. "Inquiry-Design-Model-Template." Last modified 2018. PDF. http://www.c3teachers.org/inquiry-design-model/.

DonorsChoose.org. n.d. "DonorsChoose.org: Support a Classroom. Build a Future." DonorsChoose.org. Last modified 2018. Accessed October 9, 2018. https://www.donorschoose.org/.

Edmodo. n.d. "Edmodo Homepage." Edmodo. Last modified 2018. Accessed October 9, 2018. https://www.edmodo.com/.

Educreations. n.d. "Educreations Homepage." Educreations. Last modified 2018. Accessed October 9, 2018. https://www.educreations.com/.

Feedly. n.d. "Welcome to Feedly." Feedly. Accessed October 9, 2018. https://feedly.com/i/welcome.

Friedman, Thomas L. 2007. *The World Is Flat 3:0 : A Brief History of the Twenty-First Century: The World Is Flat: A Brief History of the Twenty-First Century.* New York: Picador.

"Future Ready Librarians." n.d. Video file. n.d. Future Ready Schools: Preparing Schools for Success. Posted by Alliance for Excellent Education, February 7, 2017. Accessed August 24, 2018. https://youtu.be/B8TzLuscEgM.

Gil, Paul. n.d. "What Is Twitter and How Does It Work?" Lifewire. Last modified February 5, 2018. Accessed October 12, 2018. https://www.lifewire.com/what-exactly-is-twitter-2483331.

Google. n.d.a. "About." Google Expeditions. Accessed October 10, 2018. https://edu.google.com/expeditions/#about.

Google. n.d.b. "Classroom." Google Classroom. Accessed October 10, 2018. https://edu.google.com/k-12-solutions/classroom/?modal_active=none.

Google. n.d.c. "Forms." Google. Accessed October 10, 2018. https://www.google.com/intl/en-GB/forms/about/.

Google. n.d.d. "Google Earth." Google Play. Last modified 2018. Accessed October 10, 2018. https://play.google.com/store/apps/details?id=com.google.earth&hl=en_US.

Kahoot. n.d. "What Is Kahoot?" Kahoot! Last modified 2018. Accessed October 11, 2018. https://kahoot.com/what-is-kahoot/.

Kajeet. n.d. "Homepage." Kajeet. Last modified 2018. Accessed October 11, 2018. https://www.kajeet.net/.

Laur, Dayna, Jill Clayton, and Tim Kubik. n.d. "Project Arc." ARC. Last modified 2017. http://www.proj-arc.com/.

Microsoft. n.d. "Flipgrid Homepage." Flipgrid. Last modified 2018. Accessed October 9, 2018. https://flipgrid.com/.

Morrow, Katie. 2014. *Write to Change the World: Challenge Based Learning for Persuasive Writing.* Apple. ibook.

"New York State K-12 Social Studies Framework." 2014. University of the State of New York. http://www.nysed.gov/common/nysed/files/programs/curriculum-instruction/ss-framework-k-12-intro.pdf.

Nichols, Mark H., Karen Cator, and Marco Torres. 2016. *Challenge Based Learning Guide Take Action. Make a Difference.* Digital Promise. Digital file.

Olson, Sarah, and Bridget Crossman. "Are You at the Table? The Importance of Leadership in the Library." School Library Connection, April 2018. http://schoollibraryconnection.com/Home/Display/2143884.

Padlet. n.d. "What Is Padlet." Padlet. Last modified 2017. Accessed October 11, 2018. https://padlet.com/support/whatispadlet.

Puentedura, Ruben R. n.d. *Learning, Technology, and the SAMR Model: Goals, Processes, and Practice*. PDF. Blog available at http://www.hippasus.com/rrpweblog/archives/2014/06/29/LearningTechnologySAMRModel.pdf.

Ratzer, Mary Boyd, and Paige Jaeger. 2014. *Rx for the Common Core: Toolkit for Implementing Inquiry Learning*. Santa Barbara, CA: Libraries Unlimited, an imprint of ABC-CLIO.

Remind. n.d. "Homepage." Remind. Last modified 2018. Accessed October 12, 2018. https://www.remind.com.

Ripp, Pernille. n.d. "Home." The Global Read Aloud. Last modified 2018. Accessed October 10, 2018. https://theglobalreadaloud.com/.

Scholastic. n.d. "Scholastic Dollars." Scholastic. Assessed October 12, 2018. http://direct.www.scholastic.com/bookfairs/scholasticdollars/.

Screencastify. n.d. "Homepage." Screencastify. Last modified 2018. Accessed October 12, 2018. https://www.screencastify.com/.

SOFTONIC INTERNATIONAL S.A. n.d. "QuickTime Help and Info." Softonic. Accessed October 12, 2018. https://quicktime.en.softonic.com/mac/download.

Stripling, Barbara K., and Sandra Hughes-Hassell. 2003. *Curriculum Connections through the Library*. Westport, CT: Libraries Unlimited.

Swan, K., S. G. Grant, and John Lee. 2018. *Inquiry Design Model: Building Inquiries in Social Studies*. Washington, D.C.: National Council for the Social Studies and C3 Teachers.

"Tutorials." n.d. Flipboard. Last modified 2018. Accessed October 9, 2018. https://about.flipboard.com/tutorials/.

Wagner, Tony. 2008. *The Global Achievement Gap: Why Even Our Best Schools Don't Teach the New Survival Skills Our Children Need—and What We Can Do about It*. New York: Basic Books.

Wagner, Tony, and Ted Dintersmith. 2015. *Most Likely to Succeed: Preparing Our Kids for the Innovation Era*. New York, NY: Scribner.

WSWHE BOCES. 2011. "WISE: Inquiry Model Teacher's Guide." PDF. Accessed March 28, 2019. http://drmsmediacenter.weebly.com/uploads/3/3/4/7/3347316/wisecurriculumguide.pdf.

YouTube. n.d. "Live Streaming on YouTube." YouTube Creators. Accessed October 12, 2018. https://creatoracademy.youtube.com/page/course/livestream.

Suggested Further Reading

Alliance for Excellent Education. n.d.a. "Alliance for Excellent Education." Last modified 2018. Accessed November 21, 2018. https://all4ed.org/

Laur, Dayna, Jill Clayton, and Tim Kubik. "Project Arc." ARC. Last modified 2017. http://www.proj-arc.com/.

Morrow, Katie. *Write to Change the World: Challenge Based Learning for Persuasive Writing*. Apple, 2014. ibook.

Nichols, Mark H., Karen Cator, and Marco Torres. *Challenge Based Learning Guide Take Action. Make a Difference*. Digital Promise, 2016. Digital file.

Olson, Sarah, and Bridget Crossman. "Are You at the Table? The Importance of Leadership in the Library." *School Library Connection*, April 2018. http://schoollibraryconnection.com/Home/Display/2143884.

Ratzer, Mary Boyd, and Paige Jaeger. *Rx for the Common Core: Toolkit for Implementing Inquiry Learning*. Santa Barbara, CA: Libraries Unlimited, an imprint of ABC-CLIO, 2014.

Stripling, Barbara K., and Sandra Hughes-Hassell. *Curriculum Connections through the Library*. Westport, CT: Libraries Unlimited, 2003.

Swan, K., S. G. Grant, and John Lee. 2018. *Inquiry Design Model: Building Inquiries in Social Studies*. Washington, D.C.: National Council for the Social Studies and C3 Teachers.

WildEarth. "WildEarth Schools Project." WildEarth. Last modified 2017. Accessed October 28, 2018. https://wildearth.tv/.

Index

Page numbers followed by *t* indicate tables and *f* indicate figures.

About the Author

BRIDGET CROSSMAN is a school librarian at Lake George Elementary School, Lake George, New York, and founder and director of the not-for-profit children's literacy organization B.O.O.K.S. (Books Offer Opportunities, Kids Succeed). She is coauthor of *Six Shifts of Librarianship, Inquiry Infusion: Surviving and Thriving in 1:1 Environment,* and *Are You at the Table? The Importance of Leadership in the Library,* published by *School Library Connection.* Crossman was the recipient of the 2013 New York State Reading Association's Library Media Specialist Award.